The Westland Lysander

Airframe Detail No.9
The Westland Lysander
– A Technical Guide
by Richard A. Franks

First published in 2020 by
Valiant Wings Publishing Ltd
8 West Grove, Bedford, MK40 4BT, UK
+44 (0)1234 273434
valiant-wings@btconnect.com
www.valiant-wings.co.uk
Facebook: valiantwingspublishing

© Richard A. Franks 2020
© Richard J. Caruana – Colour Side & Top Profiles, B&W Profiles, Stencil Diagrams & Scale Plans
© Libor Jekl – Section 4

The right of Richard A. Franks to be identified as the author of this work has been asserted in accordance with sections 77 and 78 of the Copyright Designs and Patents Act, 1988.

The 'Airframe Detail' brand, along with the concept of the series, are the copyright of Richard A. Franks as defined by the Copyright Designs and Patents Act, 1988 and are used by Valiant Wings Publishing Ltd by agreement with the copyright holder.

All rights reserved. No part of this publication may be reproduced or transmitted in any form or by any means, electronic or mechanical, including photocopy, recording, or any other information storage and retrieval system, without permission in writing from the publishers.

Please note, whilst we are always happy to hear from readers, we are not in a position to enter into discussion (in person, in writing or via electronic mail) with any individual, nor to undertake or supply research/supporting material relating to this, or any of our other titles. Our apologies for this, but it is inevitable if we are to meet our production schedule each year, and all sources (excluding those from private collections) are listed in the bibliography.

ISBN: 978-1-912932-03-0

Groundcrew pack a parachute into a supply container before fitting it to the stub winglets of a Mk II of No.225 Squadron at RAF Tilshead, Wiltshire
(©Crown Copyright)

Acknowledgements
The author would like to give a word of thanks to the Aircraft Restoration Company for allowing access to their airworthy example and to Juraj Jankovic, George Papadimitriou, Nigel Perry, Bryan Ribbans and Scott Willey for their invaluable help with photographs. Special thanks must go to Libor Jekl for his excellent model build and Richard J. Caruana for his superb artwork.

Note
There are many different ways of writing aircraft designation, however for consistency throughout this title we have used the Roman numbering system for the pre-1948 period (e.g. Mk I, Mk III etc.) and another for the post-1948 period when the RAF adopted the Arabic system of numbering (e.g. Mk 1, Mk 3 etc.).

Sections

Introduction	5
1. Technical Description Detailed coverage of construction and equipment	25
2. Camouflage & Markings Colour side profiles, notes and photographs	73
3. Little Lizzie A build of the 1/72nd scale Mk III (SD) from Dora Wings by Libor Jekl	97
Appendices	104
i Lysander Kits	
ii Lysander Accessory, Decals & Masks	
iii Bibliography	
iv Lysander Squadrons	

Mk Is under construction at Yeovil

Glossary

A&AEE	Aeroplane & Armament Experimental Establishment
AACU	Anti-Aircraft Calibration Unit
AAPC	Anti-Aircraft Practice Camps
ACM	Air-Chief Marshall (RAF)
AFDU	Air Fighting Development Unit
AFS	Advanced Flying Schools
AGS	Air Gunnery School
AI	Airborne Interception (radar)
AID	Airworthiness Inspection Directorate
AM	Air Marshall (RAF)
ANS	Air Navigation School
AOC	Air Officer Commanding
AOS	Air Observer School
APC	Armament Practice Camp
APS	Armament Practice School
AVM	Air Vice Marshall (RAF)
AWOCU	All Weather Operational Conversion Unit
BEF	British Expeditionary Force
BS	British Standard
CAACU	Civilian Anti-Aircraft Co-operation Unit
CBE	Commander of the Most Excellent Order of the British Empire
CFE	Central Flying Establishment
CFS	Central Flying School
CGS	Central Gunnery School
CO	Commanding Officer
CofG	Centre of Gravity
DFC	Distinguished Flying Cross
DFM	Distinguished Flying Medal
D.H.	de Havilland Ltd
DTD	Department of Technical Directorate
EAAS	Empire Air Armament School
ECFS	Empire Central Flying School
EFS	Empire Flying School
ETPS	Empire Test Pilots' School
FAA	Fleet Air Arm
FEAFES	Far East Air Force Examining School
FCCS	Fight Command Communications School
FIU	Fighter Interception Unit
Flt Lt	Flight Lieutenant (RAF)
F/O	Flying Officer (RAF)
Flt	Flight
Flt Sgt	Flight Sergeant
FRAeS	Fellowship of the Royal Aeronautical Society
FRS	Flying Refresher School
FS	Federal Standard
ft	Foot
FTS	Flying Training School
FWS	Fighter Weapons School
G force	Equal to an acceleration of 32ft/sec/sec, which is the rate of acceleration of a body in free fall due to gravity
GP	General Purpose
Gp Capt	Group Capitan (RAF)
HQ	Headquarters
IFF	Identification Friend or Foe
Imp. Gal.	Imperial Gallon (4.546 litres)
in	Inch
ITF	Instrument Training Flight
lb	Pound
JCF	Jet Conversion Flight
JCU	Jet Conversion Unit
MAP	Ministry of Aircraft Production
Mk	Mark
Mod	Modification
MoS	Ministry of Supply
mph	Miles Per Hour
MU	Maintenance Unit (RAF)
NAS	Naval Air Squadron (FAA)
NF	Night-fighter
No	Number
(O)AFU	(Observers) Advanced Flying Unit
OCU	Operational Conversion Unit
OFU	Overseas Ferry Unit
OTU	Operational Training Unit
P/O	Pilot Officer (RAF)
PR	Photo Reconnaissance
PRU	Photo Reconnaissance Unit
RAAF	Royal Australian Air Force
RAE	Royal Aircraft Establishment
RAF	Royal Air Force
RNAS	Royal Naval Air Station
R.P.	Rocket Projectile
SAAF	South African Air Force
Sgt	Sergeant
SOC	Struck Off Charge
Sqn	Squadron
Sqn Ldr	Squadron Leader (RAF)
TT	Target Towing
TWU	Tactical Weapons Unit
UK	United Kingdom
US Gal.	US Gallon (3.785 litres)
Wg Cdr	Wing Commander (RAF)
WWII	World War II (1939-1945)
/G	Suffix letter added to aircraft serial number denoting that it carried special equipment and was to be guarded at all times

King Edward VIII ascends a ladder to view inside K6127 at A+AEE Martlesham Heath in 1936 (©British Official)

Airframe Detail No.9 – Lysander

Hectors of No.13 (Army Co-operation) Squadron during camp at Mitcham's Wood, East Anglia in the summer of 1937 (©Air Ministry)

Introduction

Brief History

Army co-operation was a long established element of RAF operations and in the late 1920s the Audax, Hardy and Hector, developed from the Hart bomber, were used in the role. The Hector was one of the types built under licence by Westlands and was only an interim design, so in April 1935 a new specification (A.39/34) was issued for a more modern type to replace the Audax/Hardy/Hector. Four companies submitted designs to meet the new specification, Avro (Type 670), Bristol (Type 148), Hawker (with an untitled biplane design) and Westlands. The Avro and Hawker designs were never built, while the Bristol 148 was an advanced monoplane design, but it (K6551) did not fly until sixteen months after the first of the Westland prototypes. Westland's new P.8 was the second design proposal from Edward W. 'Teddy' Petter B.A., who had taken on the role of Technical Director at Westlands after R.A. Bruce B.A. had retired. His first design, for a radial engine monoplane had not been accepted by the Air Ministry, as they were apprehensive of his experience and thus abilities. With the P.8 though Petter and his team spent a day with the School of Army Co-operation at RAF Old Sarum in order to understand the operational, handling and maintenance needs of an Army Co-operation type. Although there was no unanimous requirement, it was agreed that the pilot needed a good, unobscured, field of vision, while the aircraft needed to exhibit good flight characteristics, have a low stall speed and the ability to operate from unprepared small fields. Early on in the development of the basic design it was decided that to meet the handling requirements, the type would need to adopt a monoplane wing that was placed high up and was fitted with both slots and flaps. The wing featured a duralumin monospar with metal torsion box leading edge, triangulated square-section tubular members behind the spar and the torsion stresses relieved by V-shaped struts attached to the root end of the extruded hairpin cantilever undercarriage unit. To give the type safe stall characteristics, while retaining a high rate of descent, the outer leading edge slats had to be adjusted so that they opened first. To do this the profile of the trailing edge in which the slats rested (the 'venting') was varied, but it still always opened

The second Bristol Type 148 (known as the Type 148B), K6552 flew in May 1938 and was fitted with a Bristol Taurus II engine in place of the Mercury IX (and later Perseus XII) used in K6551. It was retained by the manufacturer and used for Taurus engines tests and development work'

K6127 seen fitted with a two-blade Watts propeller that was only used for taxiing trials, the fabric has not been painted and the undercarriage covers are still to be fitted

This shot taken of the Lysander prototype K6127 in 1936 shows it in its original form, with the fixed tailplane

K6127 seen with the New Type Park number 6 applied for the RAF Air Display at Hendon

A lovely shot, which was sadly damaged but it included as this original print does show K6127 with the variable incidence tailplane installed

K6127 seen flying over Westland's Yeovil airfield with a 250lb bomb attached to the universal carrier under each stub wing

K6128 the second Lysander prototype is seen here before the fuselage and wings were covered (©British Official)

with a slight bang and change in longitudinal trim and because the inboard ones were linked to the flaps, that caused the aircraft to go nose-down, which shut the slats and caused another change in trim.

Construction of the first of two P.8s (K6127) was completed at Yeovil within a year of them receiving the contract and the first taxiing trials were done on the 10th June 1936 (the type was fitted with a two-blade, fixed-pitch Watts propeller for these trials). The aircraft was then moved by road to Boscombe Down, where it undertook its first flight on the 15th with Harold Penrose at the controls. The type had a fixed tailplane, a Dowty tailwheel and had no cowling flaps, nor were the undercarriage fairings or armament fitted. A series of minor adjustments took place to the control servos and mass balance weights, it was also fitted with a Mercury IX engine driving a de Havilland three-blade variable-pitch propeller and the undercarriage fairings were installed, then on the 27th it was shown to the public for the first time, when marked with the New Type Park number '6' it appeared at the RAF Air Display at Hendon. On the 29th it was flown to Hatfield for the annual SBAC (Society of British Aircraft Constructors) Display, then after being fitted with cowl gills, armament and radio equipment on the 24th July it went on to the A&AEE at Martlesham Heath for a week of initial evaluation before it returned to Yeovil. These trials showed that the type was longitudinally unstable, so increased area of the tailplanes was needed, but this aggravated problems with trim on the glide and during landing. The tailplanes had thus far been fixed, so they were now made trimmable to a large negative angle, but this resulted in another problem during an overshoot, whereby as the throttle was opened, the aircraft pitched up before the pilot could trim the tail sufficiently to get it back on an even keel. Correcting this problem would take too much time and the type was already in production by this stage, so the A&AEE just added a note in the operating instructions that in the event of an overshoot, the pilot should only apply half power until the aircraft was retrimmed. The second prototype K6128 first flew on the 11th December 1936, powered by the Mercury XII poppet-valve radial engine. It also had all the improvements made to the first prototype, such as the cowl gills, three-blade propeller and adjustable tailplane. It also had the rear canopy sliding panel frames changed and the pilot's steps were relocated to the port undercarriage spat, while a pitot was installed on the port rear strut. During diving trials, the fabric was torn from the upper wing, but the pilot Sqn Ldr R.W. Collings returned to base safely. By this stage most of the mandatory trials had already been done using K6127, so the second prototype spent most of its life at Martlesham Heath and in 1938 went to India to undertake tropical and field trials with No.5 (Army-Co-operation) Squadron based at Miramshah. Later it was used for navigation tests with No.20 (Army-Co-operation) Squadron in Delhi and ended its days as an instruction airframe in 1940.

By May 1936 the Air Ministry had decided against any further development of the Bristol Type 148, so the Westlands design was considered the winner of the A.39/34 specification. The name Lysander was chosen for the P.8, after the Spartan soldier and politician, as per the Air Ministry's rules to give army co-operation aircraft classical names and an order for one-hundred and sixty-nine was placed.

Into Service

It only took two years from the first flight of K6127 until the type entered service with No.16 (Army Co-operation) Squadron, who received the type in June 1938. The unit was chosen because it was based at Old Sarum, so the nearby School of Army Co-operation could call on pilots of the squadron to give instruction on the new type. By the time of the Munich Crisis (30th September 1938), the squadron was fully operational. Production of the Mk I continued into 1939 with No.16 (Army-Co-operation) Squadron getting fourteen and the School of Army Co-operation nine. The

K6128 during trials in India with Audax K5582 seen to its left

second squadron to adopt the type was No.13 (Army Co-operation) Squadron, who disposed of their Hawker Hectors in January 1939 and received the first Lysander on the 23rd of the month. The squadron was then based at Odiham, but in April it moved to Duxford. Other units that received the type were No.26 Squadron at RAF Catterick, No.4 (Army-Co-operation) Squadron at Wimbourne and No.II

(Army Co-operation) Squadron at Hawkinge and by the time war broke out, there were seven Lysander squadrons, with Nos.613 and 614 RAF Auxiliary Air Force squadrons joining those already listed. By this stage most of the Mk Is had been replaced with the Perseus XII-powered Mk II and many of the older Mk Is were crated and shipped out to the RAF units in the Middle East, where there was a chronic shortage of aircraft.

During the initial 'Phoney War' period all bar No.16 (Army-Co-operation) Squadron, who remained at Old Sarum, were based in France. As the heavy snows of winter set in No.II (Army-Co-operation) Squadron was relocated to Durant, No.4 (Army-Co-operation) to Monchy Lagache, while No.16 (Army-Co-operation) Squadron moved from Old Sarum to Lympne to be nearer the French coast. The Nazi assault started on the 10th May and as the attack on Belgium had been foreseen by the Allies, Nos.II and 4 (Army-Co-operation) squadrons moved forward to Lille-Ronchin, while the remainder stayed behind to do reconnaissance and gun spotting for the BEF.

A formation of Mk Is operated by the first squadron to use the type, No.16 (Army Co-operation), seen here in May 1938

A Lysander Mk I of No.13 (Army Co-operation) Squadron taxies to its dispersal point in the snow at Mons-en-Chaussee in 1939 (©British Official)

Although a crew of No.4 (Army-Co-operation) Squadron managed to shot down a Bf 110, the squadron lost nine crews and eleven aircraft in the 10th to 23rd May period, so only five crews and aircraft returned to the UK to land at Ringway on the 25th. No.II (Army-Co-operation) Squadron dispersed two aircraft to the airfields at Abbeville, Bethune, Roncq, Lilles and Brussels. It withdrew back to the UK, landing at Bekesbourne with twelve aircraft, but continued to fly in support of the BEF and French troops as they fell back towards the coast. On the 2nd June volunteers were called for in the squadron and eight Lysanders dropped supplies to the defenders of Calais, while fifteen cannisters of small arms and anti-tank ammunition were dropped on the Citadel garrison. Losses were high though and by the time the troops were evacuated at Dunkirk, the squadron had hardly a serviceable aircraft left. No.16 (Army-Co-operation) Squadron moved from its new base at Lympne to France shortly after the 10th May assault and was involved in close reconnaissance in the area of St. Quentin. The unit lost a number of aircraft on the ground, plus more during sorties, so it was decided to withdraw the unit and return it to Lympne. The campaign in France saw 174 Lysanders sent and eighty-eight of them were lost in combat with a further thirty destroyed on the ground, either by enemy action or by having to be destroyed due to a lack of fuel. The seven squadrons involved lost 120 crews and returned to the UK with about fifty aircraft.

Back in the UK the Lysander squadrons were dispersed and in mid-summer 1940 No.26 Squadron moved to RAF West Malling and started to do survey flights of UK beaches that were though to be potential landing grounds for any Nazi invasion. It lost three Lysanders on the ground at West Malling during a bombing attack on the 18th August, then shortly afterwards moved to Gatwick to undertake anti-aircraft calibration and balloon spotting duties. They continued to do this until early 1941, when Curtiss Tomahawks started to replace the Lysander. No.13 (Army Co-operation) Squadron moved to RAF Hooton Park, whilst No.16 moved to Westland Zoyland and during the Battle of Britain period both sent detachments to coastal airfields to

A Lysander Mk II of No.13 (Army Co-operation) Squadron in France undergoing maintenance in the harsh winter of 1939-40, note the lack of fin flash and the serial number has been painted over or toned down (©British Official)

Airframe Detail No.9 – Lysander

undertake air-sea rescue duties, looking for downed pilots and dropping them a dinghy and supplies. No.4 (Army Co-operation) Squadron remained in the traditional army co-operation role and having moved to RAF Linton-on-Ouse on the 10th June 1940 it undertook tactical reconnaissance and light bombing support for ground forces that were on training manoeuvres. It moved to Clifton at the end of the year and for the next eighteen months worked in conjunction with the 11th Armoured Division doing spotting and reconnaissance until June 1942, when the Lysander was replaced by Curtiss Tomahawks.

Eighteen months after Lysander squadrons had been forced to leave France they returned, but secretly. The Special Operations Executive (SOE) had been formed not long after the fall of France to maintain contact with those fighting in Nazi German-occupied Europe. In August 1941 the first squadron, No.138 (Special

Lysander Mk I L4705 is the subject of much interest as one of the first to be delivered to No.II (Army Co-operation) Squadron at Hawkinge

Pilots of No.161 (Special Duties) Squadron at Tangmere in 1943, Sqn Ldr Hugh Verity is second from left

Duties), was formed at Newmarket. It initially used Hudsons, Whitleys and Lysander Mk IIIs, but these were later joined by Halifaxes and it maintained contact with the resistance in France by dropping supplies and occasionally delivering saboteurs. The Lysander was ideal for landing by night in hastily prepared fields. It also collected individuals that were being hunted by the Germans, or brought a resistance leader to London for debriefing. On more than one occasion a Lysander that was being used to bring someone into France was used on the return flight to bring back downed RAF airmen. As the winter or 1941-42 progressed it was obvious that the Lysanders needed to get deeper into occupied Europe, so to that end the Mk IIIA was developed via the additional of a large fuel tank under the fuselage (adopted from a Handley-Page Harrow overload tank). The type had a ladder attached to the port side by the rear fuselage and the rungs of this were painted in fluorescent paint but otherwise the aircraft were overall black. Between August 1941 and the end of 1944 around four hundred sorties were undertaken by Nos.138 and 161 (SD) squadrons and 293 agents and other passengers were taken to France, with over 500 returned to the UK.

The Middle East

Pre-war Air Ministry plans stated that only twenty-four Lysanders would be needed in the entire Middle Eastern region. Just one unit, No.208 Squadron, would operate twelve of the type in place of the Hawker Audax it had operated from Heliopolis since 1934, with the other twelve being held in reserve. Having done tropical trials with the second prototype (K6128), twenty-four aircraft (L4707 to L4730) were crated directly off the assembly line at Yeovil and shipped to Egypt, arriving in November 1938. They did not see action in the region with No.208 Squadron

Lysander Mk Is of No.208 Squadron fly near the Great Pyramids of Giza

first though, as problems in Palestine led No.6 (Army Co-operation) Squadron to evaluate two of the new Lysanders in the anti-terrorist role during the Christmas period of 1938. No.208 Squadron began to convert from the Audax from December 1938 to January 1939 and continued with its work-up on the type during the spring. By this stage war in Europe was inevitable, so the Air Ministry decided to increase the strength of Lysanders in the Middle East as well, bringing the compliment up to forty-eight aircraft. These would be operated by No.208 Squadron as well as alongside the Hardys and Gauntlets operated by No.6 (Army Co-operation) Squadron. With a plentiful supply of older Mk Is in the UK, as units there converted to the Mk II, these were earmarked for shipment to the Middle East.

A Lysander Mk II of No.208 Squadron RAF parked at El Adem airfield, Libya, shortly after its occupation on the 5th January 1940. In the foreground are the remains of one of eighty-seven wrecked Italian aircraft found on the airfield (©British Official)

Lysander Mk II, JV•E of No.6 Squadron based at Ramleh, Egypt, makes a low-level 'attack' on Australian infantry during an anti-aircraft exercise in the Western Desert (©British Official)

Initial operations in the theatre up until May 1940 were very much exercises concentrating on army co-operation duties for the inevitable contact with the enemy. These 'show of force' exercises were there to show both the locals and the enemy that a sizeable RAF force was in the region and ready to defend it, especially as suspicions ran high at this time that Italy would soon enter the conflict on the Nazi German side. When France fell on the 10th June 1940, Mussolini declared war on Britain, but in the Middle East the Italian forces were ill prepared for any assault into the east. When war with Italy was declared, No.208 squadron had thirteen Mk Is and moved forward to Sidi Barrani. The squadron's first sortie was less than impressive though, as a reconnaissance flight near Sollum for the 7th Armoured Division ended up with L4677, flown by P/O Hardiman, having to make a forced landing in the desert due to a shortage of fuel. General reconnaissance sorties by the Lysander in the region needed fighter protection, if they were to survive and as the Italian forces started their push out from Libya on the 13th September operations started to increase. Losses up until this point for No.208 Squadron had been low, but by October the attrition rate started to climb, the unit suffering its first fatalities on the 15th October when P/O D.M.B. Druce and Sgt J. F. Muldowney were killed when their aircraft was shot down. The situation was eased slightly though from November, as C Flight re-equipped with the Hawker Hurricane in the tactical reconnaissance role, although the Lysander remained with the squadron until May 1942. The next units to arrive in the Middle East with the Lysander were No.3 Squadron, RAAF, who had a single flight flying the type and No.6 (Army Co-operation) Squadron, which was preparing to move from Palestine to the Western Desert. The latter squadron's C Flight moved to Qasaba in Egypt for operational training, while the remainder continued to operate in the Palestine region doing blackout inspection, coastal flights looking for illegal immigrants and general co-operation duties with the Palestine Police. B Flight took over C Flight's role in the region from December 1940 and with the departure of No.208 Squadron in support of operations in Crete (see elsewhere), A and B Flights operated from Tobruk, while their HQ and C Flights moved from Palestine to Heliopolis. No.6 (Army Co-operation) Squadron's A Flight began to re-equip with the Hurricane at Agedabia in March 1941, but B Flight continued to use the Lysander at Barce.

However, the arrival of General Rommel and the Afrika Korps in the region forced British and Commonwealth forces to withdraw from the area and regroup/re-equip, however No.6 (Army Co-Operation) Squadron was

Lysander Mk II R1994 delivers newspapers and letters from Cairo to units operating in the Western Desert (©Department of Information)

10 Airframe Detail No.9 – Lysander

Lysander Mk II, L4808 of No.28 Squadron seen in flight over the Western Desert in 1941

ordered to stay behind and give close-support to the besieged garrison at Tobruk. The combined German and Italian assault on Tobruk started on the 11th April, with bombing attacks from the 14th and the nearby Lysander base of Barce came under regular aerial attacks with, on the 22nd April, L6875 and L6876 being destroyed on the ground and so the airfield was evacuated. The four remaining Hurricanes of No.73 Squadron left Tobruk on the 25th April, leaving No.6 (Army Co-operation) Squadron's handful of Lysanders, Hurricanes and a single Miles Magister. The situation worsened and on the 19th May the unit was ordered to withdraw, flying the four remaining Lysanders and the Magister to Maaten Bagush. By the beginning of 1942 the Lysander was being withdrawn by No.6 (Army Co-operation) Squadron, as it started to re-equip with the Hurricane Mk II and by June 1941 the unit had completely converted to the Hurricane, bring the operational life of the Lysander in the Western Desert to a close.

The Lysander was also operated by No.451 (RAAF) Squadron during 1941/42 in the Western Desert, operating the Mks I & II from Kasfareet, Aboukir, Qasaba, Landing Ground (LG) 75, 132, 128, 145 and 146, El Gubbi, LG 131 & 148, Sid Azeiz, Helioplois, Rayak and Estabel.

Crete

No.208 Squadron continued to operate in the Western Desert throughout 1940, but with the threat to Greece, it moved nine Lysanders via Crete to Phasala, arriving there on the 15th April 1941. German forces already held control of the air in the theatre, so the unit was forced to continually move to keep its aircraft safe and to offer the widest reconnaissance for the ground forces as they retreated. On the 20th April the unit withdrew to Argos, then on to Crete on the 22nd and whilst German propaganda announced the total destruction of the unit in Greece, the squadron suffered no casualties at all and only lost three Hurricanes and three Lysanders.

India & Burma

The second prototype (K6128) did tropical trials in India, being shipped to Karachi in March 1938 and later operating with No.20 (Army Co-operation) Squadron in the region. With war declared patrolling the borders of the northwest frontier was outside of what the RAF could reasonably achieve, so the Indian Air Force had to take up the task. At this stage the IAF operated the Hawker Audax and Hart in the role and there was some doubt that a 'modern' type like the Lysander would be suitable for them, however by 1941 it was decided to re-equip No.1 Squadron, Indian Air Force under the command of Sqn Ldr S. Mukerjee with the type. Forty-eight machines were shipped to the RAF depot at Drigh Road and in August 1941 No.1 Squadron IAF was withdrawn from active service to convert to the Lysander. However, by September all units operating along the northwest frontier were being prepared for service in Europe, so No.1 Squadron IAF returned to active service, leaving one Flight to continue conversion, while the rest of the unit moved 750 miles north to Peshawar. The twelve Lysanders of No.1 Squadron IAF were officially handed over at a ceremony at Peshawar on the 7th November 1941, the aircraft having been purchased by the Indian Government thanks to money donated by the Bombay War Gifts Fund. The terrain along the frontier was unforgiving and the first accident with a Lysander occurred on the 13th November when P1694 hit a boulder whilst landing at Manzai, causing it to cartwheel, thankfully without injury to the pilot. This was followed on the 22nd November by another wrecked Lysander during landing at Lahore.

The first RAF squadron in this theatre to operate the Lysander was No.28 Squadron based at Kohat in September 1941. The Lysanders were used throughout the retreat from Burma and two aircraft were specially fitted with extra fuel tanks so they could operate from the Andaman Islands. No.20 (Army Co-operation) Squadron also operated from Kohat with fifteen Lysanders from the 31st December 1941, but quickly moved to Secunderabad, then Jamshedpur and Tezpur in Assam, as the military situation in Burma worsened and eventually re-equipped with the Hurricane Mk II in the late summer of 1943.

No.1 Squadron IAF was joined by No.2 Squadron, when the later converted to the Lysander from November 1941 and it was initially intended to create ten IAF squadrons, the third using the machines relinquished by Nos.1 and 2 squadrons. No.4 Squadron started to receive the Lysander from February 1942 and from late November No.1 Squadron started a series of flights for publicity purposes and to encourage young Indians to join the IAF. Just a few such flights had taken place when Japan attacked Pearl Harbor (7th December) and on the 9th December the offensives against Kota Bahru in Malaya and the Tenasserim Peninsula in Burma began, so on the 10th No.1 Squadron was ordered to move to Burma. Such a move to a war

A Lysander Mk II of No.28 Squadron, who operated the type in India from September 1941 to December 1942

footing in Burma was impossible though, as No.1 Squadron was on detachment a long way from its home base and, as there had been no aerial opposition during its patrols along the northwest frontier, their Lysanders had never carried an air gunner. Volunteers were sought to become air gunners and after a sufficient number became available, they were hastily trained and the squadron was ready for a move to Burma. Twelve Lysanders made their way to Burma in stages, reaching the operational wartime base of Toungoo on the 1st February 1942 and joined No.28 Squadron RAF, from whom it had taken over frontier duties in mid-1940. That very first night Toungoo was bombed by the Japanese and No.1 Squadron's commander, Sqn Ldr Majumber decided they

Lysander Mk IIIA (SD), V9289 'C', of C Flight, No.357 (Special Duties) Squadron RAF based at Mingaladon, Burma, in flight

had most likely come from Mae-Haugsaum in Siam and that it was time to take some action. He flew his Lysander in the company of two No.67 Squadron Brewster Buffaloes to attack Mae-Haugsaum on the 3rd February, bombing the airfield with a pair of 250lb bombs and the attack was repeated on the 4th, only this time with all twelve Lysanders. Later, No.1 Squadron had to send half its force as a detachment to Lashio in support of the Chinese 5th Army, while the rest went to Mingaladon to support the ground forces defending Rangoon.

The situation was such though that the might of the Japanese forces led to a withdrawal back into India from late February 1942. No.1 Squadron withdrew from the Mingaladon region to Magwe and re-joined the remainder of the Lashio-detachment on the 5th March. On the 7th two Lysanders flew two pilots back to collect two serviceable Hurricanes that had been left there in the face of the Japanese advance, luckily the operation went without any Japanese fighters being in the area and the recovered Hurricanes escorted the Lysanders back to base. By the 12th March No.1 Squadron only had four serviceable aircraft left, so they handed these over to the Burmese Communications Flight, who were undertaking evacuation work and the crews flew back to India aboard a B-17. Once back at Peshawar the unit re-equipped with the Hawker Hurricane while No.4 Squadron was forming there with the Lysander. Its first four machines had arrived on the 16th February 1942 and the unit had not fully worked-up on the type before all four were detached to Kohat to quell the tribal uprising in the frontier region. Based at Miranshah the Lysanders undertook bombing attacks against the tribesmen as they undertook raids across the northwestern plains. The Hur tribe in central India began rioting as well, but this was controlled when a No.4 Squadron detachment was sent to Lyderabad. By late 1942 No.4 Squadron was supporting the 7th Indian Division in the Risalpur area but by this stage more modern types were entering the theatre in larger numbers and as a result Nos.2 and 4 Squadrons IAF and Nos.20 and 28 Squadrons RAF were re-equipped with the Hawker Hurricane.

The Lysander continued to be used in India though, this time as a target tug and for special supply duties along the Burmese Front and for general communications work. For this task a number of Mk IIIs and IIIAs were shipped to India and a few Mk IIIAs were used by both Nos.2 and 4 Squadrons until the very end of hostilities in India.

Air-Sea Rescue

The huge loss of life experienced by RAF pilots who ditched in the Channel during the Battle of Britain made it obvious that a dedicated air-sea rescue service was required instead of expecting the base from which each pilot had flown from to be responsible for their recovery, as had been the case since the outbreak of war. By the end of July 1940 No.11 Group's commander, AVM Keith Park arranged with the Army Co-operation units to allocate twelve Lysanders for searching up to 20 miles off shore for downed crews, but it was

Lysander Mk III T1696 AQ•H of No.276 (ASR) Squadron drops a dinghy pack

not until the 22nd August that these machines were officially put under the control of Fighter Command. The Lysander did not have the room or carrying capacity to use the standard Lindholme gear, but it was not long before a pack comprising four M-type dinghies, distress flares, food and water were packed into a valise and held within a SBC (Small Bomb Container) mounted on the racks under the stub wings. By May 1941 a further six Lysanders had been added to the ASR units and this allowed the coverage to be extended from the mouth of the Humber to the Isle of Man. By October

A dinghy and survival pack in an Small Bomb Container (SBC) is loaded onto the stub wings of a No.277 (ASR) Squadron Lysander, whilst the pilot looks on (©British Official)

1941 the first of four specialised units were created, with No.275 (ASR) Squadron at RAF Valley, No.276 (ASR) Squadron at RAF Harrowbeer and No.278 (ASR) Squadron at Matlask in October and No.277 (ASR) Squadron at RAF Stapleford Tawney in December.

By this stage these units operated thirty-six Lysanders and such was their coverage and success that they were nicknamed the 'Salvation Navy'. By 1942 there was a distinct shortage of Lysander spares, as the type was no longer in production, so a large quantity had to be shipped from India and the Middle East, but a replacement type was obviously needed. Into this role stepped the Boulton-Paul Defiant (See Airframe Detail No.5 ISBN 978-0-9957773-6-1), as a large number were now surplus due to the adoption of the Bristol Beaufighter (see Airframe Album No.14 ISBN 978-0-9957773-8-5) in the nightfighter role. By the end of 1942 just four Lysanders remained with the ASR squadrons and by early 1943 the type was withdrawn, marking the end of another stage in the Lysander's career.

ASR Flights

The initial rather confusing system authorised on the 14th May 1941 saw each flight allocated two Lysanders but in June 1941 this was raised to two plus one in reserve, allocated to the following establishments:
- 10 Group at RAF Exeter, Pembrey, Portreath and Warmwell
- 11 Group at RAF Kenley, Manston, Martlesham Heath and Tangmere
- 12 Group at RAF Coltishall

These were eventually broken down into the following unnumbered flights:
- **10 Group**
1. Formed at RAF Warmwell 14th May 1941, became A Flight of No.276 (ASR) Squadron 21st October 1941
2. Formed at RAF Roborough 14th May 1941, absorbed into No.276 (ASR) Squadron 21st October 1941
3. Formed at RAF Pembrey 14th May 1941, to RAF Fairwood Common 4th July 1941, became D Flight of No.276 (ASR) Squadron 21st October 1941
4. Formed at RAF Portreath 18th July 1941, became HQ and B Flight No.276 (ASR) Squadron at RAF Harrowbeer on the 21st October 1941, while C Flight was formed on the 11th November 1941 at RAF Portreath
- **11 Group**
5. Formed 14th May 1941 at RAF Martlesham Heath attached to No.613 Squadron, became A Flight No.277 (ASR) Squadron 22nd December 1941
6. Formed 18th July 1941 at RAF Hawkinge, became B Flight No.277 (ASR) Squadron 22nd December 1941
7. Formed 14th May 1941 at RAF Shoreham, moved to RAF Freiston 9th July 1941, back to RAF Shoreham 15th October 1941, became C Flight No.277 (ASR) Squadron 22nd December 1941
8. Formed in 1941 at RAF Merston, moved to RAF Westhampnett 15th November 1941, to RAF Shoreham 30th November 1941 and absorbed into the Station Flight
- **12 Group**
9. Formed July 1941 at RAF Matlask and gained two Lysanders in August, became A Flight No.278 (ASR) Squadron 1st October 1941 – *Note: this unit is often referred to (probably unofficially) as No.3 ASR Flight*
10. Formed 18th July 1941 at RAF Coltishall, became part of No.278 (ASR) Squadron 1st October 1941

From these groups and flights came Nos. 275, 276, 277 and 278 (ASR) Squadrons, for more details see Appendix IV.

Towing a Target

The slow speed characteristics made the Lysander an ideal target towing aircraft and a great many of those built both in the UK and Canada ended up in this role. The Lysander was both converted and built anew for the target towing role, with the TT Mk I, TT Mk II and TT Mk III all being conversions based upon the basic standard variants, while the TT Mk IIIA was newly built both in the UK and Canada. The rear cockpit was stripped of all unnecessary equipment including the gun and an electrically operated three-drum winch was mounted on the roll-over structure between pilot and the now, winch operator. The drum allowed a drogue target to be towed at a distance of between 1,000 to 1,250ft astern and a pair of doors in the floor allowed the operator to play out both the cable and drogues from inside the aircraft whilst it was in flight. A tubular structure below and slightly forward of the hatch included a pulley so that the cable was turned through 90° to ensure it did not foul the doors or the tailwheel, additional cables were also attached from the tips of the tailplanes to the top of the rudder to ensure the cable did not foul them either. The ability to bring the drogue back into the aircraft was of benefit as it maximised firing times over the ranges in that it could be brought back into the aircraft, detached and rolled up to be dropped

Lysander Mk II V9547 of No.277 (ASR) Squadron runs up prior to another sortie

Lysander TT Mk IIIA V9905 was the penultimate one to leave the Westland production line and is seen here at Yeovil in December 1941 (©Air Ministry)

Lysander T Mk III T1444, G•5 operated by No.5 Air Observers School based at Jurby on the Isle of Man, seen here flying just off the Manx coast

during a slow pass of the landing field, thus allowing a new drogue to be attached and towing to continue.

A number of target towing flights were created by the RAF, as follows:

- No.1 Group (TT) Flight – Formed 18th September 1941 at RAF Goxhill, moved to RAF Binbrook 10th November 1941 and redesignated No.1481 (TT) Flight on the 14th November 1941
- No.2 Group (TT) Flight – Reformed on the 30th September 1941 at RAF West Raynham and later redesignated No.1482 (TT) Flight
- No.3 Group (TT) Flight – Formed at RAF Marham 14th February 1940 (previously had been a detachment from No.98 Squadron offering target towing since October 1939) and redesignated No.1483 (TT) Flight on the 18th November 1941
- No.4 Group (TT) Flight – Formed at RAF Driffield in February 1940 from RAF Linton-on-Ouse Station Flight, operated from RAF Cottam from 29th September to 24th October 1940 due to heavy bombing raid on Driffield. Unit was amalgamated with No.5 Group (TT) Flight until 2nd April 1941 (although not using the Lysander), back to Cottam from 12th May 1941 to 28th September 1941 and redesignated No.1483 (TT) Flight on the 14th November 1941
- No.5 Group (TT) Flight – Formed 14th February 1940 at RAF Driffield (had previously operated from Finningley since October 1939 offering TT duties for 5 Group Hampden squadrons), amalgamated with No.4 Group (TT) Flight on the 2nd April 1941 and moved to RAF Coningsby, detachment to RAF Scampton 19th August to 2nd October 1941. Disbanded on the 2nd October 1941 (part used to form No.1485 (TT) Flight).
- No.6 Group (TT) Flight – Formed at RAF Abingdon 27th December 1939, task taken by RAF Bicester Station Flight from 6th March 1940 and ended February 1941 when the OTUs took on the target-towing role.
- No.9 Group (TT) Flight – Formed at RAF Valley 16th July 1941 and redesignated No.1486 (TT) Flight on the 8th December 1941
- No.10 Group (TT) Flight – Formed at RAF Warmwell 16th July 1941, to RAF Filton October 1941, back to RAF Warmwell November 1941, redesignated No.1487 (TT) Flight on the 8th December 1941
- No.11 Group (TT) Flight – Formed at RAF Shoreham 16th July 1941, to RAF Ford October 1941, back to RAF Shoreham 25th October 1941, redesignated No.1488 (TT) Flight on the 8th December 1941
- No.12 Group (TT) Flight – Formed at RAF Coltishall 16th July 1941, to RAF Sutton Bridge 2nd October 1941, to RAF Matlask 13th April 1942, redesignated No.1489 (TT) Flight on the 8th December 1941
- No.13 Group (TT) Flight – Formed at RAF Acklington 16th July 1941, redesignated No.1490 (TT) Flight on the 8th December 1941
- No.14 Group (TT) Flight – Formed at RAF Inverness/Longman October 1941, redesignated No.1491 (TT) Flight on the 8th December 1941
- No.82 Group (TT) Flight – Formed at RAF Ballyhalbert 2nd November 1941, redesignated No.1480 (TT) Flight on the 24th November 1941
- No.1481 (TT) Flight – Formed from No.1 Group (TT) Flight 14th November 1941 at RAF Binbrook redesignated No.1481 Target Towing & Gunnery Flight in January 1942, Lysanders replaced by Miles Martinets in February 1943
- No.1482 (TT) Flight – Formed from No.2 Group (TT) Flight November 1941 at RAF West Raynham, redesignated No.1482 Target Towing & Gunnery Flight in January 1942, redesignated No.1482 (Bomber) Gunnery Flight 2nd May 1942, Lysanders replaced by Miles Martinets from January 1943
- No.1483 (TT) Flight – Formed from No.3 Group (TT) Flight 18th November 1941 at RAF Newmarket, redesignated No.1483 Target Towing & Gunnery Flight 7th February 1942, redesignated No.1483 (Bomber) Gunnery Flight in July 1942, Lysanders replaced by Miles Martin from July 1943
- No.1484 (TT) Flight – Formed from No.4 Group (TT) Flight 14th November 1941 at RAF Driffield, redesignated No.1484 Target Towing & Gunnery Flight in 1942, redesignated No.1484 (Bomber) Gunnery Flight in May 1942, Lysanders had been replaced by February 1943
- No.1485 (TT) Flight – Formed 30th October 1941 at RAF Coningsby, absorbed from No.5 Group (TT) Flight and redesignated No.1485 Target Towing & Gunnery Flight in April 1942, detachment at RAF Coningsby from 1st August 1942 to 8th March 1943, to RAF Fulbeck 27th October 1942, designated No.1485 (Bomber) Gunnery Flight in February 1943, Lysanders replaced by Miles Martinets by August 1943
- No.1486 (TT) Flight – Formed from No.9 Group (TT) Flight 30th October 1941 at RAF Valley, redesignated No.1486 (Fighter) Gunnery Flight 22nd April 1942, to RAF Llanbedr 8th July 1943 and disbanded to form part of No.12 Armament Practice Camp on the 18th October 1943
- No.1487 (TT) Flight – Formed from No.10 Group (TT) Flight 30th October 1941 at RAF Warmwell, detachments to RAF Portreath Jan-June 1942, RAF Fairwood Common 4th April 1943 to 13th September 1943, RAF Exeter 2nd October 1942 to August 1943 and RAF Colerne from 1st March to 31st July 1943, redesignated No.1487 (Fighter) Gunnery Flight 22nd April 1942, to RAF Fairwood Common 13th September 1943 and disbanded to form part of No.11 Armament Practice Camp on the 18th October 1943
- No.1488 (TT) Flight – Formed from No.11 Group (TT) Flight 1st December 1941 at RAF Shoreham, to RAF Rochford 9th February 1943, No.1 Flight to RAF Shoreham and No.2 Flight to RAF Rochford 22nd April 1942, redesignated No.1488 (Fighter) Gunnery Flight 22nd April 1942, to RAF Martlesham Heath 7th June 1942 with detachments to RAF Ipswich 7th October 1942 and RAF Ford from 1st February 1943, to RAF Southend 17th August 1943 and disbanded to form part of No.17 Armament Practice Camp on the 18th October 1943
- No.1489 (TT) Flight – Formed from No.12 Group (TT) Flight 8th December 1941 at RAF Coltishall, redesignated No.1489 (Fighter) Gunnery Flight 22nd April 1942, detachments to RAF East Fortune from 12th September 1943, RAF High Ercall December 1942 to June 1943, RAF Kirton-in-Lindsey December 1942 to April 1943 and RAF Ludham December 1942-1943, to RAF Matlask 13th April 192, to RAF Hutton Cranswick to work with No.1495 Flight from

2nd June 1943, disbanded to form part of No.16 Armament Practice Camp on the 18th October 1943
- No.1490 (TT) Flight – Formed from No.13 Group (TT) Flight 8th December 1941 at RAF Acklington, redesignated No.1490 (Fighter) Gunnery Flight 22nd April 1942, re-equipped with Miles Masters and Martinets in 1942, although Lysanders were still on strength in February 1943
- No.1491 (TT) Flight – Formed from No.14 Group (TT) Flight 8th December 1941 at RAF Inverness, to RAF Tain 26th December 1941, redesignated No.1491 (Fighter) Gunnery Flight 22nd April 1942, to RAF Skaebrae 15th November 1942, to RAF Castletown 16th August 1942, to RAF Peterhead October 1943 and disbanded to form part of No.15 Armament Practice Camp on the 18th October 1943
- No.1492 (TT) Flight – Formed from No.70 Group (TT) Flight 18th October 1941 at RAF Weston Zoyland, redesignated No.1492 (Fighter) Gunnery Flight 22nd April 1942, started to re-equip with the Miles Master and Martinet throughout 1942 and no Lysanders remained on strength by early 1943
- No.1493 (TT) Flight – Formed from No.83 Group (TT) Flight 31st October 1941 at RAF Ballyhalbert, to RAF Newtownards 6th January 1943 with detachments to RAF Eglington March to 23rd August 1942, Ballyhalbert 6th April 1942 to 26th January 1943 and Kirkistown 6th April to November 1942, re-designated No.1493 (Fighter) Gunnery Flight 22nd April 1942, to RAF Ballyhalbert 26th January 1943, to RAF Eastchurch 14th April 1943 with detachments to Westhampnett 9th June to 1st July 1943, to RAF Detling 26th July 1943 under No.11 Group control, to RAF Gravesend 7th October 1943 and disbanded to form part of No.18 Armament Practice Camp on the 18th October 1943
- No.1494 (TT) Flight – Formed 18th December 1941 at RAF Long Kesh, to RAF Sydenham 13th April 1942, to RAF Ballyhalbert 16th April 1943, to RAF North Weald 5th March 1945, Miles Masters added in May 1945 and unit disbanded on the 30th June 1945
- No.1495 (TT) Flight – Formed 8th August 1942 at RAF Sawbridgeworth, to RAF Hutton Cranswick 10th July 1943 under No.12 Group control and disbanded to form part of No.16 Armament Practice Camp on the 14th November 1943
- No.1496 (TT) Flight – Was to have formed on the 11th November 1942 at RAF Hawarden, but Lysanders allocated to Nos.41 and 42 OTU instead
- No.1497 (TT) Flight – Formed 8th March 1943 at RAF Macmerry, to RAF Ayr 22nd June 1943, to RAF Shoreham 3rd July 1943 under No.11 Group control and disbanded to form part of No.17 Armament Practice Camp on the 18th October 1943
- No.1498 (TT) Flight – Formed 8th March

K6127 as the P.12 Wendover ani-invasion prototype in flight, with the 'tandem wing' and mock-up gun turret clearly visible from this angle

Another view of K6127 as the P.12 mock-up in flight, regardless of the modifications, K6127 would be reverted to standard configuration after the trials

This image from A&AEE Boscombe Down in late 1941 confirms the fitment of a functional FN20 turret, as the gun barrels can be seen projecting out the back (©Crown Copyright/A&AEE)

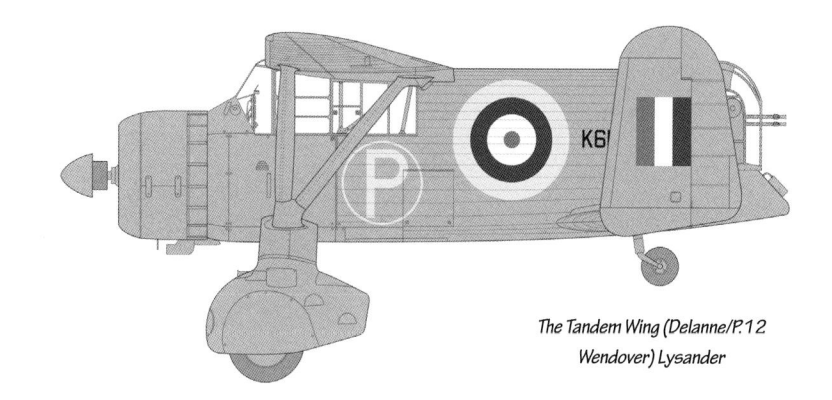

The Tandem Wing (Delanne/P.12 Wendover) Lysander

1943 at RAF Hurn, to RAF Colerne 14th August 1943, to RAF Fairwood Common 12th September 1943 and disbanded to form part of No.11 Armament Practice Camp on the 18th October 1943
- No.1500 (TT) Flight – Formed 4th May 1943 at RAF North Front initially with Lysanders, but these were all replaced by Miles Martinets by March 1944

For details of all the target towing units of the RAF see Appendix IV.

Trials & Tribulations

The Lysanders performance was such that it was used for a number of unusual experiments, including the following:

• The Tandem Wing (Delanne/P.12 Wendover) Lysander

This was an anti-invasion design intended for beach-strafing and the first Lysander prototype K6127 (with Perseus engine and cowlings of the Mk II) was fitted with an entirely new rear fuselage that was to house a gun turret. This new rear fuselage sported a wide tandem wing (not tailplanes as many will assume, it was classified as a 'wing') with twin end fin and rudder units. The initial design was created by Westlands in early 1940, and although they undertook the conversion of the rear fuselage, the new tail unit was built by Harrington's, a coach-builders based in Hove. The first flight was undertaken on the

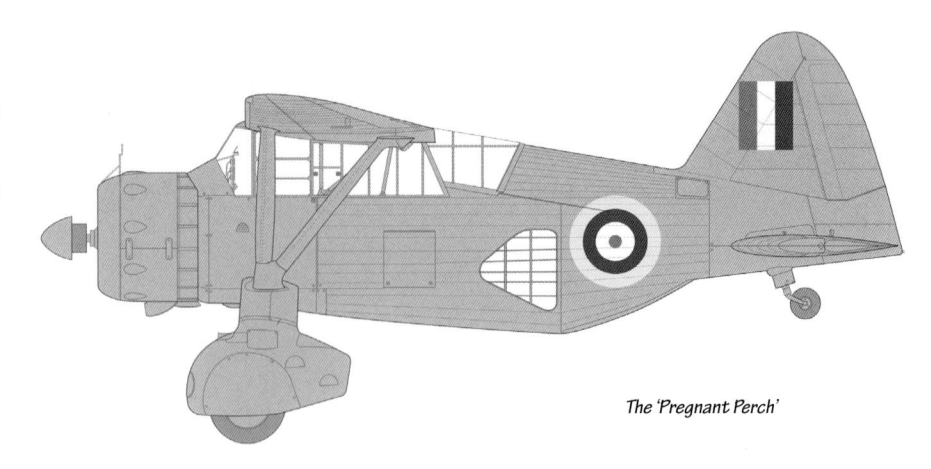

The 'Pregnant Perch'

L4637 the first production Mk I was converted to become an aerodynamic test airframe for another anti-invasion beach strafer, nicknamed the 'Pregnant Perch', it came to grief on in August 1940 after suffering engine failure and the project was abandoned

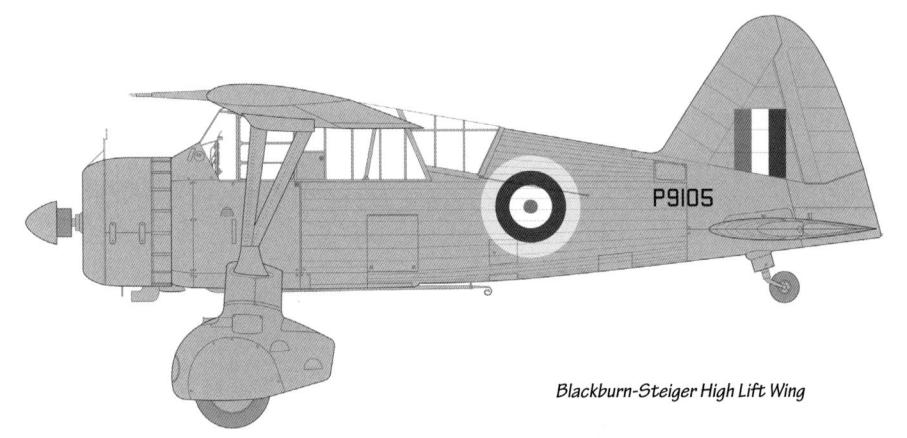

Blackburn-Steiger High Lift Wing

The Blackburn-Steiger high lift wing seen here fitted to P9105 was only ever intended for research purposes, it was never intended for a practical production application to the Lysander

27th July 1941 and Harold Penrose felt that although the rudders seemed less effective and the type exhibited a considerable move aft in the CofG (the fuselage had been shortened to 25ft 9in), it proved even more stable than a standard Lysander. In this form K6127 arrived at A&AEE Boscombe Down until October 1941, by which time the immediate threat of invasion had greatly diminished and the type was never put into production (the A&AEE report actually states that the type was purely an experiment to determine if a rear turret can be added to an existing type without "destroying the general flying characteristics", so the Air Ministry obviously never had any intention of putting the P.12 into production). Although most sources will state that the type only ever had a mock-up turret with ballast weights installed (often stating it was a Boulton-Paul unit, whilst the A&AEE report clearly states it was an 'FN-type'), images of it at A&AEE in late 1941 confirm that it was fitted with a fully functioning Fraser-Nash FN20 turret complete with four 0.303in guns. From surviving test documents however, it is not possible to state that the turret undertook firing, either on the ground or in the air. Official support for the type was withdrawn before the full handling report was ever submitted, so the airframe was then handed over to RAE Farnborough, although its subsequent use there is unknown, before it was finally struck off charge on the 13th June 1944.

• **The 'Pregnant Perch'**

This was another anti-invasion experiment, where L4673 was fitted with a ventral gun position intended for beach-strafing. The nickname came about due to the distended belly of the prototype, but the whole project was cancelled when L4673 suffered a forced landing, uphill under high tension cables, due to an engine failure with George Snarey at the controls and was written off.

• **Blackburn-Steiger High Lift Wing**

Lysander Mk II P9105 was fitted with a parallel-chord wing of reduced span built by Blackburns and designed by H.J. Steiger, purely for research purposes. The wing featured full-span slats and flaps and lateral control was achieved with wing tip spoilers. It was built around a single spar, was swept forward by 9° and only had a span of 38 feet. Once the experiments were concluded, P9105 was converted back to a production Mk II and issued to No.513 Squadron.

• **Undercarriage Experiments**

The prototype Lysander K6127 was used to test two different undercarriage systems designed to cope with operations from difficult landing strips. In one set of these trials it was fitted with castoring main wheels designed by Dowty, which allowed it to land facing into wind on an out-of-wind airstrip. Another trial saw the fitment of caterpillar tracks instead of traditional pneumatic tyres. None of these undercarriage types were ever adopted for service.

• **Retractable Undercarriage**

Westlands submitted patent GB526946 in early 1939 for two styles of retractable undercarriage for the Lysander. The first one had a sesquiplane design with the smaller stub wings located at the bottom of the fuselage and the wing support struts therefore set further outboard. The undercarriage legs (set vertically at the mid-point of the stub wing) retracted inboard to stow inside the fuselage in a recess within the fuel tank.

• **Cannon-armed**

Before it became the P.12, the Lysander prototype (K6127, with Mk II Perseus engine and cowling) was used for armament trials and fitted with two Oerlikon 20mm cannon, one above each wheel fairing, during July 1940. The guns fired just clear of the propeller arc and it was officially sanctioned for potential use against invasion barges. Most published sources to date have stated that this installation was not proceeded with, however images have come to light recently that confirm that other production airframes were fitted with 20mm cannon in this manner. It is likely that a limited number were thus modified and issued to squadron/s in the mid-1940 period, but as the threat of invasion diminished, they were most likely all converted back to standard configuration.

This well-known shot shows K6127 with the Dowty castoring main wheels attached to the standard undercarriage beam

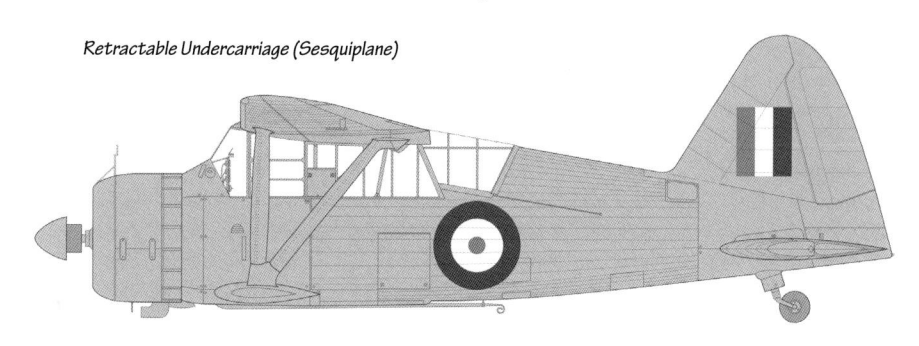

Retractable Undercarriage (Sesquiplane)

The second option was like a standard Lysander, but with the bottom section of the undercarriage legs and spats removed and retractable undercarriage legs/wheels that folded back to lay within recesses in each side of the lower fuselage (an alternative would have had them retracting into the underside of the fuselage).

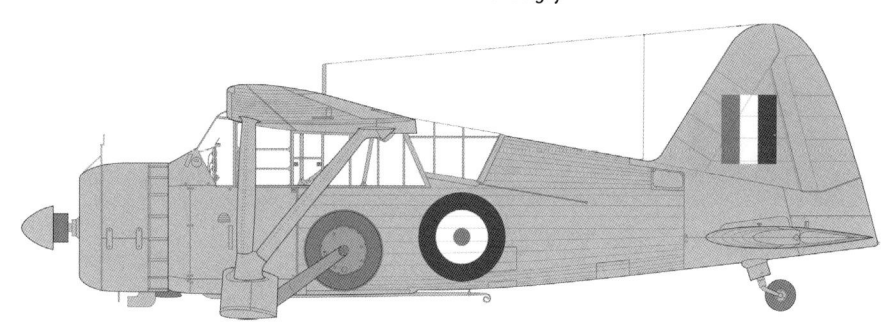

K6127 seen fitted with 20mm Hispano cannon in another anti-invasion beach-strafing project that came to naught

Four-gun Turret

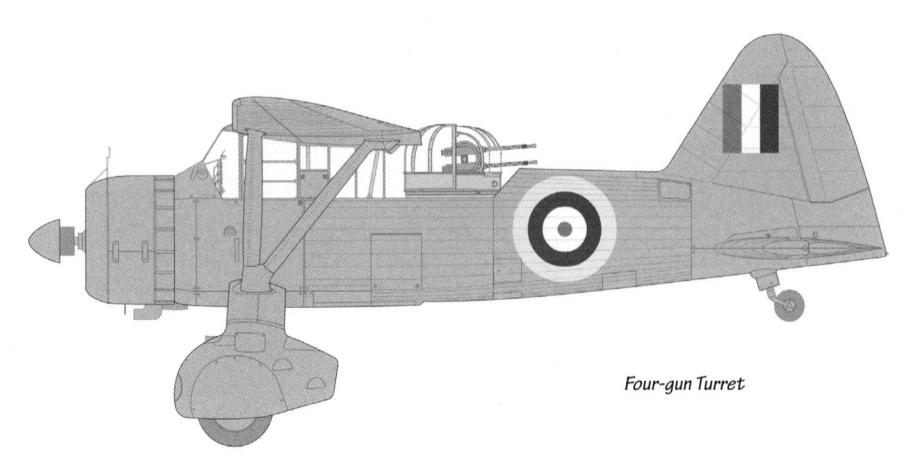

- **Four-gun Turret**

This experiment saw the fitment of a Boulton-Paul Type A, Mk III four-gun power-operated turret immediately aft of the wing, however because the wing seriously restricted the field of fire, the project never got any further than the mock-up stage in Mk II P1723.

- **Air Brakes**

A single Lysander Mk II (R9126) was fitted with a hydraulically operated bench-type air brake below each wing, these were 8ft long and 8in wide and operation of the hydraulics was via a battery and electric motor in the fuselage. It is most likely they were installed simply as

A front view of the bench type air brakes tested on a Lysander

an aerodynamic experiment rather that with any particular operational requirement in mind, although many sources state that this was yet another anti-invasion experiment. R9126 was at A&AEE Boscombe Down from September 1940 and flight testing proved that 260mph could not be exceeded in the dive, but the change in trim was so violent as to be totally unacceptable. The aircraft was returned to the manufacturer after the trials and it is assumed was returned to production Mk II standard and passed into service.

- **Enlarged Tail**

Mk III T1571 went to A&AEE Boscombe Down in June 1941 fitted with a tailplane of increased span, elevators with enlarged horn balances and larger servo tabs on the ailerons. Although the modifications made the controls much lighter, the elevators tended to overbalance and this was considered unsafe, so the installation was never adopted for production.

- **Target Tug**

Although the Lysander was modified as a target tug and put into limited production in the form, the first one to carry a winch was V9815 in February 1943. This machine was at A&AEE Boscombe Down and was fitted with the basic Type E winch on the starboard fuselage side, this winch could not pull in a drogue and cable, just the cable, so obviously it was intended to use a cable cutter.

- **Porton Down**

Five Lysanders were operated by the Special Duty Flight at A&AEE Boscombe Down for various trials at Porton Down. L4737 and L4738 arrived in October 1939, with the latter used for development of 'chemical apparatus' (e.g. gas, smoke curtains etc.). L4682 and L4691 joined in February 1940, although L4682 was severely damaged after an engine failure in March 1941 and R2613 arrived in April 1941 and remained in use until the end of 1943. Two TT Mk IIIs, T1428 and T1501, were also operated, although both were eventually lost due to heavy landings.

Production

- **Westland P.8 Lysander prototypes to Specification A.39/34**
– K6127 (first flew 15th June 1936) and K6128 (first flew 11th December 1936)
- **Westland Lysander Mk I to Specification A.36/36, 169 aircraft built**
– L4673-L4738, P1665-P1699, R2572, R2575-R2600, R2612-R2652 (with R2650 to Royal Egyptian Air Force)
- **Westland Lysander Mk II, 442 aircraft**
– L4739-L4816, L6847-L6888, N1200-N1227, N1240-N1276, N1289-N1320, P1711-P1745, P9051-P9080, P9095-P9140, P9176-P9199, R1987-R2010, R2025-R2047 plus 3106-3136 to Turkish Air Force. 61-66 to Irish Air Corps and '01' to Armée de l'Air
- **Westland Lysander Mk III, 100 aircraft built**
– R8991-R9030, R9056-R9079 and R9100-R9135. Finland received R8991 to R8999 and R9000 was supplied to Egypt.
- **Westland Lysander Mk III, 250 aircraft built**
– T1422-T1470, T1501-T1535, T1548-T1590, T1610-T1655, T1670-T1709, T1735-T1771
- **Westland Lysander Mk III, seventeen aircraft built**
– W6939-W6945 & W6951-W6960 plus a further 483 aircraft between W6675 and W6938 and W6961 and W7241 were all cancelled
- **Westland Lysander Mk IIIA, 347 aircraft built**
– V9280-V9329, V9347-V9386, V9401-V9450, V9472-V9521, V9538-V9557, V9570-V9619, V9642-V9681 & V9704-V9750. The USAAF received V9506, V9583 and V9741, V9614 was supplied to Free French forces and V9309, V9321, V9363, V9439, V9555, V9594, V9705 & V9729 were supplied to Portugal
- **Westland Lysander TT Mk IIIAs, 100 aircraft built**
– V9751-V9753, V9775-V9824, V9844-V9868 & V9885-V9906

Production (Licence)

Lysander Mk II, 75 built
– 416 to 490 (438, 439 & 440 became DG445, DG446 & DG447 respectively)

Lysander Mk III, 150 built
– 2305-2454

Conversions

- Westland Lysander TT Mk I, fourteen aircraft converted from Mk Is – R2572, R2575, R2578, R2581, R2587, R2588, R2589, R2591, R2593, R2594, R2597, R2598, R2632 & R2638
- Westland Lysander TT Mk II, five aircraft converted from Mk IIs – L6867, N1289, N1320, R9099 & R1998

Mk IIIA V9815 in flight in February 1943 being used as a target tug at A&AEE Boscombe Down (©A&AEE/Crown Copyright)

- Westland Lysander TT Mk III, seven aircraft converted from Mk Is – P1666, P1668, P1680, P1681, P1683, R2651 & R2652 plus sixteen aircraft converted from Mk IIs – N1289, N1320(*), P1715, P9109, P9110, P9111, P9113, P9114, P9115, P9117, P9123, P9125, P9126, P9128, P9130, & P9133
  *N1320 was converted to a TT Mk II, then a TT Mk III
- Westland Lysander TT Mk IIIs, twenty-eight converted from Mk IIIs – T1445, T1450, T1453, T1456, T1458, T1461, T1532, T1534, T1571, T1583, T161, T1623, T1626, T1633, T1642. T1674-T1679, T1688, T1692, T1699, T1746, T1750, T1752 and T1763 plus T1570 was on Admiralty charge as a TT Mk III
- Westland Lysander TT Mk IIIAs, four aircraft converted from Mk IIIAs – V9372, V9579, V9679 & V9726

Total Production (excluding prototypes) – 1,650

Foreign Service

The Lysander was built in Canada and supplied to a number of nations, so what follows therefore is a list of all such countries that operated the type.

Canada

Production of the Lysander was undertaken in Canada under licence by the National Steel Car Corporation Ltd, based at Hamilton, Ontario. British-built Mk II R2047 was supplied as a pattern in January 1940 and from this seventy-five Mk IIs and one-hundred and fifty Mk IIIs (2305-2454) were built. A small number were shipped to England in 1940 for use by Canadian squadrons of the RAF, but the bulk were retained in Canada for service with the RCAF as communications and target-towing duties. The very first Canadian-built Lysander, '416', was delivered on the 7th September 1939 and when Canada declared war on Germany on the 10th the initial order for Lysanders was raised to seventy-five (416 to 490). The only modifications made to these first Canadian-built examples was to improve the canopy heater and sealing, as the type was not best suited to the very cold Canadian climate.

The first RCAF unit to operate the type was No.110 (Army Co-operation) Squadron and it was also the first RCAF unit to be ordered into service abroad. It left Halifax, Nova Scotia on the 16th February 1940, leaving its aircraft behind, and arrived in Liverpool on the 26th. On the 27th February the unit arrived at Old Sarum and was issued with twelve Lysanders. Twelve Canadian-built machines were crated at Malton for supply to the RAF to replace those issued to No.110 (Army Co-operation) Squadron, but in the end only six (Nos. 434 and 436 to 440) actually reached the UK and these

Lysander Mk IIs 418, 419 and 420 of No 110 (Army co-operation) Squadron seen in initial overall aluminium scheme and in typical Canada winter surroundings (©Library and Archives Canada)

Both aluminium and camouflaged Lysanders of No 110 (Army Co-Operation) Squadron at RCAF station Ottawa, 30th January 1940 (©Library and Archives Canada)

The Canadian president, the Rt Hon W. L. Mackenzie King (centre) inspects Lysanders of No 110 (Army Co-operation) Squadron (©Library and Archives Canada)

Lysander TT Mk III 1557 being refuelled at Patricia Bay on the 14th February 1944 (©Library and Archives Canada)

were allocated serial numbers DG442 to DG447. On the 9th June 1940 No.110 (Army Co-operation) Squadron was moved to RAF Odiham and was initially used by the RAF as a specialist Lysander trials unit (having K6127 with 20mm cannon installed on strength for a time). The unit undertook anti-invasion patrols and dive bombing practice and on the 23rd August 1940 was the first unit to receive the Mk III when R9001 to R9009 were delivered, followed by more throughout 1940. By April 1941 however the unit had relinquished the Lysander (all bar four probably kept for communication duties) and flew the Curtiss Tomahawk. The second RCAF squadron to use the Lysander, No.111 (Thunderbirds) Squadron was mobilised at Rockcliffe on the 10th September 1939. Shortly afterwards the unit moved to Patricia Bay, where they were later joined by four Lysanders and these remained with the unit until January 1941. In December 1939 No.118 Squadron received Lysanders at its base at Saint John, but these had gone by August 1940 when the squadron was re-designated as a fighter squadron. This never happened though and No.118 Squadron disbanded in late September 1940.

The next unit to receive the Lysander was No.112 (City of Winnipeg) Squadron, having been mobilised on the 10th September 1939 and then moving to Rockcliffe to await service overseas. The first Lysanders were delivered in March 1940, but by the time the unit reached the UK France had already fallen and so it was left doing training duties for the remainder of that year. By early 1941 the unit was redesignated as No.2 (Fighter) Squadron, RCAF and based at RAF Digby, where it would ultimately become No.402 (Canadian) Squadron. Two brand new squadrons were created to operate the Lysander in 1941, these being No.400 (City of Toronto) Squadron, which formed at RAF Odiham on the 1st March 1941, but it was in fact No.110 (Army Co-operation) Squadron RCAF renumbered and it operated the Lysander alongside the Curtiss Tomahawk until December 1941. The second new unit was No.414 (Sarnia Imperials) Squadron at Croydon on the 12th August 1941. It operated the Lysander alongside the Tomahawk until both were replaced by the Mustang Mk I (See Airframe & Miniature No.6 ISBN 978-0-9575866-1-1) in June 1942. All the other RCAF units formed with the Lysander remained in Canada, these were Nos.121, 122 and 123 Squadron, with the latter operating as the School or Army Co operation at Rockcliffe until June 1943 and the others using the Lysander until March 1944.

The very last RCAF Lysander was not struck off charge until the 13th December 1946 with a large number being sold on the civil market in the late 1940s and this all helped to swell the number of Lysanders that survive to this day.

Lysander Mk II 429 prepares for a gunnery flight, 16th January 1940, a side caption notes it was '15° below'! (Library and Achive of Canada)

Egypt

The Egyptian government signed a contract for the supply of nineteen Lysander Mk Is for use by the Royal Egyptian Air Force. These machines were delivered between the 13th October and 15th December 1938 at a cost of £5,600 each and received the serial numbers of Y500 to Y517. They also received a single ex-Air Ministry Mk I (R2650), which became Y518 and a twentieth airframe, which was a Mk III (R9000), although it does not seem to have received a serial number in Egyptian service. They were all operated by No.1 Squadron, REAF, based at Almaza from 1940 to 1943. This unit was initially designated a General Purpose squadron, but after training

The last Mk I from Egypt's initial order, Y517, is seen here shortly after completion at Westland's Yeovil factory

New Lysander Mk Is of No.1 (Army Co-operation) Squadron REAF line up for inspection by the Director of the Air Force Brigadier Ali Islam Bey

with No.208 (Army Co-operation) Squadron who were also based at Almaza, it became operational at the end of January 1939 (commanded by Sqn Ldr S. Mahmud) as an Army Co-operation squadron. The type remained in service with the squadron until 1943, after which date the type was relegated to target-towing and searchlight co-operation duties with the same unit. By 1944 the squadron re-equipped with the Hurricane and the last Lysanders were used in convoy protection exercises, with two retained for hacks into 1945.

That was not the end of the Lysander's operational career with the REAF. As the post-war situation deteriorated and disputes occurred about the frontier of Palestine the REAF retained as many aircraft as they could. As a result, by early 1946 thirteen Lysanders remained on charge, but nine were considered beyond repair and were scrapped between October 1946 and January 1947. The remaining four were subjected to overhaul and returned to airworthiness and were allocated to the REAF Royal Flight, which later became No.3 (Communications) Squadron. In early 1948 two of these Lysanders were converted for the photo-reconnaissance role, just prior to the start of the Arab-Israeli War on the 15th May 1948. The initial phase of the conflict was over by the 11th June, resulting in a truce that would last until the 8th July and it is not known if the small group of REAF Lysanders actually undertook any sorties during this initial stage of the conflict. During the second phase, on the 9th July 1948, Air Cdre Muhammad Abd al-Munaim Miqaati was due to fly from al-Arish to Cairo-Almaza and en route he was intercepted and attacked by an Israeli Avia S-199 flown by American-born Bob Vickman. The Air Commodore, having flown the type as one of the first three in the REAF, knew how the aircraft could quickly drop, so as the rear gunner opened fire he dropped to about 100ft and the Avia, so intent on following his target, just followed, resulting in him being unable to pull out and diving straight into the sea almost alongside the Lysander. This was to be the swansong for the Lysander because by October 1948 No.3 (Communications) Squadron had no Lysanders on strength. Whilst a single example remained on strength at Almaza in a serviceable state as late as January 1950, this was probably one held in preparation for a proposed air museum, which eventually never happened due to the Egyptian 1952 Revolution and even if it did survive the revolt, all of the REAF's earlier aircraft types were destroyed in the Suez campaign in 1956.

Estonia

This country ordered ten Mk Is prior to WWII, but this was cancelled when Soviet forces occupied the Baltic states as part of the Molotov–Ribbentrop Pact from the 16th June 1940. *Modellers should note that although decal sheets are produced that claim to show Estonian examples, these are purely 'what if?'.*

LY-121 of LLv 30 at Pori in June 1941 still in the original RAF camouflage (©SA-Kuva)

LY-120 of 2/LeLv 16 during a visit to Nuroila in June 1942 (©SA-Kuva)

Finland

The story of the supply of Lysanders to this nation is somewhat confused, some sources state that nine were initially supplied from the contract with Estonia that was never fulfilled, while the contract signed on the 8th February 1940 was for the supply of seventeen at a cost of £149,311. Of these, only eleven actually reached Finland and the first nine ex-RAF Mk IIIs (R8991 to R8999, which became LY-114 to LY-122) were sent by sea to Gotenburg in Sweden on the 24th February 1940 and were then assembled at the Götaverken factory, before finally reaching Finland between the 21st March and 3rd May. The remaining eight aircraft were to be flown directly to Finland, however four of them were taken by the RAF and another was destroyed before making the flight to Finland (most likely L4678/LY-123*). Westland's therefore paid back the money (£40,263) paid for the five aircraft that were not supplied. The three remaining outstanding aircraft (L4681/LY-124, L4682/LY-125 and L4703/LY-126) were flown directly from the UK and took off on the first leg of their delivery flight on the 2nd March 1940, but LY-124, flown by Mr A. F. Anderson, had a mechanical problem and was damaged beyond repair during a forced landing in a field on Buoy Island, near Stavanger in Norway. The other two Lysanders flew in company with three Hawker Hurricanes (HU-453, HU-457 and HU-460 that had set out on the same day as the Lysanders, but from Wick) to the next

Flight leader 1st Lt V Härmälä gives a briefing to Sgt O. Kosonen and observer 1st Lt G. Kuhlberg alongside LY-119 of 2/LLv 16 at Viiksjärvi on the 17th February 1942 (©SA-Kuva)

Mechanics take the covers off the propeller of a Lysander prior to a mission at Viiksjärvi in 1942
(©SA-Kuva)

The single example ordered by France prior to the collapse of that country in 1940 and seen here prior to delivery at Westland's Yeovil factory

stop in Oslo. The Lysanders finally reached Säkylä, Finland on the 8th March 1940 still in the company of the Hurricanes.

All of these machines were operated by *Lentilaivue 16* (the 2nd Flight (2./LeLv 16) operating the Lysander), LeLv 14 (TLeLv 14) and LLv 30, with those that remained after the end of the war being used as hacks by various units, including HLeLv 21. Losses include LY-117 and LY-125 shot down 05/08/41 near Värtsilässä and LY-121 shot down 03/09/41 near Tsalkissa.

Note that LY-123 to LY-126 were Mk Is, even though LY-114 to LY-122 were Mk IIIs because the Mk Is were new-builds (from the cancelled Estonian order), while the Mk IIIs were all ex-RAF

France

The Armée de l'Air purchased a single Mk II, which received the identification number '01' prior to the fall of that nation in 1940. It was apparently shipped to France, although some sources state it was wrecked by a French pilot during a test flight at Yeovil, however this was K6127, as proven by period images. Nothing more is known of its use in France, but it is most likely it was either lost to bombing during the initial Nazi German offensive, as no record of its testing or use by a squadron can be found, or was subsequently captured and/or scrapped.

A number of machines were later transferred to Free French forces and used as follows:

Mk II – L4798, L6869, N1204 (Chad Free French Flight)
N1208, N1245, N1259 (*Escadrille Rennes, Groupe Bretagne*), N1300 (*Escadrille Rennes, Groupe Bretagne*), P1708 (*Escadrille Rennes, Groupe Bretagne*), P1713 (*Arras Escadrille, Groupe Artois*), P1735 (*Escadrille Rennes, Groupe Bretagne*), P1736 (*Béthune Escadrille, Groupe Artois*), P1738, P3638, P9059 (*Escadrille Rennes, Groupe Bretagne*), P9078, P9102, P9103 (*Groupe Artois*), P9134 (*Escadrille Rennes, Groupe Bretagne*), P9181 (*Escadrille Rennes, Groupe Bretagne*), P9197 (*Escadrille Rennes, Groupe Bretagne*), R2005 (*Béthune Escadrille*), R2036, R2040, R2043, R2045, R2046 (Free French Flight) & T1753 (*Béthune Escadrille, Groupe Artois*)

Mk IIIA – V9614
The history of the Lysanders used by French forces begins in August 1940 when a number were embarked on HMS Penland bound for French West Africa (AOF – *Afrique Occidentale Française*). where they were used to create *3e* and *4e Escadrilles of Groupe de Bombardment 1* in Egypt. Here they were used by *Escadrille Rennes of Groupe Bretagne* in support of General Leclerc's Saharan forces during the 1941-42 period. The *Groupe Artois* was created on the 1st January 1942 and included *Escadrilles Béthune and Arras*; they received six Lysanders and seven Ansons and were tasked with monitoring the Gulf of Guinea. On the 27th February 1944, these Lysanders was removed from operational service and sent to North Africa to form *Escadrille Spéciale 56* (Special Squadron No. 56) after some necessary modifications.

During the spring of 1943, the *Groupe de Bombardement Bretagne* received its first Lysander, which it used until November before re-equipping with the Martin B-26 Marauder. In 1944, all airworthy Lysanders

An unidentified Lysander of the Free French forces over Chad or the neighbouring countries (via J-J Petit)

L1713 is pushed into the hangar at Pointe Noire AB in 1943, this aircraft belonged to Escadrille Arras, the second flight of Groupe Artois (via J-J Petit)

were grouped in North Africa where in Algiers they were transformed for special missions: the fuel capacity was increased to allow flights of over 900 miles (1,500 km) and three seats were installed for passengers. They were then regrouped into a unit for special missions over central Europe whilst based in Corsica, often alongside RAF Halifax squadrons. Some French pilots who had previously flown the Lysander in the UK as part of No.138 (SD) Squadron joined the Corsican flight to carry out similar missions in the Alps in South-Eastern France around the Vercors region.

Ireland

Six Mk IIs (61-66) were ordered (costing £6,250 each) by the Irish Air Corps on the 8th June 1939 and these were delivered between the 15th June and 11th July 1940. Two (Nos.61 and 66) were converted to target towing in September 1944. All of these machines bar No.63 and three lost in accidents, remained in service until they were struck off charge in November 1946. No.63 remained in service with the IAC the longest, not being struck off charge until April 1947.

Latvia

Like Estonia, Latvia ordered the Mk I (twelve) prior to WWII, but this was cancelled when Soviet forces occupied the Baltic states as part of the Molotov–Ribbentrop Pact from the 16th June 1940.

Portugal

Two Mk Is (L4731 to L4733) were ordered by Portugal from the first production batch, but these were cancelled before any were supplied. Later eight Mk IIIAs (V9309, V9321, V9363, V9439, V9555, V9594, V9705 and V9729) were purchased by Portugal and shipped to Lisbon on the SS Cumberland in September 1943. These machines were part of a large batch that had originally been intended for delivery to No.2 SFTS at Pretoria, South Africa. They were operated by the Portuguese Army Aviation's reconnaissance & liaison squadron BA3, based at Tancos and 361 *Grup de Reconhecimento e Informacao*.

Turkey

Thirty-six Mk IIs were ordered for the Turkish Air Force on the 29th June 1939. These were allocated serial numbers 3101 to 3136, with the first being delivered on the 8th January and the last on the 12th April 1940. They were all operated from the airfield at Yesilkoy, although little more is known about their service life.

Few images seem to exist of the IAC Lysanders, this one shows a line-up of machines, the nearest with its engine running

Factory-fresh 3112, one of thirty-six (3101-3136) delivered to Turkey during Feb-March 1940

USAAF

Three Mk IIIAs (V9506, V9583 & V9741) were allocated to the USAAF, for evaluation purposes. A further twenty-five T Mk IIIAs were transferred to the USAAF in 1942 and were retained for use by USAAF units in the UK until all those that were still airworthy were returned in 1945.

Yugoslavia

This nation ordered two Lysanders, but they were never actually delivered.

Lysander Mk IIIa V9817 assigned to the 3rd Gunnery & Tow Target Flight, 8th Air Force (some sources list this as belonging to the 2025th Gunnery Flight)

Survivors

As we write this, the following complete examples of the Lysander survive around the world:

United Kingdom
- Lysander Mk III, R9125 on static display at the Royal Air Force Museum Hendon, London
- Lysander Mk III, V9552, part of The Shuttleworth Collection, Old Warden, Bedfordshire – Airworthy*

Many sources list as ex-2355, but only a small number of parts from that airframe were used in the restoration

- Lysander Mk IIIA, V9312 with the Aircraft Restoration Company, Imperial War Museum Duxford – Airworthy
- Lysander Mk IIIA, ex-RCAF 1558 marked as V9673 on static display at the Imperial War Museum Duxford, Cambridgeshire

Note: The Lysander Mk III (SD) currently displayed at the Tangmere Military Aviation Museum is a full-size replica built by Gate Guards Ltd in 2015 for use in the film 'Allied'

Canada
- Lysander Mk IIIA, RCAF 2349 statically displayed at the Canadian Museum of Flight, Langley, British Columbia
- Lysander Mk IIIA, RCAF 2363, Canadian Warplane Heritage Museum, Hamilton, Ontario – Airworthy
- Lysander Mk IIIA, RCAF 2365, Vintage Wings of Canada, Gatineau, Quebec – Airworthy
- Lysander Mk IIIA, RCAF 2367* owned by Harry Whereatt, Assinboia, Saskatchewan

Also reported by some as 2366

- Lysander Mk III, RCAF 2374* marked as R9003 statically displayed at the Canadian Aviation and Space Museum, Ottawa

Made from three airframes, the vast majority from V9415

- Lysander Mk IIIA, RCAF 2445 in storage at the Reynolds-Alberta Museum, Wetaskiwin, Alberta
- Lysander Mk IIIA, C/No.Y1399 under restoration in Uxbridge, Ontario (fuselage only. wings are from RCAF 2404)
- Lysanders Mk IIAs 2341, 2344, 2376 and 2381 (fuselage only) are all the late Ed Zalesky's estate and are presumed in storage

USA
- Lysander IIIA, ex-RCAF 2346 marked as N7791 suspended from the roof of the the Steven F. Udvar-Hazy Center, National Air and Space Museum, Chantilly, Virginia
- Lysander IIIA, C/No.1244 marked as V9545 stored at the Fantasy of Flight, Polk City, Florida
- Lysander Mk III, C/No.1176 owned by Bristol Heritage Collection, Nashville, Texas but on display at Pima Air & Space Museum, Tuscon, Arizona (*bare fuselage frame, one wing and parts only*)

India
- Lysander Mk IIIA, ex-RCAF 1589, on static display at the Indian Air Force Museum, Palam, Delhi

Belgium
- Lysander Mk III, ex-RCAF 2442 under restoration to airworthy condition with Sabena Old Timers, Zaventem, Flemish Brabant
- Lysander TT Mk III V9562* on static display at the Royal Museum of the Armed Forces and Military History, Brussels

Used parts from RCAF 2341, 2360 & 2442 in restoration to static condition

- Lysander Mk IIIA, ex-RCAF 2364, owned by Eric Vormezeele, Brasschaat, Belgium but on loan to Broken Wings Museum, Belgium

France
- Lysander Mk IIIA, ex-RCAF 2375 in storage with the *Musée de l'Air et de l'Espace* at Dugny AB, Paris – *Note that this airframe was sent to Portugal for restoration, but rejected because much of the wooden/fabric fuselage is now sheet metal*
- Lysander Mk IIIA, *Musée de l'Air et de l'Espace*, Paris-le-Bourget – Destroyed in hangar fire 17th May 1990
- Lysander Mk IIIA, two incomplete fuselage frames (ex-Canadian Warplane Heritage, Nos.040 and 184) are owned by Philippe Denis, Montpellier, stored for restoration project.

Specifications
Engine:
- Mk I – Bristol Mercury XII 890hp nine-cylinder, air-cooled, supercharged radial engine
- Mk II (inc. Canadian built) – Bristol Perseus XII 905hp nine-cylinder, air-cooled radial, supercharged, sleeve-valve engine
- Mk III – Bristol Mercury XX 870hp nine-cylinder, air-cooled, supercharged radial engine
- Mk III (Canadian built) – Bristol Mercury XXX 870hp nine-cylinder, air-cooled, supercharged radial engine
- Mk IIIA – Bristol Mercury XXX 870hp nine-cylinder, air-cooled, supercharged radial engine
- TT Mk IIIA – Bristol Mercury XXX 870hp nine-cylinder, air-cooled, supercharged radial engine

Propeller:
- All – de Havilland 11ft diameter, two-pitch, three-blade

Span: All – 50ft 0in
Length: All – 30ft 6in
Height: All – 14ft 6in

Undercarriage:
  Main: Dowty internally-sprung wheels with Dunlop pneumatic brakes, 9ft 9in track
  Tail: Fixed Dowty Ecta oleo pneumatic unit (no brakes), castoring through 180°

Weight:
- Mk I   Empty – 4,044lb
            Max. Take-off – 5,920lb
- Mk II   Empty – 4,160lb
            Max. Take-off – 6,030lb
- Mk III   Empty – 4,365lb
            Max. Take-off – 6,330lb (Mk IIIA(SD) 10,000lb)

Fuel & Oil:
- All   Fuel – 95Imp. Gal.
            Oil – 9Imp. Gal.

Performance:
- Mk I – 211mph at sea level, 219mph at 10,000ft & 218mph at 15,000ft
- Mk II – 206mph at sea level, 230mph at 10,000ft & 224mph at 15,000ft
- Mk III – 209mph at sea level, 207mph at 10,000ft & 196mph at 15,000ft

Rate of Climb:
- Mk I – 3.4 min to 5,000ft, 6.9 min to 10,000ft, 11.9 min to 15,000ft and 28.7 min to 20,000ft
- Mk II – 3.3 min to 5,000ft, 6.9 min to 10,000ft, 11.5 min to 15,000ft and 19.7 min to 20,000ft
- Mk III – 4.1 min to 5,000ft, 8 min to 10,000ft, 13.9 min to 15,000ft and 20.5 min to 20,000ft

Service Ceiling:
- Mk I & II – 26,000ft
- Mk III – 21,500ft

Armament:
- Mk I & II: Two fixed Browning 0.303in machine guns mounted in spats above the wheels with 500rpg plus Mk I reflector gunsight in cockpit. One Lewis Mk IIIG or Mk IIIE 0.303in machine gun on a Fairey mounting in the rear cockpit with eight 97-round ammunition drums
- Mk III: Two fixed Browning 0.303in machine guns mounted in spats above the wheels with 500rpg plus Mk I reflector gunsight in cockpit. Two Browning 0.303in machine guns on a mount in the rear cockpit

Note: As the Lysander was built and tested using Imperial measurements, so we have refrained from offering Metric conversions in the above data.

Section 1
Technical Description

Ex-RCAF 2346 marked as N7791 and suspended from the roof of the the Steven F. Udvar-Hazy Center, National Air and Space Museum, Chantilly, Virginia (©S. Willey)

Lysander Mk IIIA, ex-RCAF 1558 marked as V9673 at the Imperial War Museum Duxford, Cambridgeshire (©G. Papadimitriou)

Lysander Mk III marked as R9003 statically displayed at the Canadian Aviation and Space Museum, Ottawa (©G. Papadimitriou)

Lysander Mk IIIA, airworthy with the Canadian Warplane Heritage Museum, Hamilton, Ontario (©G. Papadimitriou)

The only genuine British-built airworthy Lysander is V9312 owner and operated by the Aircraft Restoration Company, Imperial War Museum, Duxford (©ARCo)

The Shuttleworth Collection's airworthy Mk III V9552, based at Old Warden, Bedfordshire (©J Jankovic)

What follows is an extensive selection of images and diagrams that will help you understand the physical nature of the Westland Lysander.

1.0 – Fuselage, Cockpit Interior & Canopy
   1.1 – Forward Fuselage
   1.2 – Cockpit Interior
   1.3 – Canopy
   1.4 – Main & Aft Fuselage

2.0 – Undercarriage
   2.1 – Main
   2.2 – Tailwheel

3.0 – Tail
   3.1 – Vertical Fin & Rudder
   3.2 – Horizontal Tailplane & Elevator

4.0 – Wings & Controls
   4.1 – Wings
   4.2 – Control Surfaces, Flaps & Slats

5.0 – Engine, Cowling & Propeller
   5.1 – Engine
   5.2 – Cowling & Exhaust
   5.3 – Propeller

6.0 – Armament & Ordnance
   6.1 – Fixed Armament
   6.2 – Flexible Armament
   6.3 – Turret Armament
   6.4 – Ordnance

7.0 – Miscellaneous
   7.1 – Camera
   7.2 – Radio & Misc. Electrical
   7.3 – Long range Tank
   7.4 – Parachute Container
   7.5 – ASR Equipment
   7.6 – Target Towing Winch & Glider Towing
   7.7 – Desert Equipment & DDT Spraying

All photographs ©R.A. Franks unless otherwise stated.

1.1 Forward Fuselage

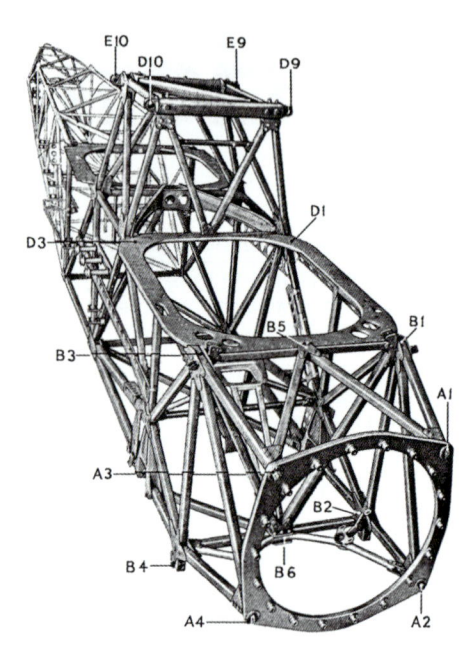

Although this diagram shows the entire fuselage structure, it highlights the forward section with the engine mount (©Crown Copyright)

This close-up from a period image shows the various panels around the engine mount

Here is the same region on the RAF Museum's example with the engine and cowl flap ring in situ – note the hot air vent on the upper decking ahead of the windscreen (©J. Jankovic)

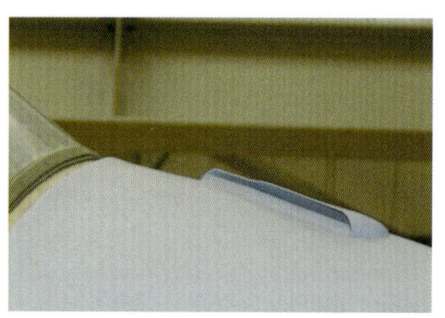

Situated on the lower starboard side, just aft of the undercarriage leg is this mounting bracket, during the war this was used to mount the message pick-up hook, but it's not fitted to the ARC's airworthy example (©N. Perry)

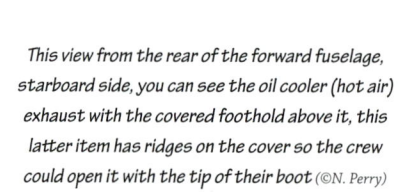

This is the hot air vent on the upper decking ahead of the windscreen on the starboard side of the RAF Museum's example

This view from the rear of the forward fuselage, starboard side, you can see the oil cooler (hot air) exhaust with the covered foothold above it, this latter item has ridges on the cover so the crew could open it with the tip of their boot (©N. Perry)

A nice overall shot of the RAF Museum's example during restoration, you can see the hot air vent ahead of the windscreen on the upper decking and the various removable panels alongside the front and rear cockpits (©J. Jankovic)

This is the underside of the forward fuselage on the RAF Museum's example with the covers removed, so you can see the various ancillaries – the support frame uses the pick-ups for the undercarriage beam (©J. Jankovic)

Airframe Detail No.9 – Lysander

1.2 Cockpit Interior

Although this image is often listed as the instrument panel etc. of a Mk I or Mk II, the lack of any bomb fusing controls in the left-hand side of the main panel plus various other revisions, means that is is most likely the first prototype either in initial form or one of its later incarnations for various trials such as the P.12 etc. (©Air Ministry)

This instrument panel period image does not comply with any of the illustrations from the manuals, the compass set up in the middle of the panel being the main change, the 'Designed & Built by Westland Aircraft Ltd, Yeovil' engraved above it make us think that this is the instrument panel of the second prototype K6128, as it was more akin to production and was used for service trials, so that explains the bomb fusing boxes on the left, but the overall difference in layout elsewhere (©Air Ministry)

Instrument panel in the Mk I viewed from port side (©Crown Copyright)

A. Sub-panel (blind flying panel)
B. Main (instrument) panel
C. Airspeed indicator
D. Artificial horizon
E. Rate of climb indicator
F. Sensitive altimeter
G. Direction indicator
H. Turn and bank indicator
J. Triple pressure brake gauge
K. Time of flight clock
L. Fuel pump pressure gauges
M. Boost pressure gauge
N. Cylinder temperature indicator
P. Engine RPM indicator
Q. Oil pressure gauge
R. Oil temperature
S. Propeller pitch control
T. Carburettor cut-out control
U. Rudder bar adjustment control
V. Cockpit ventilation control
W. Priming pump and control cock
X. Oil heating control
Y. Cockpit heating control
Z. Air intake shutter control
AA. Compass
AB. Engine controls
AC. Cowling gills control

Instrument panel of the Mk II, viewed from the port side (©Crown Copyright)

1. Engine magneto switch No.1
2. Engine magneto switch No.2
3. Triple brake pressure gauge
4. Instrument (blind) flying panel
5. Reflector sight master switch
6. Terminal block
7. Gunsight bead mounting
8. Reflector sight dimmer switch
9. Engine RPM indicator
10. Fuel pressure gauge
11. Boost pressure gauge
12. Cylinder temperature gauge
13. Oil pressure gauge
14. Oil temperature gauge
15. Carburettor priming pump
18. Cover over engine starting push button
19. Starting magneto switch
25. Engine data plate
26. Oil heating control
32. Cockpit heating control
34. Camera sight cover control
35. Instrument panel dimmer switch for starboard lamp
36. Cockpit cooling control
37. Control column
38. Compass
39. Data card holder
40. Control column spade grip
41. Instrument panel dimmer switch for port lamp
42. Rudder bar adjustment control
43. Airscrew pitch control
44. Carburettor cut-out control
45. Bomb fusing tail switch
46. Bomb fusing nose switch
47. Bomb jettison master switch
48. Flap over bomb jettison push button
49. Bomb jettison switch box
50. Master fuel cock control handle
51. Bomb selector switch boxes
52. Bomb container jettison switch box
53. Flap over container jettison push button
54. Brake control lever
55. Gun and camera gun firing button [round style Mk I and II]
56. Firing button safety socket
57. Time of flight clock
58. Brake lever locking catch
59. Reconnaissance flares switch
60. Flares switch arrow to instruction label

Airframe Detail No.9 – Lysander **27**

Instrument panel of the Mk II, viewed from the starboard side – see previous illustration on page 27 for key items not listed here (©Crown Copyright)

16. Carburettor priming pump
17. Compass Lamp dimmer switch
20. Navigation lamps switch
21. Pressure head heating switch
22. Gun heating switch
23. Gunner's attention push button
24. Morse key
27. Morse signalling switch box
28. Emergency flares release control
29. Gill control indicator sleeve
30. Gill control stationery pointer
31. Air intake shutter control
33. Rudder bar pedal and toe strap

Pilot's cockpit port side of the Mk II (©Crown Copyright)

49. Bomb jettison switch box
50. Master fuel cock control handle
51. Bomb selector switch boxes
61. Armour-plated panel port control ring
62. Seat cover
63. Folding armrest
64. Microphone socket
65. Camera sight for oblique photography in port window
66. Flap locking control lever (if fitted)
67. Bomb firing switch
68. Window release tab on port window
69. Throttle control lever
70. Mixture control lever
71. Pilot's control quadrant
72. Friction device handwheel
73. Landing lamp switch
74. Map and computer stowage cases
75. Footstep
76. Camera controller wedge plate
77. Leg straps
78. Fuel content gauge lamp switch
79. Tail adjusting gear handwheel
80. Tail adjusting gear indicator
81. Cushion
82. Shoulder straps

This shot with the covers off on the port side, shows how the internal structure and wiring can be seen from the exterior – this is the RAF Museum's Mk IIIA (©J. Jankovic)

Pilot's cockpit starboard side of the Mk II (©Crown Copyright)

17. Compass Lamp dimmer switch
20. Navigation lamps switch
21. Pressure head heating switch
22. Gun heating switch
23. Gunner's attention push button
24. Morse key
25. Engine data plate
27. Morse signalling switch box
28. Emergency flares release control
29. Gill control indicator sleeve
30. Gill control stationery pointer
33. Rudder bar pedal and toe strap
62. Seat cover
75. Footstep
81. Cushion
82. Shoulder straps
83. Compass data card holder
84. Hinged writing pad holder
85. Writing pad fasteners
86. Pencil stowage
87. Elastic band
88. Wireless remote controller and switch
89. Folding arm rest
90. Armour plate panel starboard control ring
91. Gill control instruction label

This shot with the covers off on the starboard side, shows how the internal structure and wiring can be seen from the exterior – this is Shuttleworth's example, viewed looking forward

28 Airframe Detail No.9 – Lysander

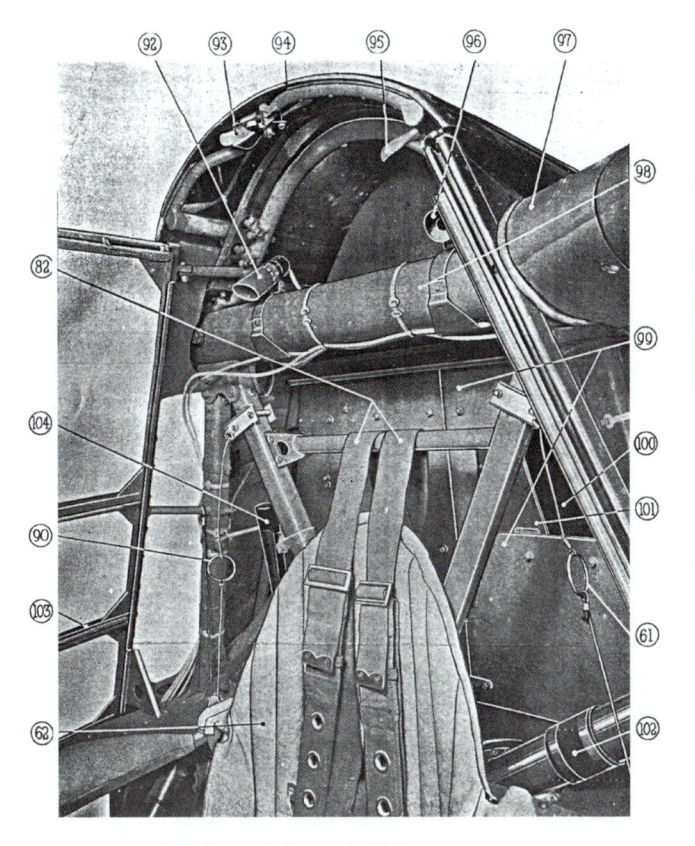

Rear view of pilot's cockpit, Mk II (©Crown Copyright)

61. Armour-plated panel port control ring
82. Shoulder straps
90. Armour plate panel starboard control ring
92. Instrument panel starboard lamp
93. Sliding roof centre catch
94. Sliding roof
95. Sliding roof port hatch
96. Instrument panel port lamp
97. Port wing leading edge
98. centre-section front spar
99. Armour plated bulkhead
100. Aperture in armour plated bulkhead
101. Sliding panel
102. Fuel tank filler neck
103. Starboard sliding window
104. Axe stowage

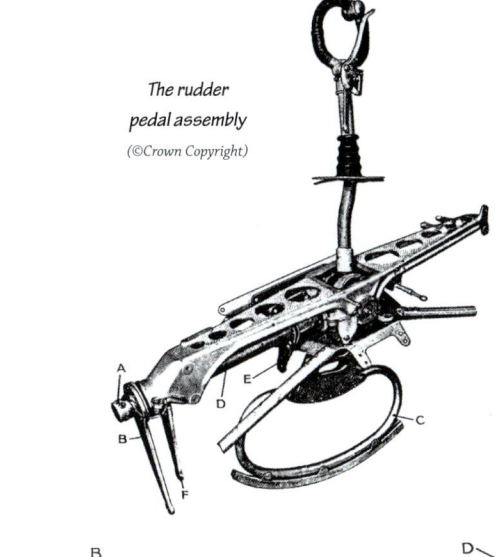

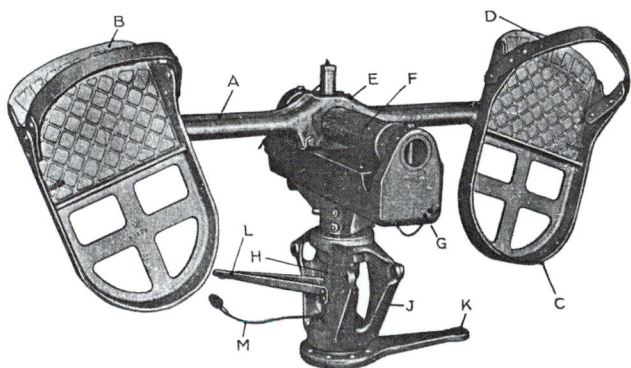

The rudder pedal assembly (©Crown Copyright)

The control column assembly (©Crown Copyright)

The is the main instrument panel of NASM's example, which shows you some of the differences in a Canadian-built machines, plus some modifications made when this aircraft was airworthy. The GM2 reflector gunsight in the tubular frame at the top of the panel is accurate for all wartime machines once the ring and bead was replaced (©NASM)

The main instrument panel of the Mk III and IIIA, viewed from the port side (©Crown Copyright)

9. Control column
11. Brake control and parking lever
12. Gun selector control button [oblong style, used by Mk III series]
13. Triple pressure gauge
15. Rudder bar control knob
21. Carburettor air intake heat control knob
22. Carburettor slow-running cut-out control knob
26. Engine starting push button
27. Master fuel cock control
28. Fuel priming pump
29. Three-way priming cock
30. Fuel pressure gauge
33. Oil heating control knob
34. Oil temperature gauge
36. Engine RPM indicator
37. Dimmer switch for instrument panel floodlamp – port
38. Dimmer switch for instrument panel floodlamp – starboard
41. Compass lamp
43. Cockpit heating control knob
44. Cockpit cooling control knob
46. Landing light switch
48. Gun sight socket
49. Gun sight dimmer switch
50. Gun sight terminal block
51. Ring sight
52. Bomb selector switches
53. Bomb nose fusing switch
54. Bomb tail fusing switch
55. Bomb jettison master switch
56. Flap over bomb jettison push button
57. Bomb container jettison switchbox
58. Flap over container jettison push button
59. Bomb jettison switchbox
65. Camera sight cover control
71. Panel for bomb distributor
72. Flying instrument panel
73. Boost gauge
74. Cylinder temperature gauge
75. Starting magneto switch
77. Morse key
79. Flap over R.3002 push buttons
80. Compass
81. Compass deviation card holder
82. Aperture for clock
83. Main magneto switches
84. Bomb distributor plug
85. Rear occupant's attention push button
86. A.S.I. correction card holder
87. Air temperature gauge
88. Airscrew pitch control knob
89. Computer stowage case
90. Map case

Airframe Detail No.9 – Lysander 29

The main instrument panel of the Mk III and IIIA, viewed from the port side – see previous illustration on page 29 for key items not listed here (©Crown Copyright)

14. Rudder bar footplate
35. Oil temperature gauge
47. Forced landing flare release
76. Navigation and pressure head heating switchbox
78. Identification switchbox

This is the same region in ARC's airworthy Mk IIIA, to give you an idea of the colours etc. (©N. Perry)

Port side of the pilot's cockpit for the Mk III and Mk IIIA (©Crown Copyright)

4. Window release tab
5. Footplate
6. Pilot's seat
8. Armrests
10. Tailplane adjusting handwheel
15. Rudder bar control knob
16. Tailplane position indicator
17. Bomb firing push button
18. Mixture lever
19. Throttle friction control handwheel
20. Throttle lever
22. Carburettor slow-running cut-out control knob
27. Master fuel cock control
31. Fuel contents gauge illumination switch
46. Landing lamp switch
52. Bomb selector switches
53. Bomb nose fusing switch
54. Bomb tail fusing switch
55. Bomb jettison master switch
56. Flap over bomb jettison push button
59. Bomb jettison switchbox
63. Armour plated panel port control ring
64. Camera controller wedge plate
65. Camera sight for oblique photography (in port window only)
80. Compass
84. Bomb distributor plug
88. Airscrew pitch control knob
89. Computer stowage case
90. Map case
91. Telephone-microphone socket
97. Leg straps
98. Shoulder straps

Starboard side of the pilot's cockpit for the Mk III and Mk IIIA (©Crown Copyright)

4. Window release tab
5. Footplate
6. Pilot's seat
7. Pilot's seat adjusting handwheel
8. Armrests
21. Carburettor air intake heat control knob
23. Gill control indicator sleeve
24. Gill control indicator pointer
25. Gill control handle
26. Engine starting push button
29. Three-way priming cock
33. Oil heating control knob
35. Oil temperature gauge
42. Dimmer switch for compass lamp
43. Cockpit heating control knob
47. Forced landing flare release
63. Armour plated panel starboard control ring
65. Camera sight cover control
67. Hinged writing pad holder
68. Writing pad fasteners
69. Pencil stowage
70. Elastic band
75. Starting magneto switch
76. Navigation and pressure head heating switchbox
77. Morse key
78. Identification switchbox
85. Rear occupant's attention push button
86. A.S.I. correction card holder
92. Engine data plate
93. Gill control indicator plate
94. Wireless remote controller
95. I.C.W. switch
96. Harness release control knob
97. Leg straps
98. Shoulder straps

30 Airframe Detail No.9 – Lysander

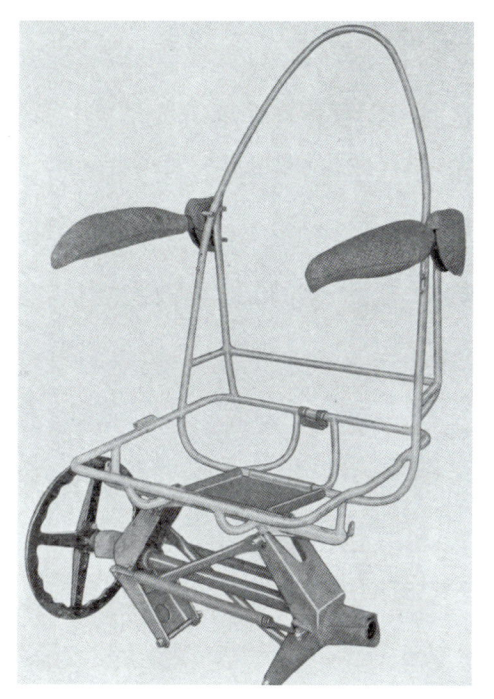

The framework for the pilot's seat, seen here in the Mk I manual (©Crown Copyright)

The pilot's seat with all the cushions and straps in place, this is from the Mk II manual (©Crown Copyright)

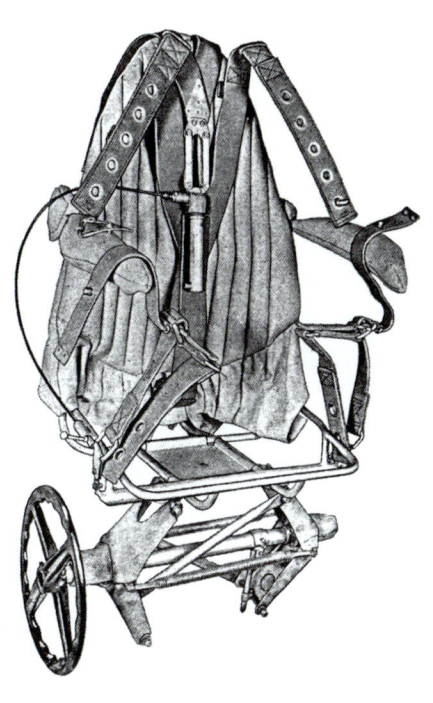

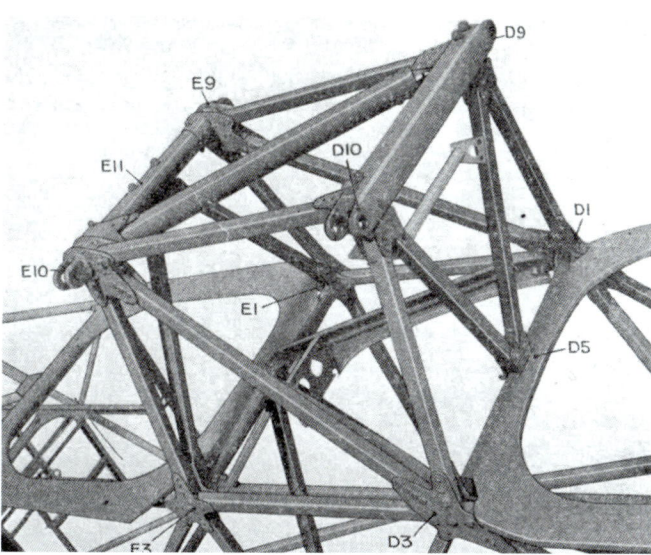

This is the superstructure between the pilot and observer, with the wing pick-ups at each upper corner (©Crown Copyright)

Here is the same region in ARC's airworthy example and as you can seem, although British-built, the beams at the top of the superstructure are tubes, not box-section as seen in the previous illustration, so you have to be careful getting too pedantic about details! (©Crown Copyright)

Although this is not 100% accurate, it's a representation of the sliding map table in the mid-section above the main fuel cell in NASM's ex-Canadian example (©NASM)

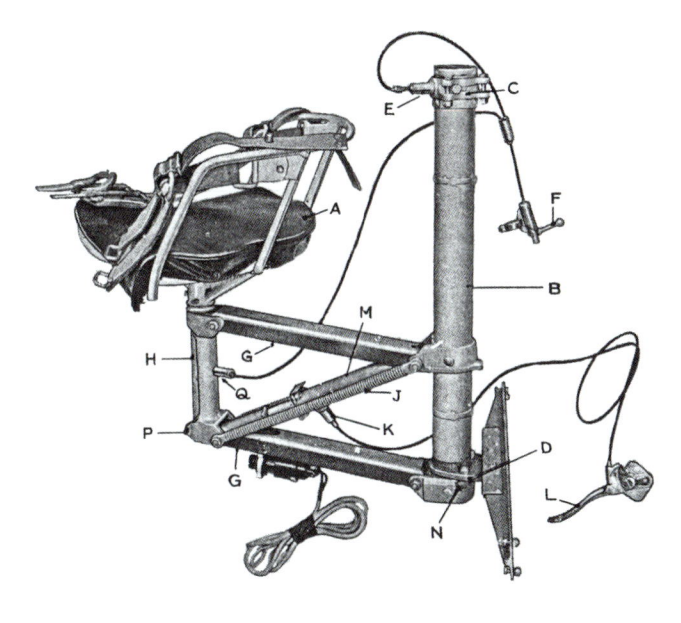

This is the gunner's seat in the rear cockpit and applies to the Mks I to III, but not Special Duties versions, which had this removed (©Crown Copyright)

Airframe Detail No.9 – Lysander   **31**

Forward portion of the rear cockpit, view to port and applicable to all bar the Special Duties version (©Crown Copyright)

1. Floodlamp
2. Dimmer switch
3. Spare bulb holders
4. Cockpit heating control
5. Instruction label
6. Engine starting battery
7. Engine starting external power supply socket
8. Fuel tank
9. Fuel contents gauge
10. Fuel contents gauge floodlamp
11. Port runner for chart-board sliding desk
12. Fire extinguisher
13. Seat traverse locking plunger
14. Seat traverse pillar mounting
15. Cockpit heating duct
16. Magazine stowage peg
17. Seat tension springs
18. Hinged sliding floor panel
19. Bomb-aimer's hinged recording panel
20. Bombsight instruction label
21. Adjustable seat
22. Harness straps
23. Seat structure
24. Bomb firing switchbox
25. Magazine stowage peg
26. Gun mounting cross member
27. First aid stowage
28. Parachute stowage frame
29. Parachute spring-loaded retaining flap

Forward portion of the rear cockpit, view to starboard and applicable to all bar the Special Duties version (©Crown Copyright)

14. Seat traverse pillar mounting
16. Magazine stowage peg
17. Seat tension springs
19. Bomb-aimer's hinged recording panel
21. Adjustable seat
22. Harness straps
23. Seat structure
30. Fuel tank dipstick
31. Signal cartridge stowage rack
32. Chart-board illumination dimmer switch
33. Camera motor supply socket
34. Seat traverse and rotation lock control
35. Microphone socket
36. Holdall stowage
37. Electrical instrument panel
38. Floodlamp
39. Dimmer switch
40. Wireless remote controller
41. Charge regulating switch instruction label
42. Magazine stowage peg
43. Elevator and rudder dual control attachments
44. Ivorine writing tablet
45. Watch holder
46. Starboard runner for chart-board sliding desk

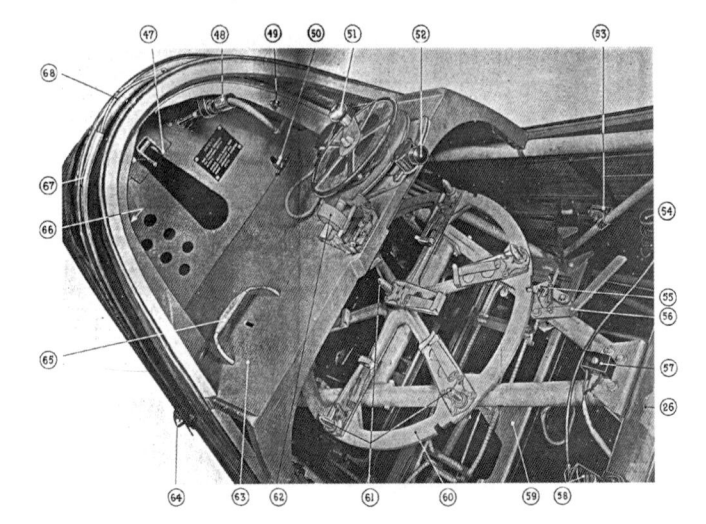

Aft portion of the rear cockpit, view to port and applicable to all bar the Special Duties version (©Crown Copyright)

26. Gun mounting cross member
47. Gun barrel stowage clip
48. Fixed aerial lead-in cable connection
49. Fixed aerial cable stowage clip
50. Trailing aerial guide bracket
51. Trailing aerial winch
52. Winch brake control
53. Fixed aerial lead-in cable socket
54. Tapping key
55. Turntable trip lever locking catch
56. Turntable trip lever
57. Terminal block
58. Seat height adjustment control lever
59. Wireless crate
60. Magazine stowage turntable
61. Magazine stowage pegs
62. Gun arm stowage catch
63. Cockpit decking
64. Sliding roof retaining catch
65. Empty link and case bag stowage
66. Gunner's attention lamp
67. Sliding roof
68. Roof catch release cable

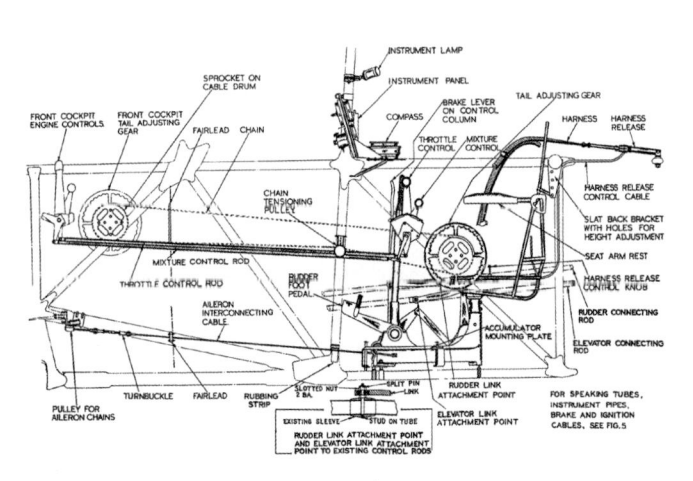

This diagram shows the dual controls that could be installed in the rear cockpit to use the Lysander as a trainer (©Crown Copyright)

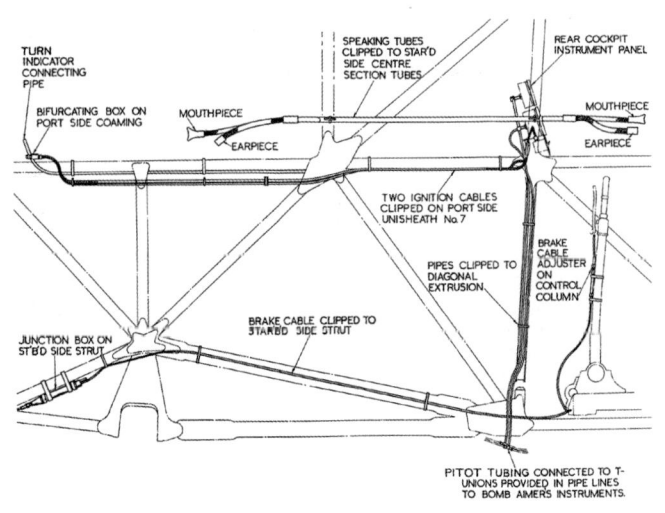

This is the cable and pipework associated with the dual control conversion (©Crown Copyright)

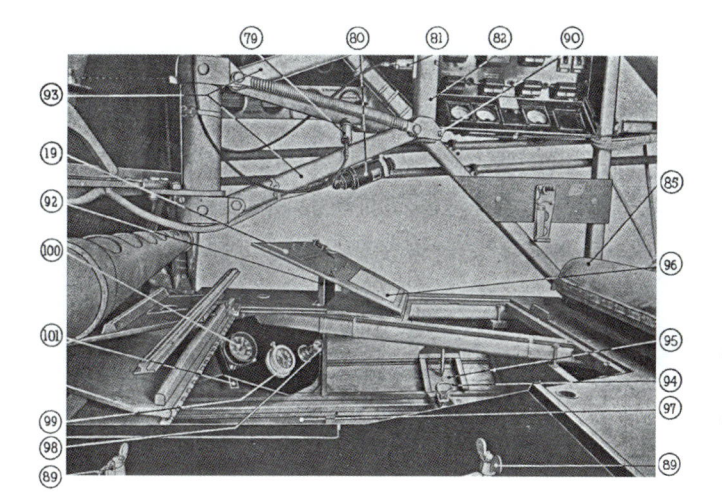

This is the bomb aimer's position in the underside of the rear cockpit area, viewed to port (©Crown Copyright)

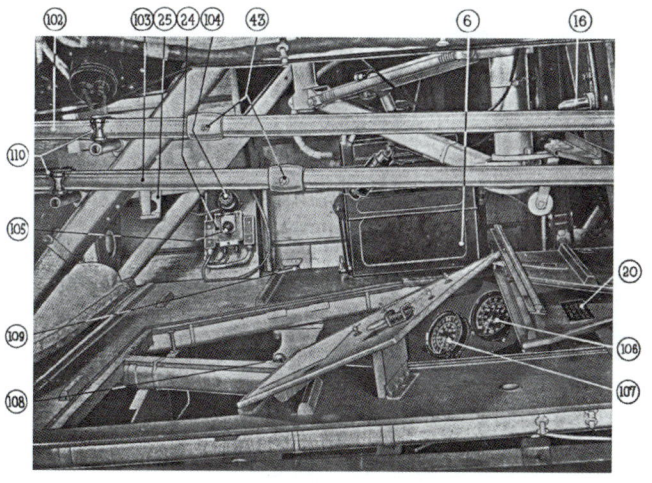

This is the bomb aimer's position in the underside of the rear cockpit area, viewed to starboard (©Crown Copyright)

6. Engine starting battery
16. Magazine stowage peg
20. Bomb sight instruction label
24. Bomb firing switchbox
25. Magazine stowage peg
43. Dual control attachments
102. Rudder control transmitting tube
103. Elevator control transmitting tube
104. Dimmer switch for floodlamp (80)
105. Bomb firing push button
106. Air speed indicator
107. Altimeter
108. Bombsight mounting
109. Port inspection door rear catch
110. Transmitting tubes roller guide
19. Bomb-aimer's hinged recording panel
79. Seat plunger for height adjustment
80. Bombsight floodlamp
81. Seat rotation locking plunger
82. Seat bearing support
85. Hinged panel as bomb-aimer's chest-rest
89. Battery holding-down bolts
90. Seat rotation friction adjuster
92. Folding support for panel (19)
93. Parallel motion seat supports
94. Windshield retaining catch
95. Windshield catch external access cover
96. Ivorine writing tablet
97. Bomb-aimer's transparent slidable windshield
98. Bomb-aimer's attention lamp
99. Watch in holder
100. Air temperature thermometer
101. Thermometer warning label

Special Duties: This is the frame for the pilot's seat, again in the RAF Museum's example, you can see the additional fuel tank in the mid-section, behind the pilot's back (©J. Jankovic)

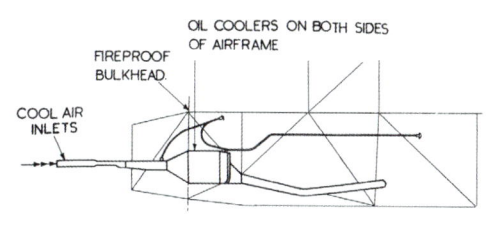

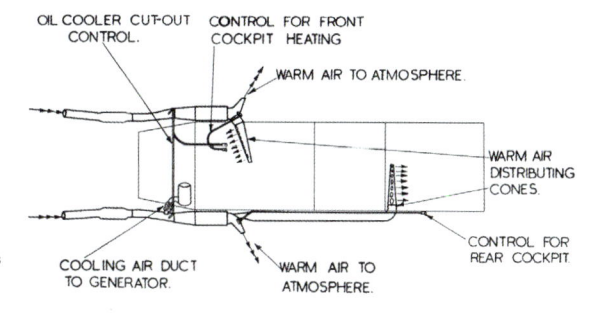

Special Duties: This is an overall shot from the port side of the instrument panel etc. in the RAF Museum's example, the blind flying panel and various other elements are sadly missing, but it gives an overall feel for the SD-series cockpit (©J. Jankovic)

This shows the cockpit heating system and it is applicable to all variants (©Crown Copyright)

Airframe Detail No.9 – Lysander **33**

Special Duties: A view forward in the rear compartment, showing the feed pipe from the additional tank going to the starboard side. The round framework on the starboard cockpit ledge is to hold a vacuum flask (©J. Jankovic)

Special Duties: The bit everyone wants clarification on with the SD version, this is the bench seat that replaced the gunner's seat/mount and as you can see it is a simple wooden unit with two hinges, the rearmost ones you can see hinges the whole unit up and back, the others are underneath midway along the hinged piece and these allow the resulting flap to be folded in half to clear the tank feed above and thus allow it to be stowed flat on the rear section. Note the call button on the cockpit ledge, the flask holder towards the front and the intercom lead socket covered in tape hanging down from the distribution panel (©J. Jankovic)

1.3 Canopy

A close-up of a period image of RCAF Mk II 418 after an accident on the 19th February 1940, you can also see the quilted back cushion and harness on the pilot's seat plus the basic ring sight mounted on the framework above the instrument panel (©Library and Archive Canada)

This shot shows the windscreen on the Shuttleworth's example from the port side (©J. Jankovic)

This head-on shot of NASM's example highlights things like the reflector gunsight fitted to later machines – the rear-view mirror is not something we have seen in any period images, so it was probably an addition prior to its restoration to airworthiness (©S. Willey)

A close-up of the starboard side of the mid-section on the RAF Museum's example during restoration, you can see the structure that acts as both roll-over frame and pick-up for each wing, plus the big fuel tank in between the cockpits (©J. Jankovic)

This is the port side of the mid-section of the canopy on the RAF Museum's (©J. Jankovic)

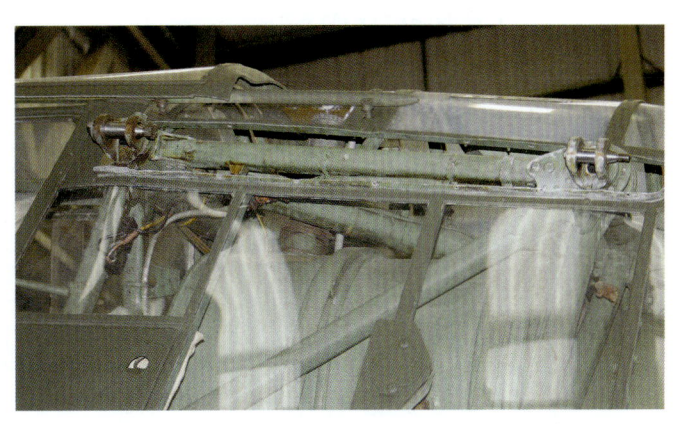

A close-up of the wing pick-ups on the port side of the RAF Museum's example, you can see the filler neck for the central fuel tank just poking up above the upper canopy, just below the rail for the upper forward sliding section

This view from the back of the starboard side of the rear canopy on ARC's example, the rail is visible along the bottom and the overall tight fit of the sliding element is evident (©N. Perry)

This is the starboard side of the rear canopy section on the Shuttleworth's example with it slid fully backwards

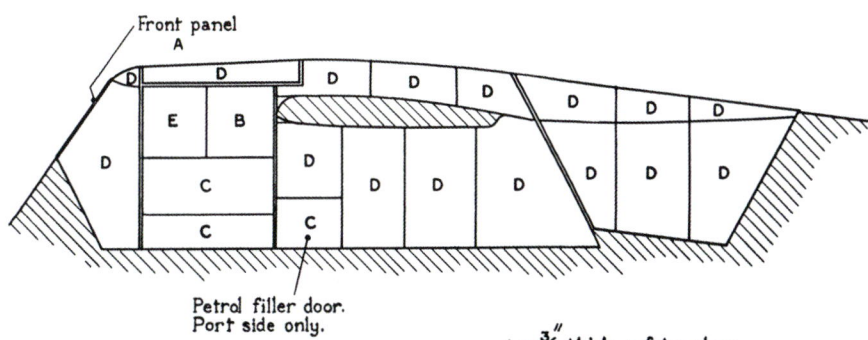

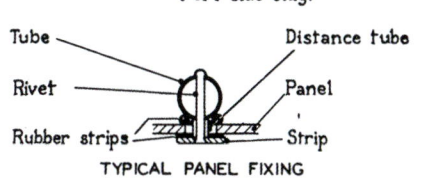

A – 3/16" thick safety glass
B – 5%" thick transparent cover
C – 3%" thick transparent cover
D – 2¼%" thick transparent cover
E – 6%" thick transparent cover

This diagram shows the various panels in the windscreen and canopies, their thicknesses and how the frames/glass are mounted (©Crown Copyright)

This shot inside the ARC's airworthy Mk III allows you to see the space where the extra fuel tank was in the SD version and over in the lower right-hand corner, the neck for the fuel filler for the main tank in the lower portion of the mid-cockpit region (©N. Perry)

Airframe Detail No.9 – Lysander **35**

1.4 Main & Aft Fuselage

Front portion of the rear fuselage, starboard side
(©Crown Copyright)

83. Message hook winch panel catch
84. Hinged panel as gunner's footrest
102. Rudder control transmitting tube
103. Elevator control transmitting tube
119. Camera aperture sliding panel
121. Camera mounting
129. Rear fuselage armour-plating starboard bolts
130. Rear fuselage armour-plating port bolts
131. Wireless remote controller stowage
132. T.R. 1091 four-pin L.T. supply socket
133. Motor generator supply socket
134. T.R. 1091, six-pin power supply socket
135. Power tray draw bolts
136. Detachable power unit crate
137. Crate mounting sliding tray
138. Detachable wireless unit crate
139. Crate retaining catches
140. Sliding frame catch release handle
141. Fuselage footstep bracket
142. Catches retaining bracket
143. Observer's anchorage strap stowage
144. Message hook actuating cable
145. Message hook
146. Message receiving aperture
147. Catch on flap carrying message hook winch
148. Enclosed footstep to rear cockpit
149. Emergency rations stowage
150. General electrical services battery
151. Battery cables dummy terminals
152. Light-series carrier electrical connection

This is a clear image from the manual showing the main fuel tank (©Crown Copyright)

A period image of the starboard side of a production Mk I with the access panels removed, so you can see things like the radio equipment and (below and slightly aft of it) the F.24 camera that were not present in the previous image. You can also see the main fuel tank and the reflector gunsight sitting above the Vickers K gun in the rear cockpit (©Air Ministry)

This shot shows the same area but on a later TT Mk III, so it has the winches above and aft of the main fuel tank and the support and pulley below the fuselage (©Westlands)

Even with the removable panel on the starboard side back in place there is still a pronounced panel line all around

36 Airframe Detail No.9 – Lysander

This is the rear fuselage upper decking (wooden) structure, you can see the two stowage compartments in the rearmost section
(©Crown Copyright)

Rear portion of fuselage, starboard side
(©Crown Copyright)

67. Sliding roof
102. Rudder control transmitting tube
103. Elevator control transmitting tube
123. Catch on hinged panel for access to carrier mounting
124. Light series carrier for flares or sighters
129. Rear fuselage armour-plating starboard bolts
130. Rear fuselage armour-plating port bolts
150. General electrical services battery
151. Battery cables dummy terminals
152. Light series carrier electrical connection
153. Fin
154. Ballast weights
155. Engine starting handle stowage
156. Rear fuselage stowage locker cover
157. Fixed aerial lead-in cable connection
158. Parachute flares release chutes
159. Controls locking tubes stowage
160. Lift-the-dot fastener on stowage bag
161. Fuselage fairings in raised position to clear carrier
162. Ballast weights
163. Lower end of stowage bag
164. Lower end of flare release chute
165. Hinged transparent fairing
166. Tail lifting bar cross tube
167. Catch on hinged flap covering lifting bar aperture
168. Tailplane leading edge
169. Tailwheel compression strut

Here you can see the rear stowage locker on the port side of the Shuttleworth's example, as well as the lack of the bay forward of it (©J. Jankovic)

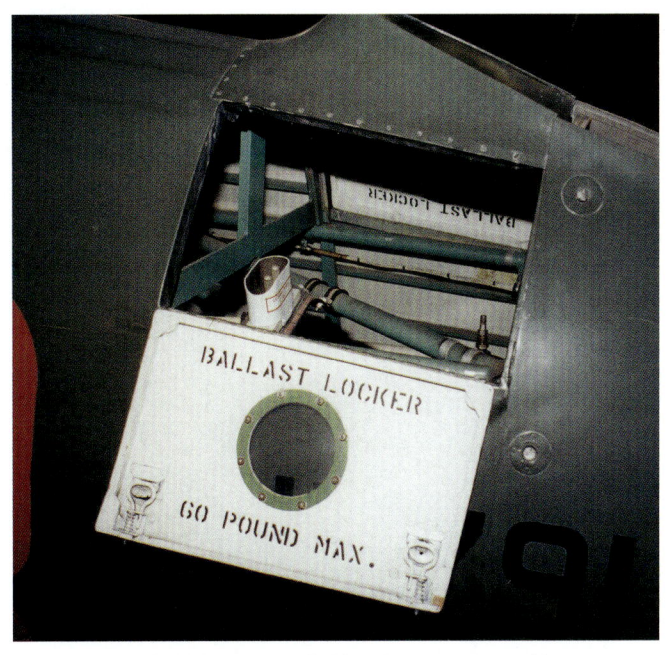

This is the rear fuselage stowage (165 on the previous diagram) bay open in NASM's example, it lacks the forward locker (156 in the previous diagram) and it only has a round clear portal, unlike British-built machines, which had the whole door transparent (©S. Willey)

Airframe Detail No.9 – Lysander **37**

British and early Canadian-built examples had the aft bay fitted with transparent panels on both sides (later Canadian ones adopted a clear porthole on each side and a solid one ahead of it), inside are the ballast weights to the left and the starter handle on the floor, it was probably clear to make post-flight checks easier (©N. Perry)

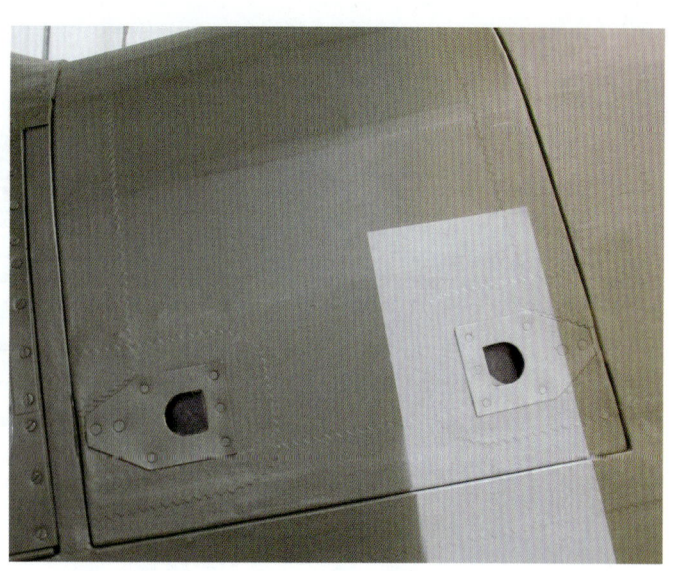

This is the forward stowage bay on ARC's airworthy British-built example, it lacks the clear porthole seen in the original diagram, but it has no aerial lead-in etc., so the porthole was probably just omitted (©N. Perry)

This combined couple of shots of RCAF examples shows the clear panel seen on early machines ('421' seen on the right) and the round clear porthole on later ones ('473' on the left)

This shot of the restored example at Hamilton, Ontario, confirms the solid front and round porthole in the rear access panels seen on later Canadian machines (©G. Papadimitriou)

This is the forward bay on the RAF Museum's example, as you can see it also conflicts with the maintenance diagram in that it lacks the clear porthole, but this may be specific to the Special Duties Mk IIIA (©J. Jankovic)

This (arrowed) is the hinged cover over the tail lifting bar cross tube, 166 in the maintenance diagram

38 | Airframe Detail No.9 – Lysander

Front portion of rear fuselage, port side

6. Engine starting battery	102. Rudder control transmitting tube
7. Engine starting external power supply socket	103. Elevator control transmitting tube
12. Fire extinguisher	109. Port inspection door rear catch
14. Seat transverse pillar mounting	111. Port inspection door front catch
15. Cockpit heating duct	112. Port hinged inspection door
17. Seat tension soring	113. Hinged door support
19. Bomb-aimer's hinged recording panel	114. First aid outfit
27. First aid stowage case in door frame	115. Hinged door support
80. Bombsight floodlamp	116. Fire extinguisher striking lever
82. Seat bearing support	117. Starter current fuse box with 10 amp fuse
89. Battery holding-down bolts	118. Battery cables dummy terminals
90. Seat rotation friction adjuster	
96. Ivorine writing tablet	

Here is the hinged access panel at the front of the port side of the rear fuselage (©J. Jankovic)

Rear portion of rear fuselage, port side

67. Sliding roof	123. Catch on hinged panel for access to bomb carrier mounting
97. Bomb aimer's slidable transparent windshield	124. Light series carrier for flares or sighters
119. Camera aperture sliding panel	125. Inspection panel catch
120. Camera aperture for oblique photography	126. Camera aperture for vertical photography
121. Camera mounting	127. Identification lamp inspection panel
122. Aperture for trailing aerial fairlead	128. Camera aperture sliding panel

In this shot of the RAF Museum's example during restoration, whilst not having things like the battery, camera and radio, it does nicely illustrate the armour plate added to protect the rear cockpit occupants from ground fire etc. (©J. Jankovic)

There is no large removable panel on the port side of the mid/rear fuselage, just the two hinged panels illustrated in previous diagrams, but you can see the prominent rear canopy rail (©J. Jankovic)

Airframe Detail No.9 – Lysander **39**

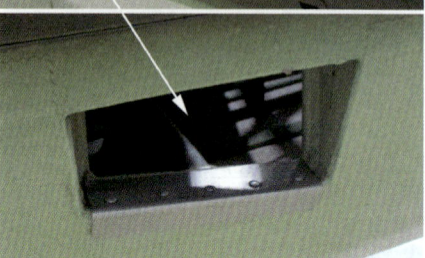

Moving to the underside, here is the front section under NASM's example, the two doors are unique to target towing machines, the cut-out in the front edge was where cable came though to go into the pulley on the structure below (not fitted now) so it could turn through 90° to clear the fuselage and tailwheel; see the previous maintenance manual diagram of the 'rear portion of rear fuselage, port side' for the panels etc. common on British-built Mk I–III (©S. Willey)

On the starboard side of the mid-fuselage of all but the SD versions was this hand/footstep at about midway up and, below and aft slightly, an open footstep (©N. Perry)

This view from underneath NASM's Canadian-built example allows you to see the shape and structure of the tubular lower footstep (©S. Willey)

With all the Special Duties Mk IIIs and the Canadian-built target tugs, the lower (open) footstep was replaced with an external tubular version, as seen here on the Shuttleworth's example

All Special Duties Lysanders had an access ladder added to the port fuselage side, as there were no access hand/footsteps originally, this can be seen here on the Shuttleworth's example – in WWII the rungs were painted with radium-luminous paint to allow those using it to see each rung even on a dark night (©J. Jankovic)

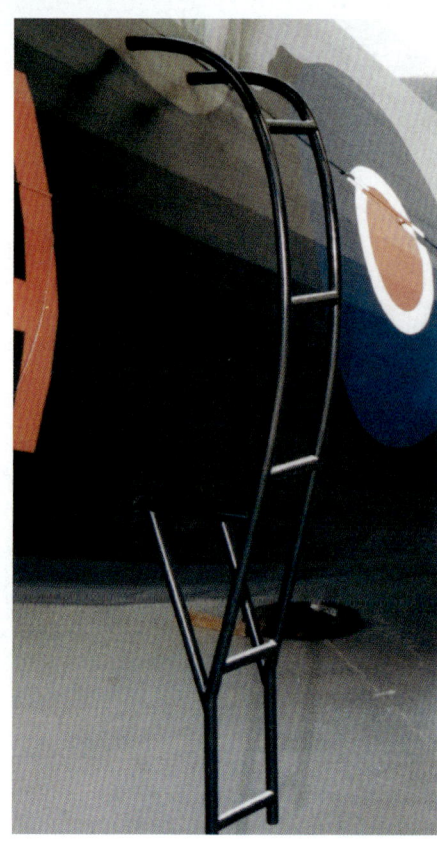

This shot from the front of the version on display at Duxford allows you to see the shape and anchor points for the SD ladder – note that as far as we are aware, all such ladders on preserved examples are modern reproductions

40 Airframe Detail No.9 – Lysander

2.1 Main Undercarriage

An odd shot I know, but you don't often get to see an original British-built Lysander's undercarriage beam, but this shows the RAF Museum's example and as you can see it is a single-piece unit, a feature that is unique to British-built machines (©J. Jankovic)

This image from the maintenance manual shows the undercarriage unit and how it attaches to the forward fuselage (©Crown Copyright)

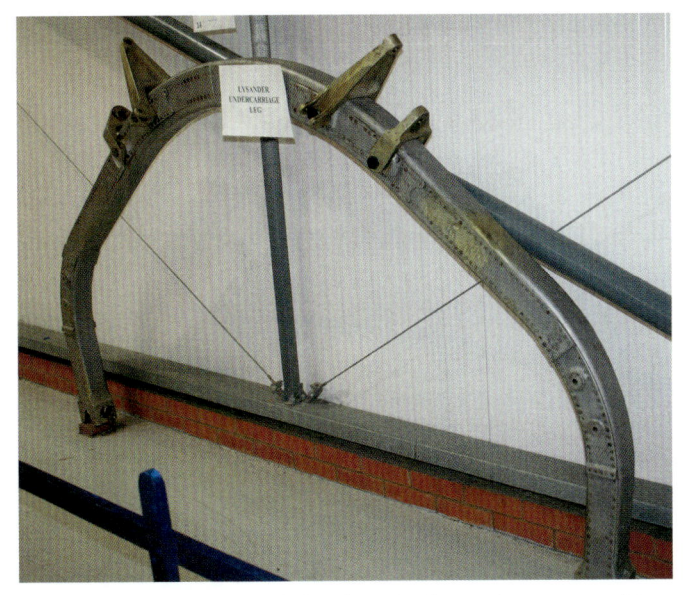

Here in contrast is a Canadian-built undercarriage beam and as you can see it is not a single-piece and has various panels rivetted to the front (and back) faces

A closer look at this Canadian-built undercarriage beam highlights those insert panels

Here is a close up of the pick-up brackets at the top on either side of the undercarriage beam, these are similar for both British and Canadian-built machines; the latter is shown here

Here you can see the undercarriage beam under, and viewable through a removable panel, in the forward fuselage on the RAF Museum's example during restoration

Airframe Detail No.9 – Lysander **41**

The upper section of each undercarriage leg is covered with this fairing, the hinged section gives access to the ammunition chutes for the fixed forward-firing 0.303in machine-gun and in this view, you are looking from the top downwards, so the main wheel spat would be attached at the bottom (©Crown Copyright)

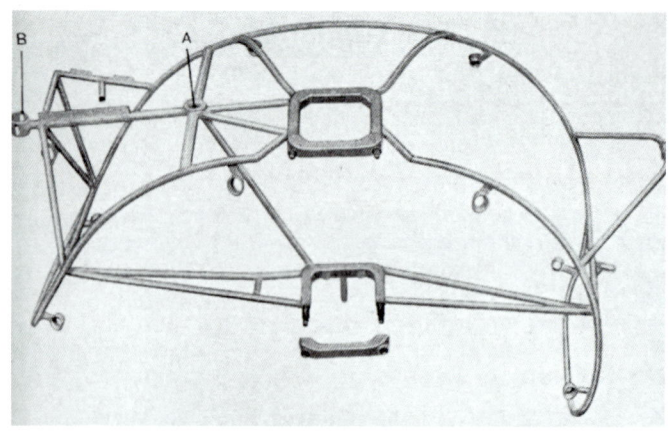

The spat is fitted around this framework above the wheel (©Crown Copyright)

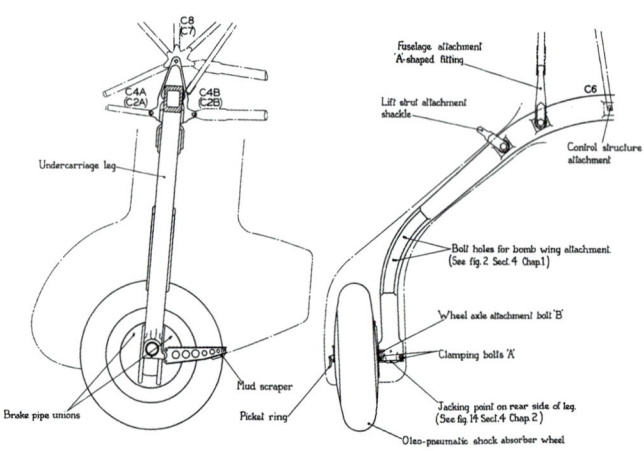

This diagram shows the overall main undercarriage arrangement and attachment (©Crown Copyright)

This close-up from a period image shows the wheel hub cover detail, you can just make out the remains of the 'Dowty' stencil opposite to the Dunlop one and you can see the oval loops that are attachments for the outer cover

This shot of the Lysander at Duxford before it was hung from the roof, shows the wheel hub detail with the outer cover removed. You can just make out the vertical cylinder of the Dowty internally-sprung hub

The sprung hub was very much of its era, as the weight and low sink-rate of planes then allowed this sort of limited damper travel. This diagram from the manual, shows what goes to make up each unit

(©Crown Copyright)

A. Brake.
B. Wheel.
C. Inner bearing.
D. Large hub casting.
E. Small hub casting.
F. Spring loaded dashpot.
G. Axle sleeve.
H. Spider plate bearing.
J. Spider plate.
K. Thrust cap.
L. Brake rim.
M. Cover plate.

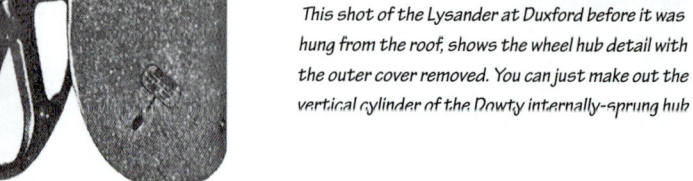

42 Airframe Detail No.9 – Lysander

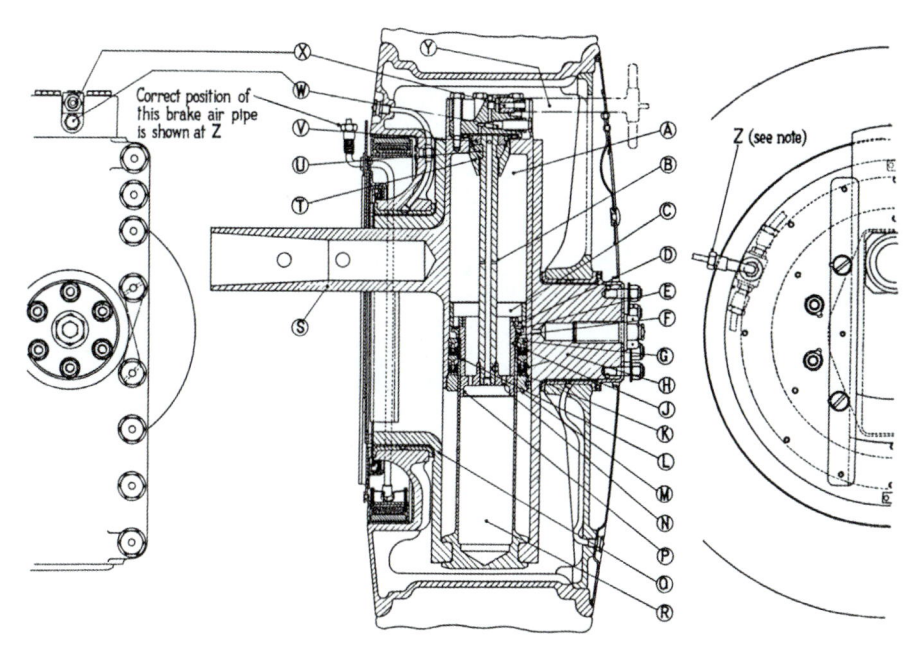

This diagram shows the construction of the internally-sprung wheel hub (©Crown Copyright)

This head-on shot of the port leg of NASM's machine clearly shows the layout of the landing light in relation to the fixed machine-gun port (©S. Willey)

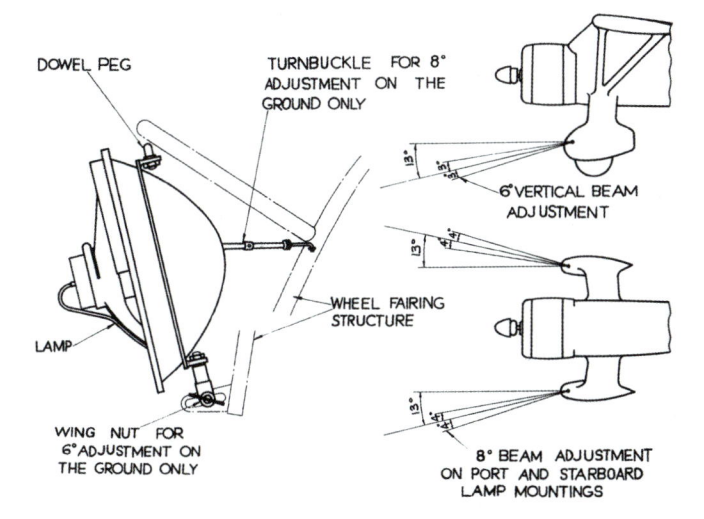

This diagram shows how the landing light in each undercarriage spat could be adjusted (©Crown Copyright)

The inside of the port leg of NASM's machine, shows the removable cover over the wheel and the hinge to the cover for the landing light (©S. Willey)

A quick look up underneath the NASM machine allows you to see the wheel cut-out and the shape of the wheel covers as they curve underneath (©S. Willey)

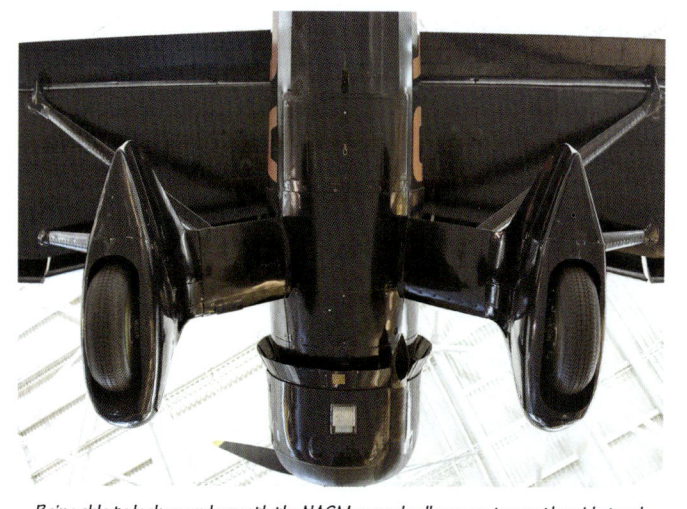

Being able to look up underneath the NASM example allows you to see the wide track of the undercarriage and the fairings etc. on the fuselage underside (©S. Willey)

Airframe Detail No.9 – Lysander **43**

Overall view of the outer face of the port undercarriage leg spat on the ARC airworthy example, you can see the footstep with hinged cover, the cover on the wheel and, access panel for the gun and the footstep on the upper front edge (©N. Perry)

This is a close-up of the footstep on the top, front edge of the wheel spat (©N. Perry)

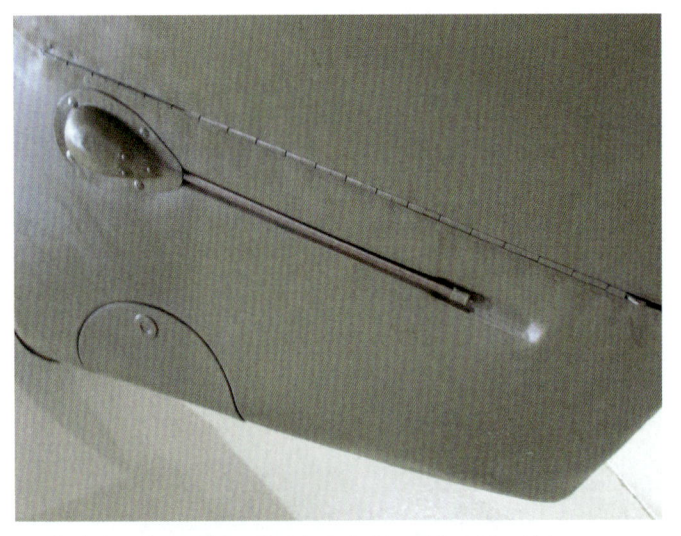

On the inner face of the starboard spat is this aerial mast inset into a recess (©N. Perry)

This is the upper section of the port leg on the ARC example, showing the fairing with the wing support strut and the dzus fasteners for the hinged panel that allows access to the ammunition bays (©N. Perry)

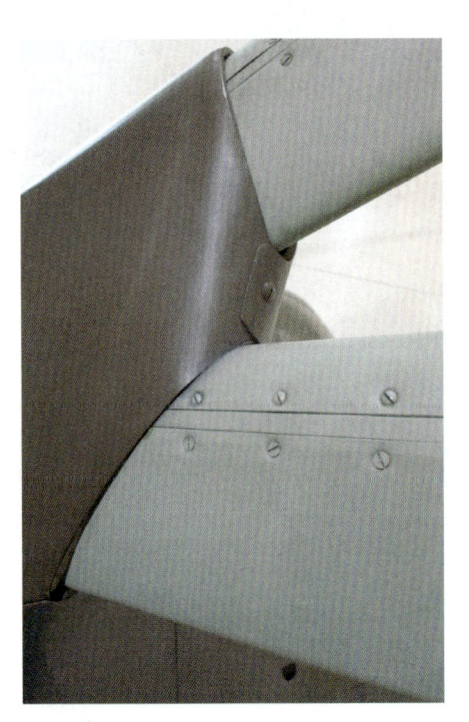

This is the upper edge of the undercarriage to wing strut fairing and you can see how the lower section is in two parts, secured with the screw in the middle (©N. Perry)

This shot of the RAF Museum example shows the pick-up on the undercarriage beam for the wing support struts

44 Airframe Detail No.9 – Lysander

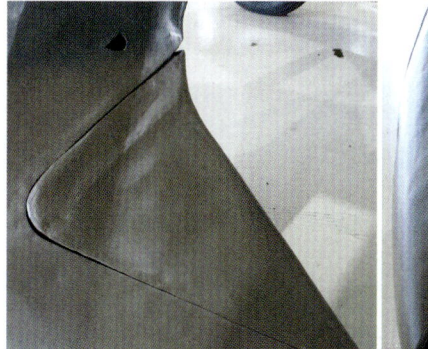

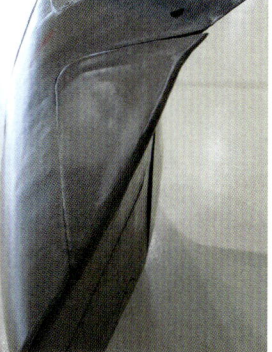

These two shots show the hinged access panel at the back of each spat that allows access to the fixed machine-gun; see the armament section for an image of this in the open position (©N. Perry)

This shows how the port for the fixed forward-firing machine-gun was covered with a doped linen patch, to keep the airflow out until the gun is fired (©N. Perry)

These two photos show the front (left) and underside (right) views of the intake that can be found on the port undercarriage leg fairing leading edge, it hinges open and closed and took air for cockpit ventilation (©S. Willey/R.A. Franks)

An unknown number of Canadian Lysanders (this is '459') were fitted with skis, this shot shows the port leg with the hydraulic damper leg for the ski attached to the outside of the undercarriage beam, you can see the tube in the end of the beam that usually takes the wheel axle (©Library & Archive Canada)

Some of the Lysanders operated by the Finnish Air Force had skis installed, these were of local manufacture and were fitted using the existing undercarriage beam, so they could have the wheel covers fitted, as see here with an example at Viiksjärvi in February 1942 (©SA-kuva)

One of the experiments done with the undercarriage of the Lysander was this one, when K6127 was fitted with castoring main wheels designed by Dowty, which allowed it to land facing into wind on an out-of-wind airstrip but it was never adopted for service

Airframe Detail No.9 – Lysander **45**

2.2 Tailwheel

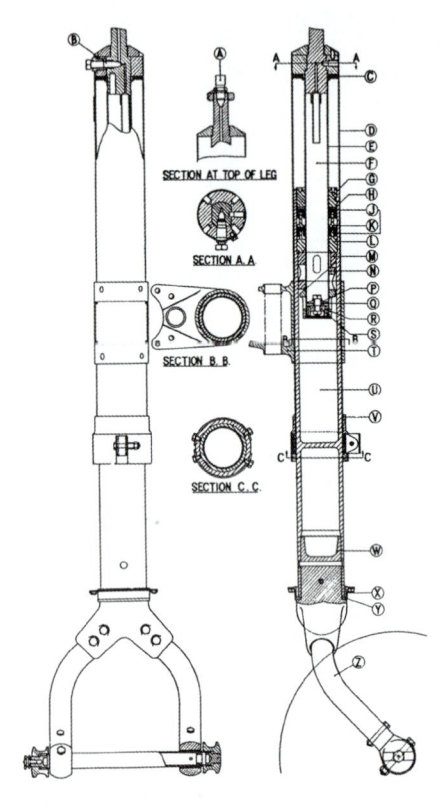

This sectional diagram shows all the components of the tailwheel shock absorber (©Crown Copyright)

This diagram from the maintenance manual shows the shock absorber of the tailwheel and applies to all variants (©Crown Copyright)

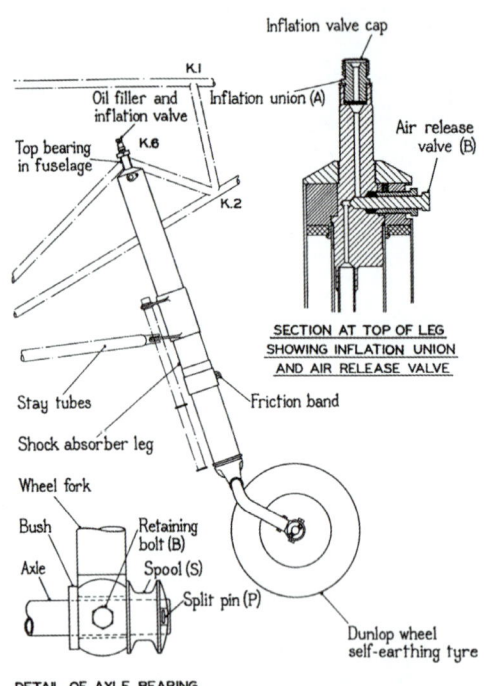

The British and Canadian-built Mk I and IIs had a cover on the upper portion of the (Dowty) tailwheel leg, as seen here on this close-up of Mk II N1256, LX•M of No.225 (Army Co-operation) Squadron

This shot shows the Dowty tailwheel strut, yoke and tyre in situ within the framework at the rear of the RAF Museum's example (©J. Jankovic)

Here is a closer look at the twin-contact tyre fitted to the tailwheel of the RAF Museum's example during restoration (©J. Jankovic)

These front and side views show K6127 with the same (Dowty) strut etc., but the lower yoke and upper cover were bigger, with the former covering much of the wheel

British and Canadian-built Mk IIIs initially had the cover, but later this was removed and most are seen in period images with the exposed Lockheed hydraulic shock absorber visible, as seen here on ARC's airworthy Mk III (©N. Perry)

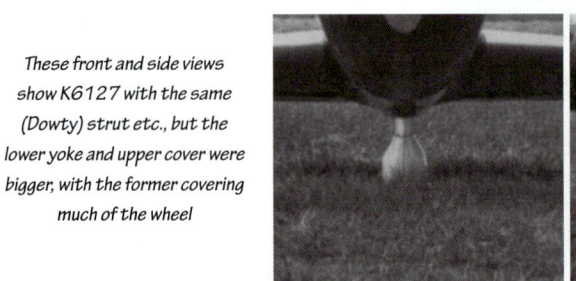

In these two shots of the tailwheel of NASM's example you can clearly see where the original cover around the Lockheed shock absorber has been cut away (its edges can be seen up inside the fuselage) – the shock seems to be set a little close to the underside, so the oil level may be low, as most period images show the leg extended further (©S. Willey)

46 | Airframe Detail No.9 – Lysander

3.1 Vertical Fin & Rudder

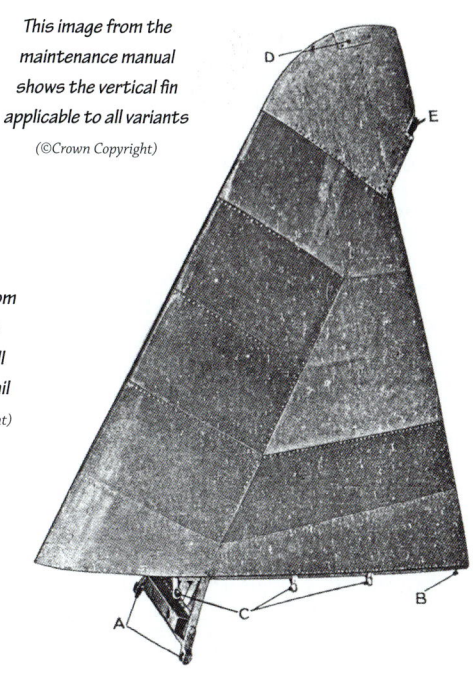

This image from the maintenance manual shows the vertical fin applicable to all variants (©Crown Copyright)

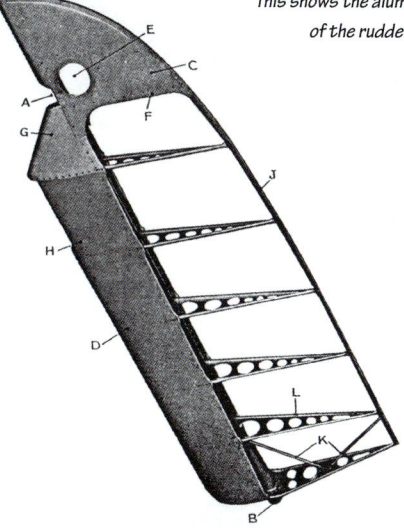

An overall image from the maintenance manual showing all elements of the tail unit (©Crown Copyright)

This shows the aluminium internal structure of the rudder (©Crown Copyright)

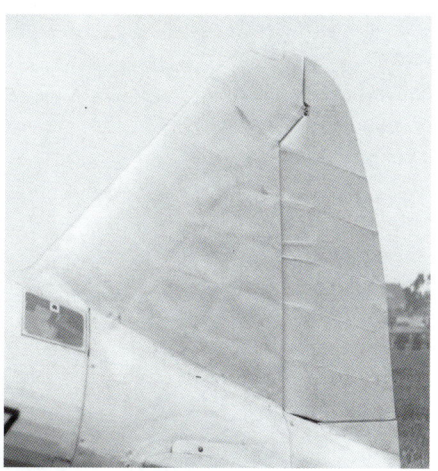

This close-up of prototype K6127 shows the skins on the vertical fin, the rather uneven tapes around the front of the rudder and the stitching along each rib

The sun angle allows this close-up of a flight of No. 16 (Army Co-operation) Squadron Mk Is to highlight the ribs of the rudder (©British Official)

At the very top of the vertical fin is a small panel that gives access for the aerial lead anchor point, seen here on NASM's example, although the lead itself is not fitted, just the initial link/loop assembly (©S. Willey)

This is the RAF Museum's example during restoration with the tail cone removed so that allows you to see how the vertical fin and rudder mount onto the fuselage tubular structure as well as the rod linkage for the rudder. The oblong patches at the base of the rudder are over manufacturer and modification plates that are affixed inside the rudder structure (©J. Jankovic)

The port side of the fin and rudder on the Shuttleworth's example, note the raised strips of linen over the stitches and the inspection panel that appears as a dull round patch

On the starboard side of the fin and rudder on the Shuttleworth's example you can see the aerodynamic elongated bulge below the fin/rudder hinge line, this covers the rod linkage for the rudder inside the tail cone

3.2 Horizontal Tailplane & Elevators

This close-up of K6127 in its initial form shows the fixed tailplane originally fitted to it

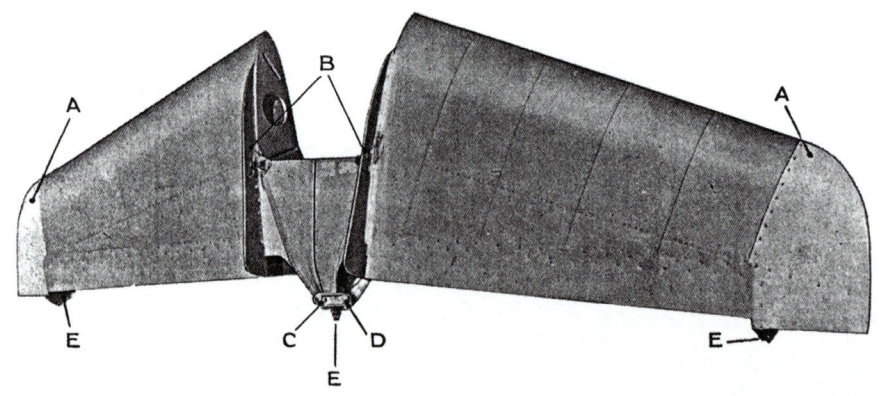

The tailplane structure as illustrated in the maintenance manual (©Crown Copyright)

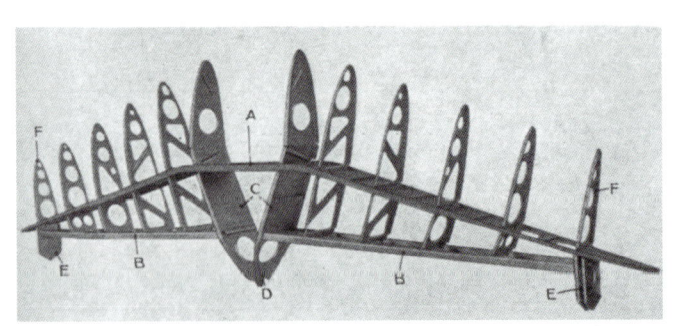

This is the internal structure of the tailplane (©Crown Copyright)

The tail incidence on all production machines was adjustable and this image from the maintenance manual shows the control wires and jack responsible for this (©Crown Copyright)

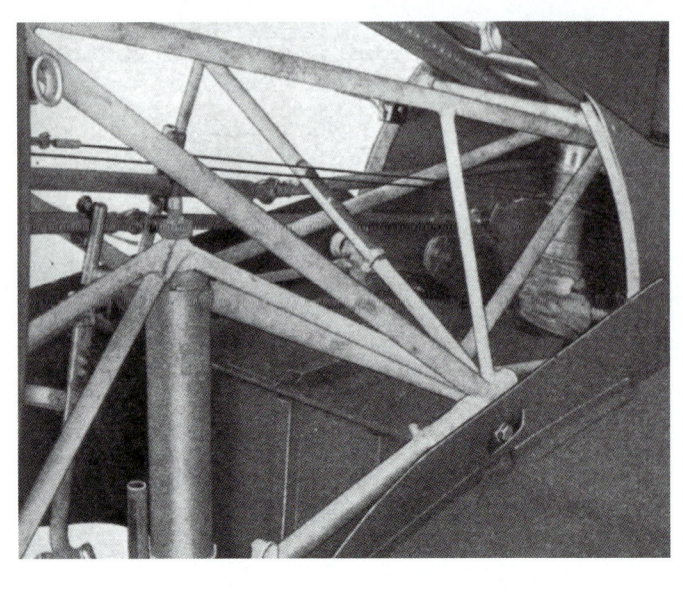

Airframe Detail No.9 – Lysander

The only real sign of the tailplane incidence mechanism on the exterior is this plate on the inboard end of each tailplane with the elongated hole and bolt in its centre, as seen here on the RAF Museum's example during restoration

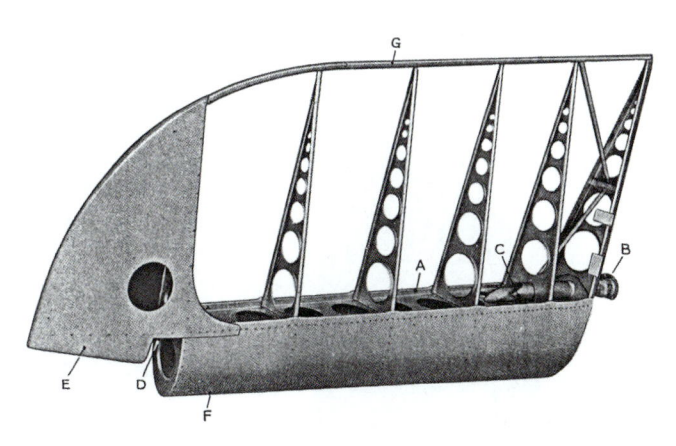

This image from the maintenance manual shows the internal structure of the elevator and applies to all variants (©Crown Copyright)

A view straight up underneath NASM's example allows you to see the gaps inboard of each elevator and around the pivot for the incidence mechanism pivot towards the front of each tailplane (©S. Willey)

The outboard hinge on the elevator is covered with this hinged metal flap, which you can see on ARC's airworthy example results in drag marks across the paintwork directly behind it (©N. Perry)

The extreme tip of the tail cone contains a formation light with clear cover and bulb, as seen here on NASM's example (©S. Willey)

Usually hidden behind the tail cone are the rudder and elevator cams and control rods, seen here on the RAF Museum's example during restoration

Airframe Detail No.9 – Lysander

4.1 Wings

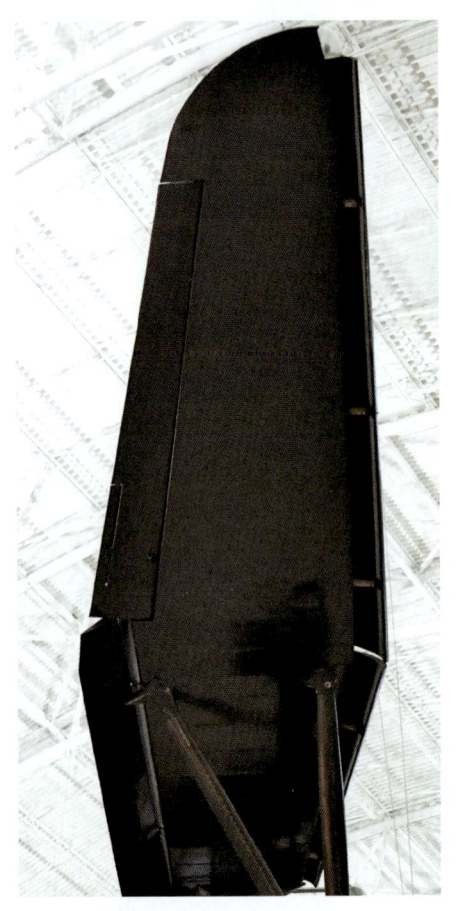

An overall view of the underside of the starboard wing of NASM's example (©S. Willey)

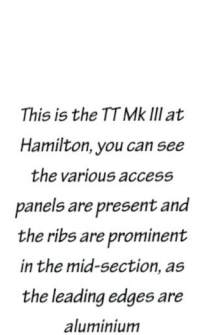

It is difficult to see details on the black undersides of NASM's example, so here is the outer section (outboard of the struts) of the starboard wing of the RAF Museum's example before it too was repainted in a Special Duties (black) scheme. All the round access panels are metal, as are their mounting frames, but the rest is all fabric covered giving a smoother finish with raised stitches that seems common in period images of British-built machines (©J. Jankovic)

This is the TT Mk III at Hamilton, you can see the various access panels are present and the ribs are prominent in the mid-section, as the leading edges are aluminium (©G. Papadimitriou)

NASM's example was rebuilt to airworthiness, so it has some deviations from an original, all the round access panels seem to be missing and thus covered. The ribs are very prominent, so probably used an aluminium strip on the main fabric through which the ribs were stitched, then the lot was covered with strips of fabric, this seems to be common in period images of Canadian-built machines (©S. Willey)

This image from the Mk II maintenance manual shows the outer bays of the wing – note that British-build machines had wooden ribs, whilst Canadian ones had the ribs in aluminium (©Crown Copyright)

Another image from the Mk II maintenance manual, this time showing the inboard bays of the wing (©Crown Copyright)

50 Airframe Detail No.9 – Lysander

This period image shows a complete wing with flaps, slats and ailerons prior to covering

This final image from the Mk II maintenance manual, shows the wing joints at the inboard root (©Crown Copyright)

This image from the Mk II maintenance manual, shows the 'lift strut bays', which means the mid-region where the support struts mount (©Crown Copyright)

The British-built Mk Is were fitted with the early style two-prong pitot, as seen here on left fitted to L4729 from the first production batch. Canadian-built Mk IIs also had the same style pitot, as seen on the right fitted to '418' with a little inset of the same aircraft viewed from the front starboard side

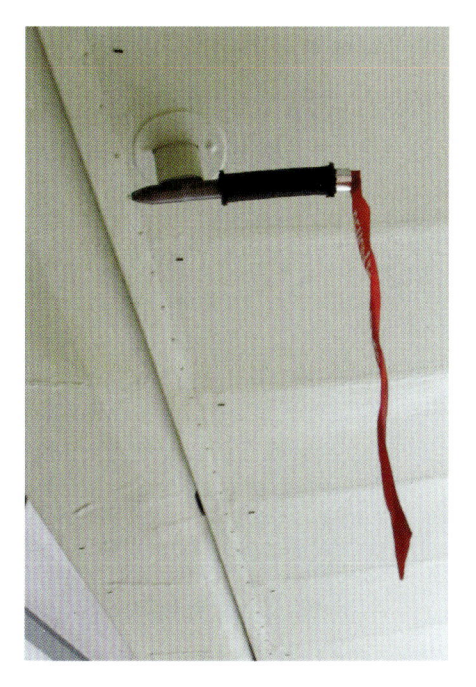

A pitot is fitted under the port wing, at about mid-way along the aileron and just inboard of its hinge line, as seen here on The Aircraft Restoration's airworthy example (©N. Perry)

The style of the pitot on NASM's example is different from those seen on British- and early Canadian-built examples, but looks similar to that used on later (Mk III) Canadian-built machines, the image to the left shows it front below/rear, that on the right from the front and you can also see the aerial antenna outboard of it on the upper surface of the wing (©S. Willey)

Airframe Detail No.9 – Lysander **51**

This gives an overall shot of the support struts under the port wing of the Shuttleworth's airworthy example – note the flap linkage built into the rear strut's top fairing (©J. Jankovic)

Each wing tip has an inboard light, this is the red light on the port side (green for starboard) of NASM's example; the light/bulb holder is of Canadian design, British-built machines used the same style holder as used for things like formation lights (©S. Willey)

This shot of the starboard wing of NASM's example shows the shape of the covers on the pick-ups between the struts and wing underside, with the flap linkage built into the back of the rear one (©S. Willey)

Here is a close-up view of the rear wing support strut and the flap linkage within it on the Shuttleworth's example

With a lighter colour used for the undersides, as here on the Aircraft Restoration Company's airworthy example, you can see that the struts are made by rolling a single piece and then riveting along the underside (©N. Perry)

This is the inboard linkage for the landing flap on ARC's example (©N. Perry)

52 Airframe Detail No.9 – Lysander

4.2 Control Surfaces, Flaps & Slats

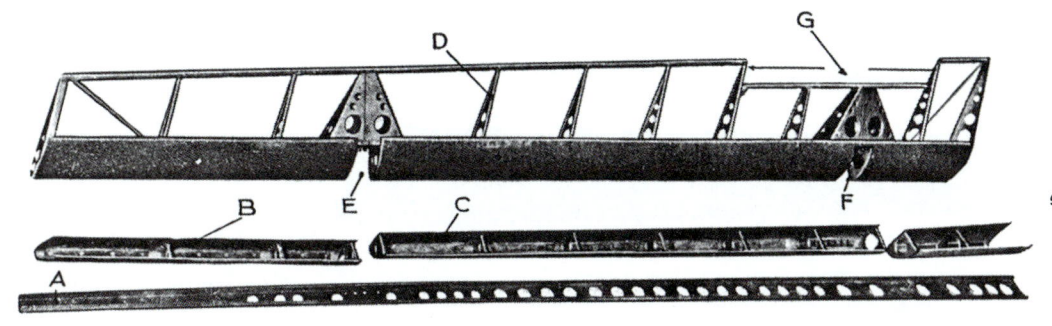

This diagram from the maintenance manual shows the construction of the aileron, with E and F being the cut-outs for the hinges and G the gap for the trim tab (©Crown Copyright)

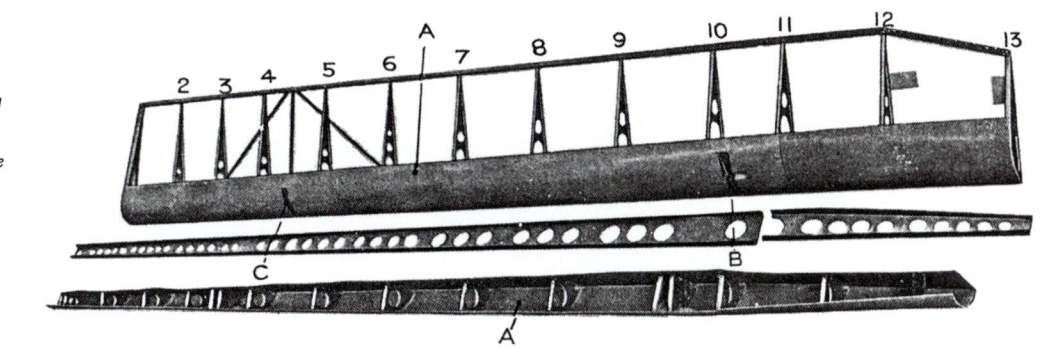

This maintenance manual diagram shows the construction of the landing flap, with B and C being the cut-outs for the hinges (©Crown Copyright)

Here you can see the underside of the aileron on the RAF Museum's Mk III, the line of holes along the trailing edge are drains, so any water that condenses inside can get back out; you can also see the British-style pitot (©J. Jankovic)

This shot of NASM's example shows the trim tab and details such as the rib tapes used to cover all the stitching to the leading edge, which is aluminium (©S. Willey)

An overall view of the upper surface of the landing flap on Shuttleworth's airworthy example. The round patches you can see are over inspection holes that allow the hinges to be checked without the need to remove the entire fabric covering

An overall view, looking inboard, of the starboard flap on the Aircraft Restoration Company's airworthy example. The 'W/T' stencils denote bonding (e.g. earthing) of the components (©N. Perry)

Airframe Detail No.9 – Lysander 53

This image from the maintenance manual shows the inner and outer faces of the inboard slats (©Crown Copyright)

This maintenance manual image shows the inner and outer faces of the outer slats (©Crown Copyright)

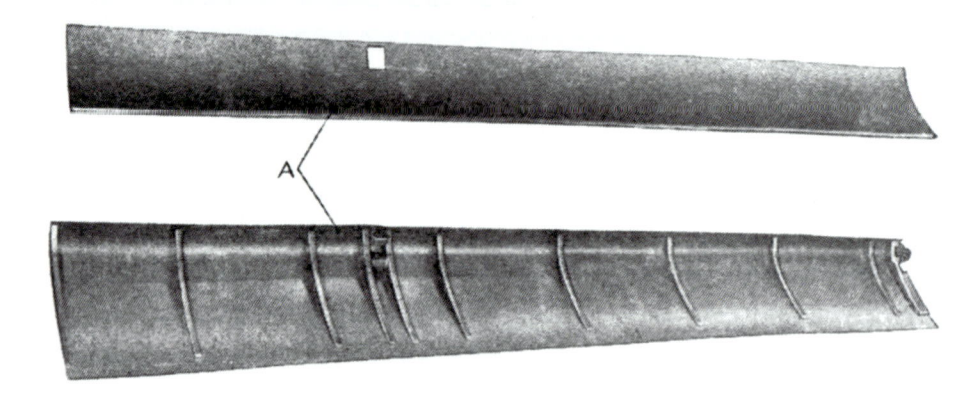

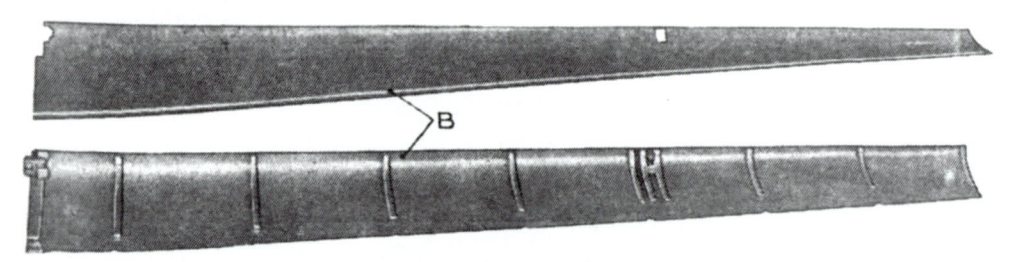

This shot of the Aircraft Restoration Company's example shows the port inboard slat in the extended position viewed from a higher vantage point (©N. Perry)

This shot of the Shuttleworth's airworthy example shows it with the inner sections of the slats extended on the starboard wing

Here you can see the inner and outer slats of NASM's example, with both in the extended position (©S. Willey)

This shows the extreme tip region of the outer slat on NASM's example, again in the extended position (©S. Willey)

54 Airframe Detail No.9 – Lysander

5.1 Engine

This image from the Mk I maintenance manual shows the starboard side of the Mercury engine installation (©Crown Copyright)

This shot shows the port side of the engine in the RAF Museum's Mk IIIA (©J. Jankovic)

This is the rear section of the port side of the engine installation on the RAF Museum's Mk IIIA, showing the domed bulkhead and the ring that holds the cowl flaps (©J. Jankovic)

This is the starboard side of the engine installation in the Shuttleworth's airworthy example, note that a couple of the cowl flaps have been removed, allowing you to see the simple long plates on which they fit

Looking into the back of the cowling, you can see the tops of the cylinders plus the flat brackets that hold the cowl flaps – these just slid into slots at the top and bottom of each bracket, they are not rivetted but screwed in place (©J. Jankovic)

Inside the front of the cowl you have the collector ring around the outside, with inlet pipes from each cylinder exhaust outlet plus the large intake for the oil cooler. Note also the two-part baffle plates between each cylinder to force the air into the cooling fins of the cylinder

(©J. Jankovic)

Airframe Detail No.9 – Lysander | 55

An overall view of a Mercury XXV preserved in Lisbon (©G. Papadimitriou)

A closer look at the cylinder head and the baffle plates on the preserved Mercury XXV in Lisbon, the exhaust and inlet valve springs can be seen as well as the inlet and exhaust outlets, which are blanked off in this instance (©G. Papadimitriou)

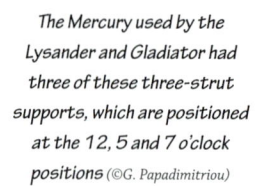

The Mercury used by the Lysander and Gladiator had three of these three-strut supports, which are positioned at the 12, 5 and 7 o'clock positions (©G. Papadimitriou)

In this head-on view of NASM's example you can see the support strut at the top and either side; note that the four holes in the upper collector ring are not standard (©S. Willey)

This shot shows the reduction casing etc. of the Aircraft Restoration Company's airworthy example (©N. Perry)

Although a bit heavy on the contrast (due to the manual having been originally duplicated, not printed), this photo from the Mk II manual shows the port side of the Perseus installation unique to the variant (©Crown Copyright)

Again, a bit heavy on the contrast, this photo shows the starboard side of the Perseus installation in the Mk II (©Crown Copyright)

5.2 Cowling & Exhaust

This is the port side of the cowling on the Aircraft Restoration Company's airworthy Mk IIIA V9312, note the two retaining plates and the bulges over the cylinder head gear of the Mercury engine (©N. Perry)

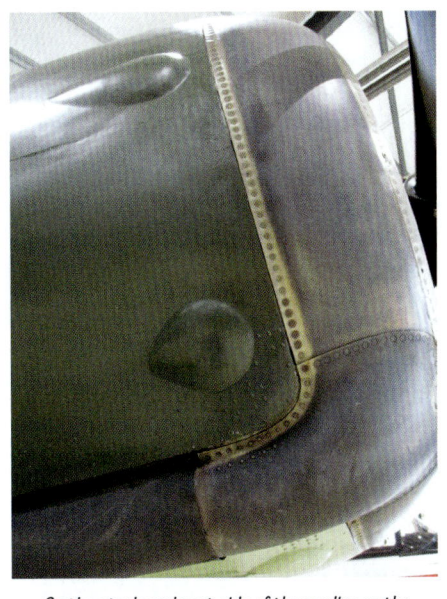

On the starboard port side of the cowling on the Aircraft Restoration Company's airworthy Mk IIIA V9312, you can see that the lower bulge is of a different size and shape to the remainder (©N. Perry)

This is the starboard side of the cowl on the Shuttleworth's airworthy example and being a Canadian built example, you will note that the lower bulge is larger and flatter than that seen on UK-built V9312

Inside the cowls you can see their two-part construction, the bulges over the cylinder heads and the reinforcing around the retaining fasteners

The big rivetted plates you will find on both sides of the cowl (port midway and starboard low down) cover these retaining clips, which once engaged can be tightened to secure the cowl, then the cover secured over them via dzus fasteners

Some Canadian-built Mk IIs adopted this revised collector ring, which incorporated intakes for the cabin (upper port) and carburettor intake (lower edge), these allowed cold air to go through these 'hot' pockets and thus be heated. You can also see that the oil cooler intakes are an elongated D-shape, not round
(©Library and Archives Canada)

Inside the front of the cowling, on either side, are intake tubes for the oil coolers that are situated on either side of the fuselage. You can also make out the collector ring at the front of the cowl, with individual inlet pipes from the exhaust outlet of each cylinder (©J. Jankovic)

Airframe Detail No.9 – Lysander **57**

A closer look at the intake 'trumpet', this time on the RAF Museum's example, plus you can see the combination of rivet types (and screws) used around the collector ring (©J. Jankovic)

This view inside the front of the cowl, on NASM's example, shows the shape of the intake 'trumpet' further back, as it flattens slightly to go between the cylinders, plus its bracket attachment to the edge of the cowl and the support struts from the engine to the collector ring (©S. Willey)

This shot of the Shuttleworth's example clearly shows the intake at the front of the cowling running along the fuselage side, with the oil cooler block situated at the back and the exhaust behind it, the latter item is why you have the outlet slot on either side of the fuselage, just forward and below the cockpit

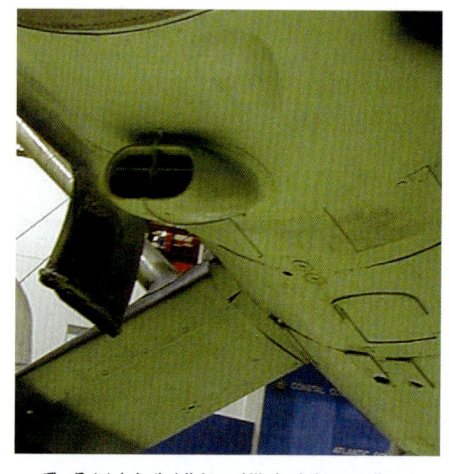

The British-built Mk Is and IIIs had this small oval carburettor intake under the cowling (©B. Ribbans)

Here is the oil cooler, which is situated on either side of the forward fuselage (©Crown Copyright)

The Perseus-powered Mk II adopted a much larger carburettor intake, that was squarer. You can also see that the Perseus did not need the bulges in the cowlings to clear the cylinder heads, due to its sleeve valve nature and thus no valve stems, cams or push rods at the top of each cylinder (©Library and Archives Canada)

This period image of the cowls off of an RCAF Mk II clearly shows the Perseus engine with its flat cylinder heads. Note also the bulges on the collector ring caused by intakes built into them, plus the flexible hoses running off at the bottom, the upper one going to cockpit and the lower one to the carburettor intake to feed hot air into it (©Library and Archives Canada)

Here you can see the square-style intake, fitted here to the Aircraft Restoration Company's airworthy Mk IIIA – the bottle and pipe are to catch oil (both are removed before running the engine), as it drips out of the overflow pipe that projects alongside the intake (©N. Perry)

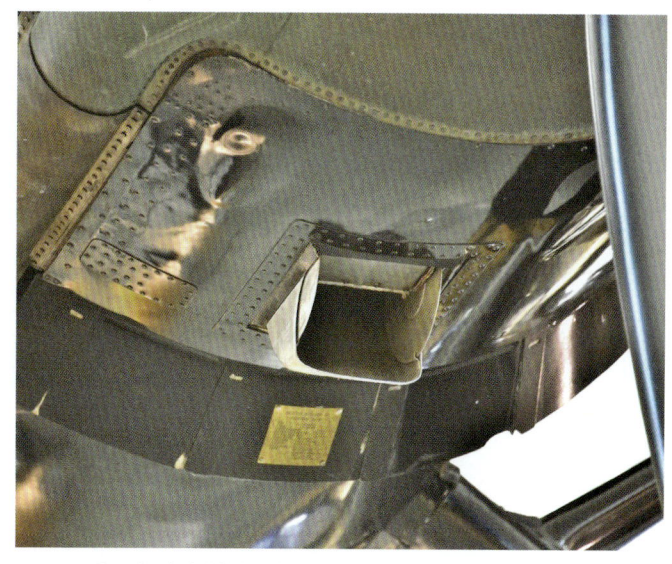

Canadian-built Mk IIIs adopted this adjustable carburettor intake, which had a section that rotates so that the intake can be closed off, reducing the amount of cold air being taken in during start-ups and running in the below-zero temperatures experienced in Canada – this is NASM's example (©S. Willey)

Here is a similar intake on the Shuttleworth's airworthy example, it does not have the rotating shutter element, it's fixed, so it's probably a revision to fly the type in the milder climate of Europe

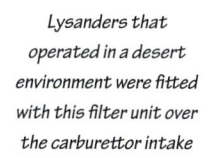

Lysanders that operated in a desert environment were fitted with this filter unit over the carburettor intake
(©Crown Copyright)

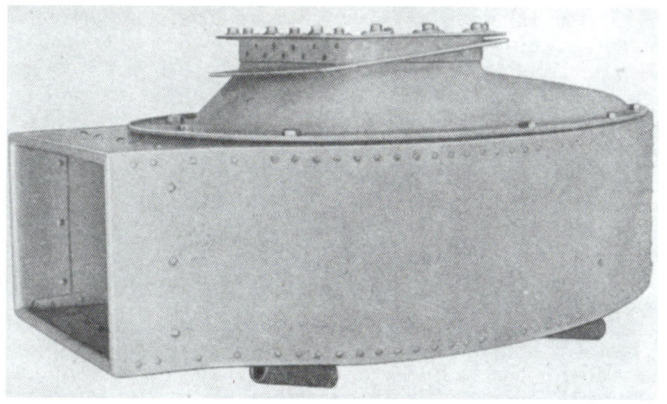

This close-up from a period image shows the desert filter unit in place, the pipe at the front seems to be common and is the oil drain pipe seen alongside the intake on previous images

There are numerous styles of exhaust stack fitted to the Lysander, this shows K6127 when used to test the fitment of 20mm cannon, but it nicely shows the standard type/length of exhaust used by most British machines and the early Canadian-built examples

Here is a close-up of the initial style of exhaust, seen on the Shuttleworth's example with the cowlings off, so you can see how the pipe is separate from the rest of the cowls

Airframe Detail No.9 – Lysander **59**

Looking up into the exhaust outlet on NASM's example allows you to see its elongated shape
(©S. Willey)

This shows the long exhaust fitted to Mk II '459' on the 7th August 1941 (©Library and Archives Canada)

Here is another long exhaust, this time on R9003 at the Canada Aviation & Space Museum, Ottawa, which is a composite rebuilt from three airframes. Note the intake in the front and the feed pipe at the rear, this latter item is probably for cockpit heating
(©G. Papadimitriou)

5.3 Propeller

An overall view of the three-blade, controllable-pitch bracket-type de Havilland propeller on the Shuttleworth's example (©J. Jankovic)

Here you can see the propeller hub with the spinner removed, once again on the Shuttleworth's example

Here you can see the detail visible of the propeller boss once the spinner is attached and seen here on the airworthy example operated by The Aircraft Restoration Company (©N. Perry)

Airframe Detail No.9 – Lysander

6.1 Fixed Armament

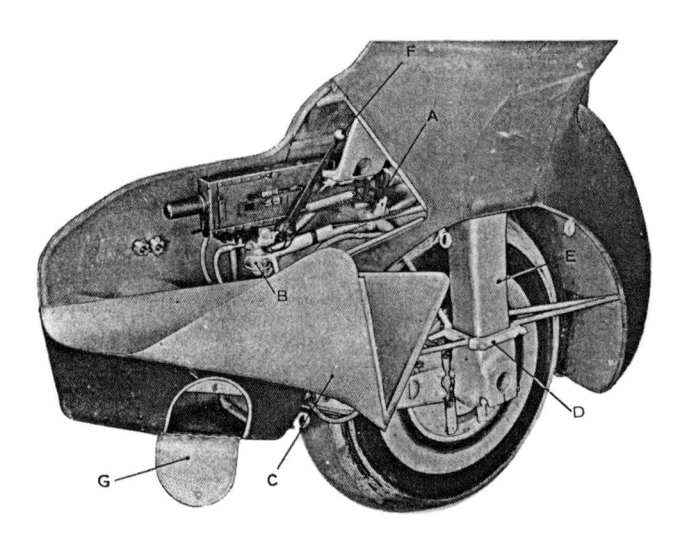

This diagram shows the fixed armament in the undercarriage spat
(©Crown Copyright)

A. Front gun hinge
B. Adjustable trunnion
C. Inner hinged access panel
D. Wheel fairing framework
E. Extruded type undercarriage leg
F. Gun loading lever
G. Empty link and cases container access cover

This period images shows ground crew checking the guns on a RCAF Lysander after target practice at Lake Deschenes 18th January 1940
(©Library and Archives Canada)

The forward-firing guns were initially sighted using a simple ring sight in the cockpit and bead sight mounted on a structure above the front of the engine cowling, as seen here on Mk II '418' of the RCAF after an accident whilst being flown by F/O Anderson on the 19th February 1940 *(©Library and Archives Canada)*

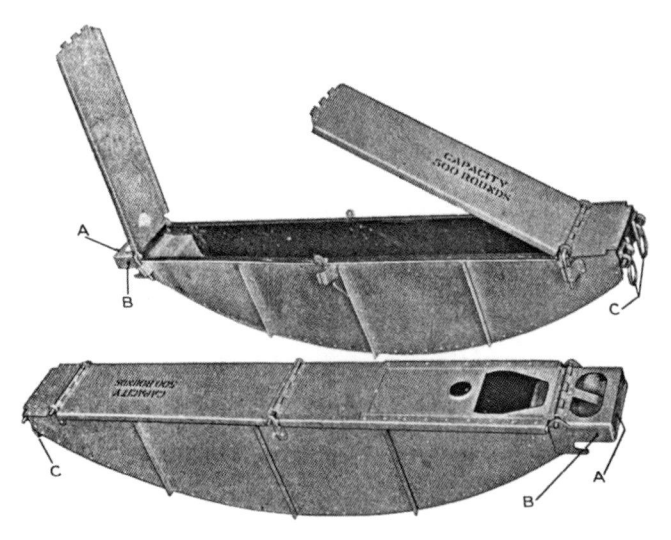

These are the ammunition boxes for the fixed 0.303in guns in each undercarriage leg *(©Crown Copyright)*

Initially the Lysander used a simple ring and bead sight, but from 1938 they adopted the Barr & Stroud GM2 sight as shown, where it was called the Fixed Gun Reflector Sight Mk II
(©Crown Copyright)

This posed shot shows armourers loading ammunition into the chutes to feed the spat-mounted machine guns on an Indian Air Force Lysander *(©British Official)*

Airframe Detail No.9 – Lysander 61

The prototype K6127 was used to test the fitment of Hispano 20mm cannon to each side for use as a potential anti-invasion beach strafer (©British Official)

This shot of a RCAF Lysander Mk II shows what look like two gun ports in the undercarriage legs, but the upper one is just an air intake
(©Library and Archives Canada)

Just to prove that K6127 was not the only installation of 20mm cannon to the Lysander, this image shows Mk II P1684 UG•A of No.16 (Army Co-operation) Squadron in June-July 1940. Such fitments would have been converted back to standard aircraft by early 1941 when the threat of invasion diminished (via Internet)

6.2 Flexible Armament

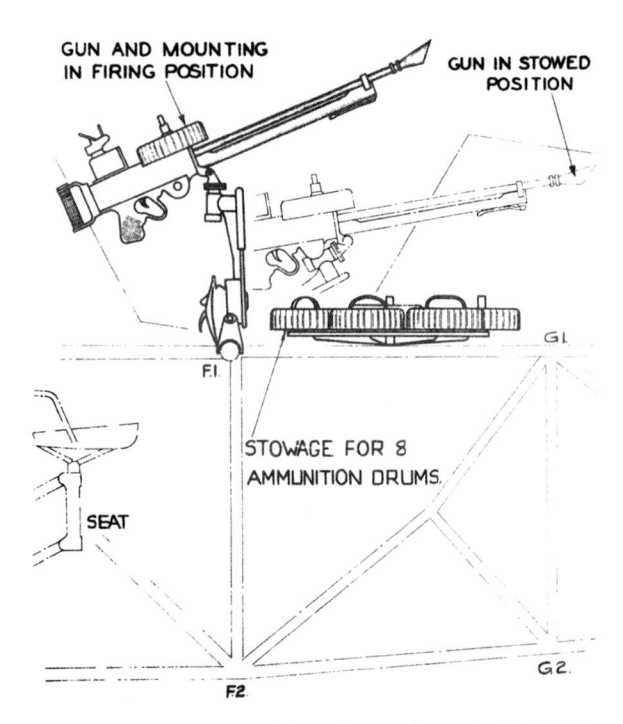

This diagram from the manual shows the original mount for the 0.303in machine-gun in the rear cockpit, along with the eight ammunition drum turntable (©Crown Copyright)

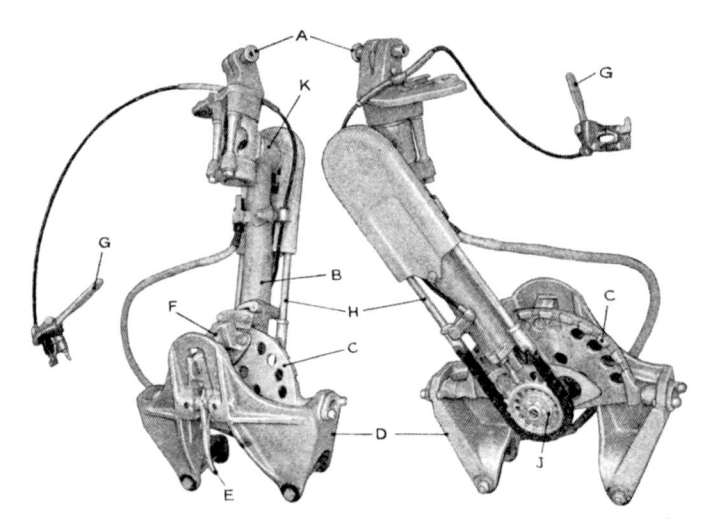

These two images from the manual show the front and back of the flexible gun mounting (©Crown Copyright)

This shot of LY-116 of 2/LeLv 16 with its pilot 2Lt Väinö Terho and gunner Sgt Kurt Sögerård allows you to see the Vickers K extended with an ammunition drum in place and the reflector gunsight on top
(©SA-kuva)

62 | Airframe Detail No.9 – Lysander

This period image by Westlands shows a flexible gun mount that is not like the Fairey-designed one seen on production machines, so we suspect this is one of the prototypes. You can however see eight ammunition drum turntable and just make out the R1091 radio receiver underneath the turntable (©Westlands)

This close up of an RCAF Lysander Mk II clearly shows the twin Browning machine-gun installation and the ammunition feeds to bins on either side (©Library and Archives Canada)

This diagram from the manual shows the aft portion of the rear cockpit, viewed to starboard, with the machine-gun mount etc. prominent (©Crown Copyright)

26. Gun mounting cross member
37. Electrical instrument panel
38. Floodlamp
39. Dimmer switch
40. Wireless remote controller
41. Charge regulating switch instruction label
51. Trailing aerial winch
52. Winch brake lever
54. Tapping (Morse) Key
55. Turntable trip lever locking catch
56. Turntable trip lever
57. Terminal block
60. Magazine stowage turntable
61. Magazine stowage pegs
62. Gun arm stowage catch
63. Cockpit decking
69. Vickers-K gun
70. Detachable magazine
71. Gun arm pivoting head
72. Rockable gun arm
73. Release lever for stowage of gun arm
74. Gated segment
75. Gun arm traverse control locking catch
76. Empty link and case bag
77. Bag retaining catch
78. Gun arm traverse control release lever

The twin Browning installation in a Mk III or IIIA with the Mk IIIA reflector gunsight visible (©British Official)

Airframe Detail No.9 – Lysander **63**

6.3 Turret Armament

K6127 as the P.12 Wendover (tandem wing) anti-invasion prototype, which initially only had this unarmed version of the turret fitted and seen here rotated through 180° so you can see the access doors

Here you can see K6127 as the P.12 at Boscombe Down, but now fitted with guns and a complete FN20 turret (©A&AEE/Crown Copyright)

Mk II P1723 was used for the mock-up installation of a Boulton-Paul Type A Mk III four-gun powered turret (©Westlands)

To give you a better idea of the detail in the FN 20 turret, here is a close-up of the starboard side of one in the rear of a Whitley (©Air Ministry)

This shows the Boulton-Paul Type A Mk III turret itself within the fuselage of P1723

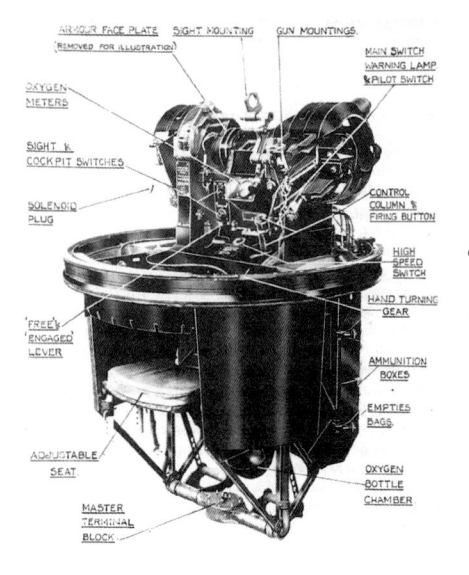

This photo from the manual shows the main components of the BP Type A turret, seen here with the cupola and guns removed (©Crown Copyright)

This diagram from the manual shows the upper portion of the B.P Type A turret (©Crown Copyright)

1. Ratchet control
2. Cupola doors release lever
3. Call light switches
4. Call lights
5. Rear gun trunnions
6. Armour plate
7. Oxygen delivery meter
8. Oxygen regulator valve
9. Oxygen supply meter
10. Reflector sight bracket
11. Supporting posts
12. Main panel lamp
13. Safety lever
14. Main switch
15. Warning lamp
16. Transfer switch
17. Manual control handle
18. Cupola door
19. Gun firing button
20. Control column
21. Socket for manual control handle
22. Operating lever
23. High-speed switch
24. Intercommunication socket lead
25. Disengaging gear lever
26. Panel lamp dimmer switch
27. Sight lamp switch
28. Side panel lamp
29. Side panel lamp dimmer switch

64 Airframe Detail No.9 – Lysander

6.4 Ordnance

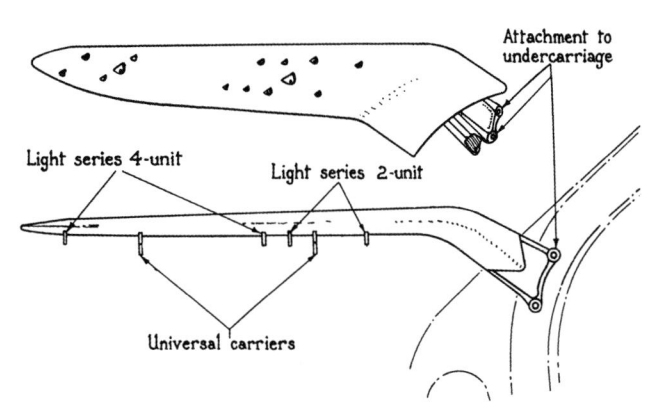

The Lysander was not intended as a bomber, although it had the capacity to carry small size bombs on the 'bomb wing' stub attached to each undercarriage leg *(©Crown Copyright)*

This is the skeletal structure within the 'bomb wings' *(©Crown Copyright)*

This official image shows a Type A Mk IID turret, which is similar to the Mk III used in P1723, note that the tubes you can see going across under the front of the turret ring, with diagonal ones on either side, are part of a ground stand that this turret was obviously in when photographed, but which has been partially removed from the negative *(©Crown Copyright)*

This period photograph shows a Universal Carrier attached to their specific attachment lugs on the 'bomb wing' *(©British Official)*

This is a Light Series 4 bomb rack attached to the outer pick-ups of the bomb wing – you can see why they were nicknamed a 'toast rack' *(©Air Ministry)*

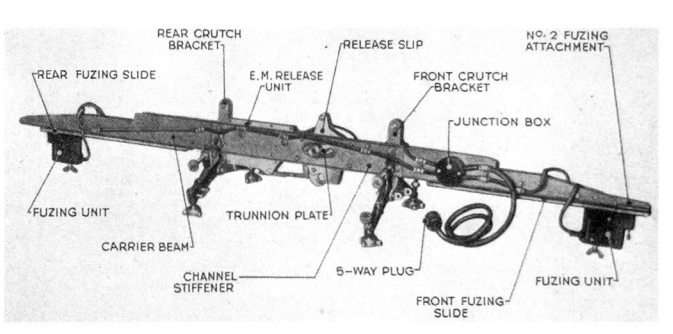

This is the Universal Bomb Carrier Type E.M./E.F. No. 1 Mk II, as used by the Lysander *(©Crown Copyright)*

A posed shot of RCAF technicians working on two Universal Bomb Carriers fitted to the stub wing of a Lysander in August 1940 *(©RCAF)*

Airframe Detail No.9 – Lysander **65**

A RCAF No.110 (Army Co-operation) Squadron Lysander is armed with practice bombs on the outer Light Series bomb rack – these bombs look to be around the 11.5lb version (©RCAF)

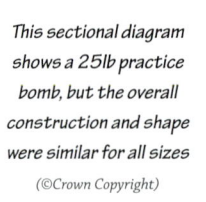

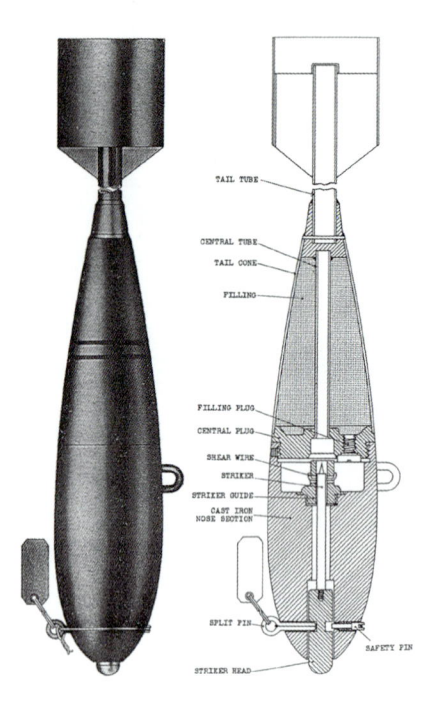

This sectional diagram shows a 25lb practice bomb, but the overall construction and shape were similar for all sizes
(©Crown Copyright)

This shot of an RCAF Lysander shows 20lb HE bombs on the outer Light Series bomb rack and a 120lb GP bomb on the inner Universal Bomb Carrier. Note the arming linkage to the fusing piston on the 120lb bomb and the arms on the outer bomb rack that prevent the spinners on the nose of the HE bombs from turning and thus arming them until each bomb is actually dropped (©RCAF)

These diagrams show a 20lb HE Mk I bomb, as could be carried by the Lysander; note the diagram on the left shows the type with the pistol exposed (©Crown Copyright)

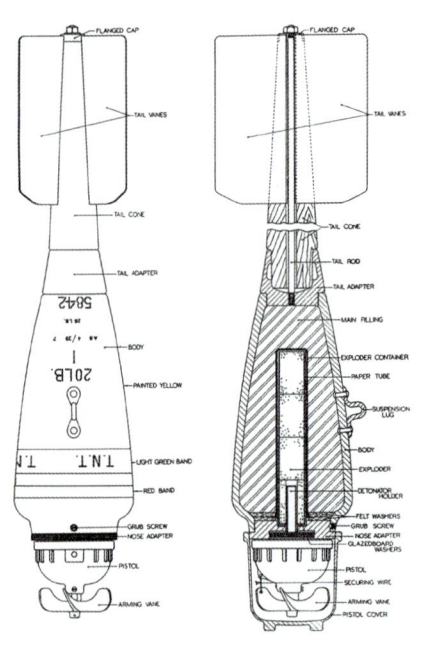

ASR squadron Lysanders would carry smoke-float flares on the rack under the rear fuselage and depicted here being loaded onto Mk IIIA, V9547 BA•E, of No.277 Squadron at RAF Hawkinge (©Air Ministry)

A lovely colour sectional diagram of the 'Smoke-Float Aircraft Navigation Mk I' flare as carried by ASR Lysander's
(©British Official)

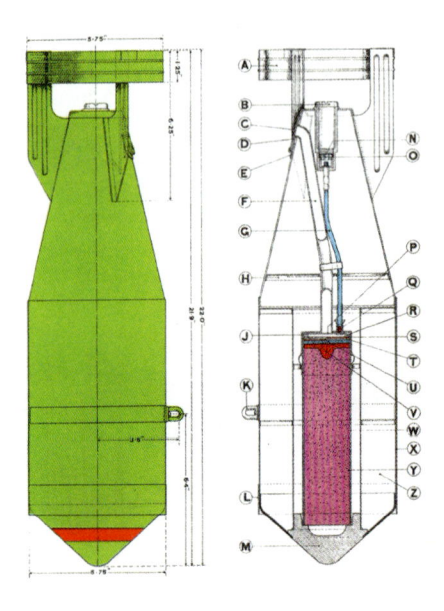

66 Airframe Detail No.9 – Lysander

The Mk I and Mk II could carry up to 250lb of bombs underneath the fuselage and here armourers working on such bombs in front of an Indian Air Force Lysander Mk II (©British Official)

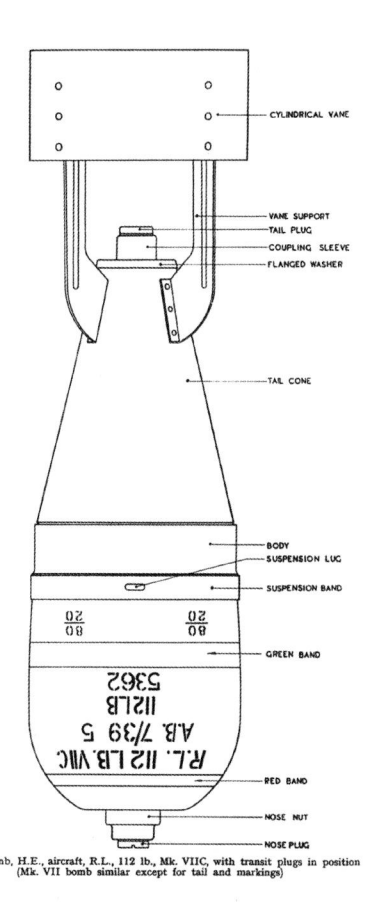

Bomb, H.E., aircraft, R.L., 112 lb., Mk. VIIC, with transit plugs in position (Mk. VII bomb similar except for tail and markings)

The Lysander could also carry the 112lb RL type bomb, as depicted here in Mk VIIC form, although these tend to only be seen in the pre and early war periods (©Crown Copyright)

The Lysander could also carry an SCI (smoke curtain installation) container on the Universal Carrier under each stub wing, as seen here on Mk IIIA V9311

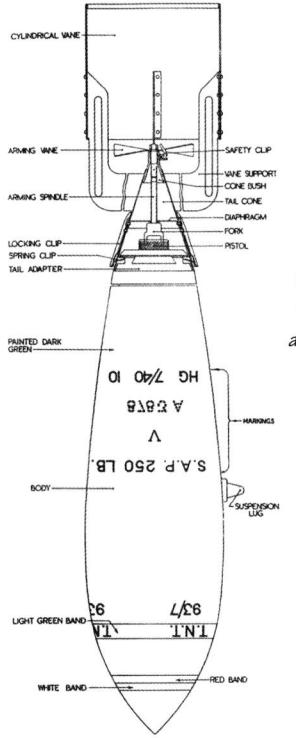

250lb bomb types that could be carried by the Lysander included the AS, GP, HE and SAP, the latter is depicted here in this period diagram (©Crown Copyright)

Bomb, H.E., aircraft, S.A.P., 250 lb., Mk. V, with tail in position

We could not find a clear image of a single SCI container, so this shows one of three tested-fitted on a Barracuda, but it does show it in greater detail than the shot of one carried by V9311 (©A&AEE/Crown Copyright)

Airframe Detail No.9 – Lysander **67**

7.1 Camera

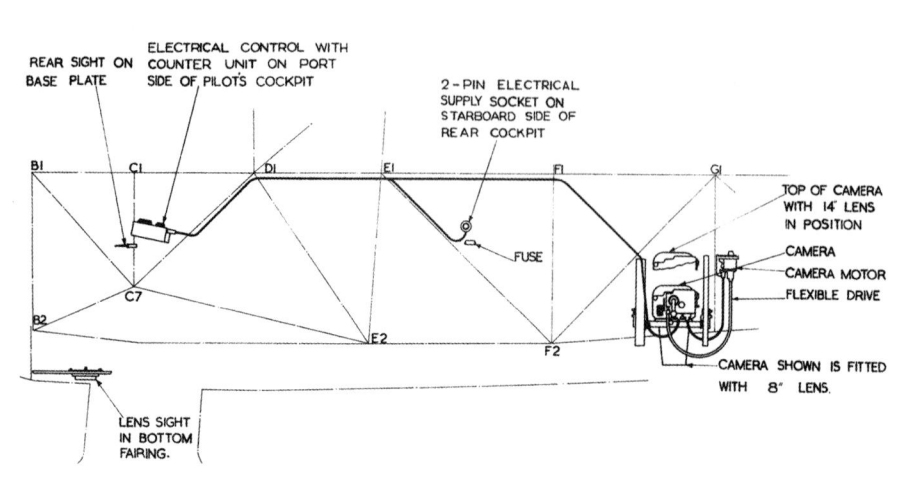

This diagram from the Mk II manual shows the F.24 camera installation (©Crown Copyright)

Here is the external view of the oblique F.24 camera in a Canadian Lysander (©Library and Archives Canada)

This period image of ground crew removing a F.24 camera from Lysander Mk IIIA, V9437, AR•V of No.309 (Polish) Squadron at Dunino, Fife, gives you an idea of how the camera is accessed from underneath (©British Official)

This photograph shows the obliquely mounted F.24 camera in a Canadian Lysander, circa 1940, viewed from the inside (©Library and Archives Canada)

This posed picture states that it shows ground crew installing camera equipment into a Lysander Mk II of No.225 Squadron at RAF Tilshead, Wiltshire. The airman on the right holds the F.24 camera with 8in lens, while the the airman on the left holds the camera motor unit. You can also see the battery up inside the fuselage, in front of the first airman's head (©British Official)

Here you have an RCAF version of the previous image, with a technician fitting a F.24 camera into the fuselage. The image also nicely shows the Canadian radio fit, visible on the ledge in front of the technician's head and the bomb rack just visible under the rear fuselage (©RCAF)

68 Airframe Detail No.9 – Lysander

7.2 Radio & Misc. Equipment

Canadian Lysanders were fitted with a different set of radio equipment to RAF examples, as seen here with the AR.2A (receiver) on the left and the AT.1.A (transmitter) on the right
(©Library and Archives Canada)

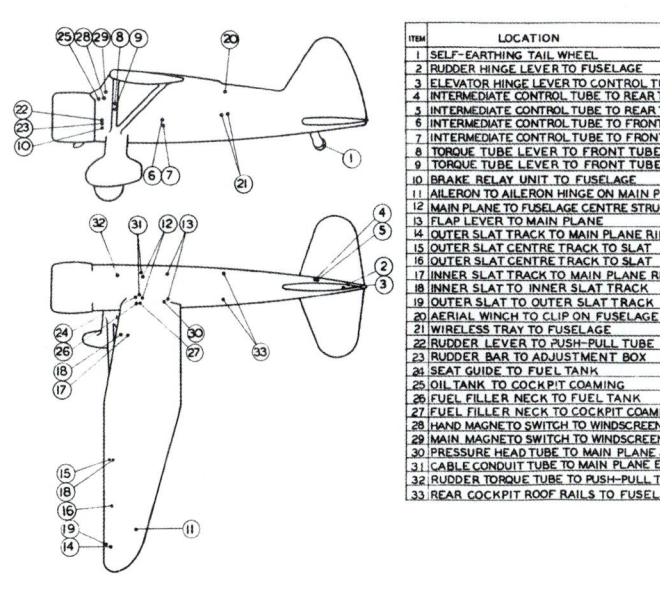

ITEM	LOCATION
1	SELF-EARTHING TAIL WHEEL
2	RUDDER HINGE LEVER TO FUSELAGE
3	ELEVATOR HINGE LEVER TO CONTROL TUBE
4	INTERMEDIATE CONTROL TUBE TO REAR TUBE
5	INTERMEDIATE CONTROL TUBE TO REAR TUBE
6	INTERMEDIATE CONTROL TUBE TO FRONT TUBE
7	INTERMEDIATE CONTROL TUBE TO FRONT TUBE
8	TORQUE TUBE LEVER TO FRONT TUBE
9	TORQUE TUBE LEVER TO FRONT TUBE
10	BRAKE RELAY UNIT TO FUSELAGE
11	AILERON TO AILERON HINGE ON MAIN PLANE
12	MAIN PLANE TO FUSELAGE CENTRE STRUCTURE
13	FLAP LEVER TO MAIN PLANE
14	OUTER SLAT TRACK TO MAIN PLANE RIB
15	OUTER SLAT CENTRE TRACK TO SLAT
16	OUTER SLAT CENTRE TRACK TO SLAT
17	INNER SLAT TRACK TO MAIN PLANE RIB
18	INNER SLAT TO INNER SLAT TRACK
19	OUTER SLAT TO OUTER SLAT TRACK
20	AERIAL WINCH TO CLIP ON FUSELAGE
21	WIRELESS TRAY TO FUSELAGE
22	RUDDER LEVER TO PUSH-PULL TUBE
23	RUDDER BAR TO ADJUSTMENT BOX
24	SEAT GUIDE TO FUEL TANK
25	OIL TANK TO COCKPIT COAMING
26	FUEL FILLER NECK TO FUEL TANK
27	FUEL FILLER NECK TO COCKPIT COAMING
28	HAND MAGNETO SWITCH TO WINDSCREEN BOLT
29	MAIN MAGNETO SWITCH TO WINDSCREEN BOLT
30	PRESSURE HEAD TUBE TO MAIN PLANE JOINT
31	CABLE CONDUIT TUBE TO MAIN PLANE END RIB
32	RUDDER TORQUE TUBE TO PUSH-PULL TUBE
33	REAR COCKPIT ROOF RAILS TO FUSELAGE

Sadly, there is no clear diagram or image in any of the manuals showing the radio transmitter and receiver units, this bonding diagram though does show the location of the radio, marked as '21', which is the earthing of the radio tray (©Crown Copyright)

7.3 Long Range Tank

This is the front view of the RAF Museum's Lysander SD long range tank, you can see the sanding on the front aerodynamic cover, along with the strap retaining it and, on the top, the filler point

A nice clear image of the long range tank on Shuttleworth's Lysander Mk III, this is a mock-up, but very accurate (©J. Jankovic)

This view shows the rear portion of the ex-Harrow fuel tank used by the clandestine Lysanders and seen here on the RAF Museum's example during restoration. The rearmost section is just an aerodynamic shape held on by the metal strap you can see just behind the vent pipe visible at the top

A starboard side shot of the tank under The Shuttleworth's example, which allows you to see the front and rear attachment struts and straps, the support bars running aft from the front strut and the rear filler cap and (right at the back) the breather pipe

Again this is The Shuttleworth's example, but from this angle you can see the front retain struts/straps, the 'V' brace in the middle and, at the front, the filler and feed pie going up into the underside of the forward fuselage

Airframe Detail No.9 – Lysander

7.4 Parachute Container

This posed image shows a Lysander pilot in full flying gear and sitting on his parachute pack, seated alongside the port stub wing of his aircraft with a Mk VB parachute container on the inboard Universal Carrier (©Air Ministry)

This view from the rear of these Mk VB Parachute Containers shows the parachute packs built into the back of the container and the lanyard from it to the Universal Carrier that will deploy the chute once the containers drops a set distance from the carrier (©Air Ministry)

The carriage of two Mk VB parachute containers was not unusual with the Lysander and this close-up views shows such an installation and confirms that there were also two bracing struts between the inner and outer Universal Carriers, albeit as two separate horizontal tubes with the inboard ones as a 'V' (©British Official)

This RCAF Lysander Mk II carries four Parachute Containers, at Dartmouth, Nova Scotia on the 19th April 1941 (©Library and Archives Canada)

7.5 ASR Equipment

In this period image ground crew fold up a dinghy with rations etc. inside to load into the SBC [Small Bomb Container] for an ASR Lysander. The valise (into which the dinghy etc. will go) can be seen on the ground on the far right, while the SBC is alongside it on its left [upside down] (©British Official)

Here a dinghy inside a valise is loaded up into a SBC (Small Bomb Container) fitted to a universal carrier on the inboard pick-up of the stub wing on a No.277 (ASR) Squadron Lysander based at RAF Stapleford Tawney (©Air Ministry)

In this posed image shows two ground crew raising the SBC to the Universal Carrier on an ASR Lysander, you can clearly see the tube at the top of the SBC that is held by the pick-ups (the ground crewman at the front is holding one set of pick-up jaws apart) of the carrier (©British Official)

This is the previous posed photograph but taken from the front (©British Official)

7.6 Target Towing Winch & Glider Towing

This shot up underneath NASM's Lysander, shows the doors plus the cut-out in the front edge for the strut and pulley arrangement (©S. Willey)

This image shows the winch drums in the rear cockpit, with the pulley for cable visible at the bottom edge

FUSELAGE JOINT H.1.
RELEASE HOOK MOUNTING.
RELEASE HOOK.
FUSELAGE JOINT K.2.
PULLEY.
PILOT'S RELEASE CONTROL KNOB.
RETURN SPRING.
FAIRLEADS.
CONTROL RUN IN FUSELAGE

This close-up of the starboard side of a TT Mk III during construction shows the tubular structure and pulley (arrowed) below the fuselage that redirected the cable from the winch inside through 90° to play out behind the aircraft (©Westlands)

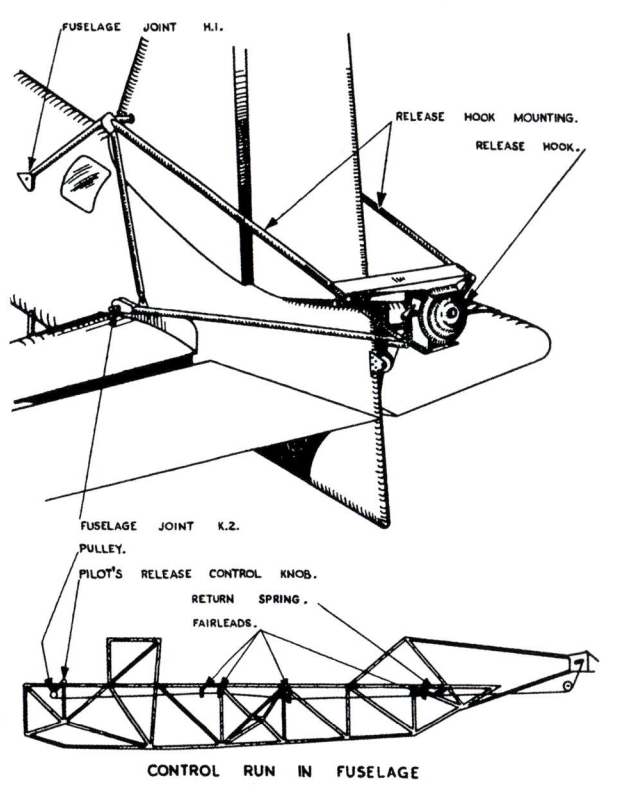

Although not used all that often, the Lysander could be adapted for towing gliders via this bridle attached to the rear fuselage (©Crown Copyright)

7.7 Desert Equipment, DDT Spraying & Access Panels

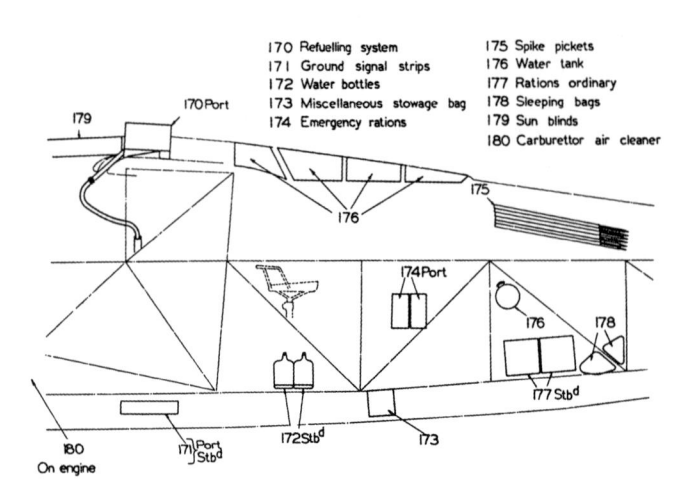

170 Refuelling system
171 Ground signal strips
172 Water bottles
173 Miscellaneous stowage bag
174 Emergency rations
175 Spike pickets
176 Water tank
177 Rations ordinary
178 Sleeping bags
179 Sun blinds
180 Carburettor air cleaner

This diagram from the manual shows the location of desert quipment in the Lysander

This shot shows a Lysander being used by the RAF Anti-Malaria Control Unit in Sicily, as it sprays DDT over swamps in an effort to eradicate malaria-carrying mosquitoes – you can see the special hopper unit underneath the fuselage
(©British Official)

A ground crew member loads bags of DDT into smoke dispensing equipment, adapted for use as an anti-mosquito spray under the fuselage of a Westland Lysander in Sicily, as the pilots look on
(©British Official)

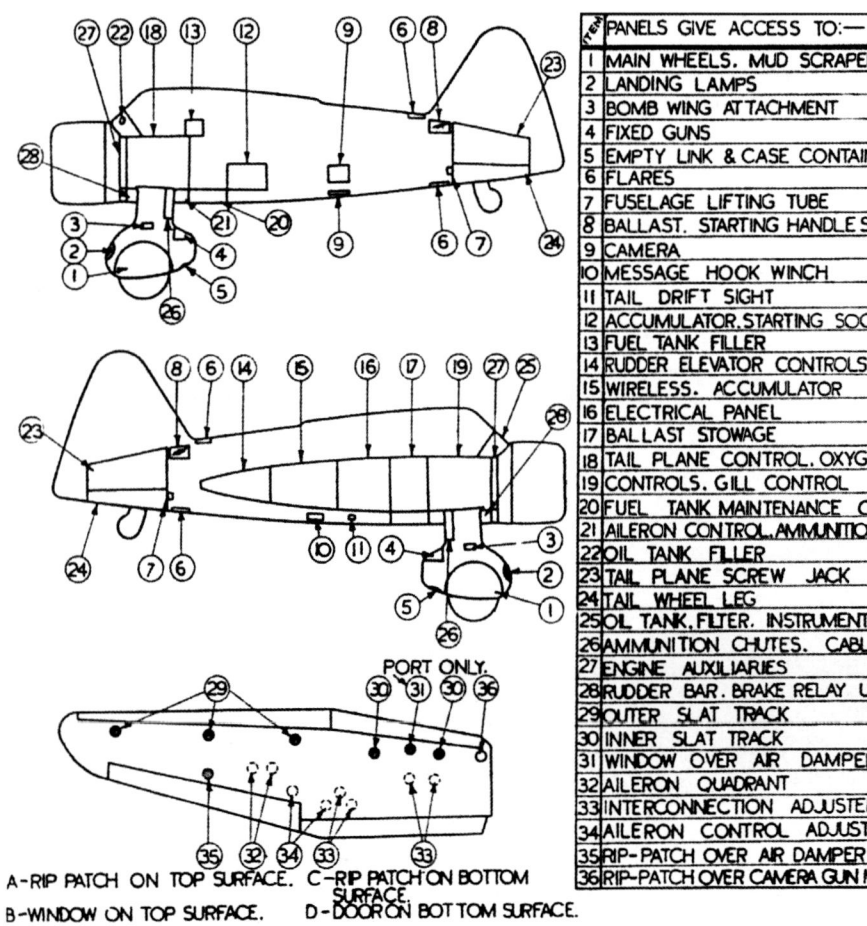

	PANELS GIVE ACCESS TO:—
1	MAIN WHEELS. MUD SCRAPERS
2	LANDING LAMPS
3	BOMB WING ATTACHMENT
4	FIXED GUNS
5	EMPTY LINK & CASE CONTAINER
6	FLARES
7	FUSELAGE LIFTING TUBE
8	BALLAST. STARTING HANDLE STOWAGE
9	CAMERA
10	MESSAGE HOOK WINCH
11	TAIL DRIFT SIGHT
12	ACCUMULATOR, STARTING SOCKET
13	FUEL TANK FILLER
14	RUDDER ELEVATOR CONTROLS
15	WIRELESS. ACCUMULATOR
16	ELECTRICAL PANEL
17	BALLAST STOWAGE
18	TAIL PLANE CONTROL. OXYGEN
19	CONTROLS. GILL CONTROL
20	FUEL TANK MAINTENANCE COCK
21	AILERON CONTROL, AMMUNITION BOXES
22	OIL TANK FILLER
23	TAIL PLANE SCREW JACK
24	TAIL WHEEL LEG
25	OIL TANK, FILTER. INSTRUMENTS.
26	AMMUNITION CHUTES. CABLES
27	ENGINE AUXILIARIES
28	RUDDER BAR. BRAKE RELAY UNIT
29	OUTER SLAT TRACK B
30	INNER SLAT TRACK B
31	WINDOW OVER AIR DAMPER B
32	AILERON QUADRANT D
33	INTERCONNECTION ADJUSTERS D
34	AILERON CONTROL ADJUSTERS D
35	RIP-PATCH OVER AIR DAMPER C
36	RIP-PATCH OVER CAMERA GUN MTG. A

A - RIP PATCH ON TOP SURFACE.
B - WINDOW ON TOP SURFACE.
C - RIP PATCH ON BOTTOM SURFACE.
D - DOOR ON BOTTOM SURFACE.

This diagram from the manual shows the various access panels on the airframe and applies to all British-built Lysanders (©Crown Copyright)

Lysander Prototype, K6127 marked as '6' for the New Types Park at the Hendon Air Display, 1937
Aluminium overall with all lettering in black. Type A roundels in six positions

Section 2

Camouflage & Markings

The Lysander had a varied career and as such carried quite a few schemes in its life. Most of these are well documented with period images, plus most of the official Air Diagrams etc. still exist, so you can make a pretty good case for each scheme. That said, the whole subject of camouflage and markings is massive and you can write volumes about it, speculating on what 'was' and 'was not', but we will try and keep it concise. Just remember, nothing is an absolute when it comes to camouflage and markings.

Prototypes

Both K6127 and K6128 were supplied in an overall aluminium scheme, with Type A roundels applied either side of the fuselage, just below the rear edge of the rear canopy and above and below each wing, situated well outboard, only just inboard of the tip. The serial number was applied in either side of the rear fuselage in 8in high black characters, these were on a hypothetical line projecting forward from the leading edge of the horizontal tailplane. When K6127 was displayed at Hendon it carried the New Type Park number '6' in a large black character on either side of the rear fuselage, between the roundel and serial number.

Later the serial number was also applied on either side of the rudder, again in 8in high black characters (written with the 'K' above the '6127'), as well as under each outer wing panel. These latter markings were applied so that it could be read from the trailing edge

K6127 in its original form (note the shape of the tail cone, due to the original fixed tailplane), in overall aluminium with bare metal cowlings, Type A roundels on both fuselage and wings and the New Type Park number '6'

K6127 in its revised form with the variable incidence tailplane, seen in overall aluminium with bare metal cowling and Type A roundels on both fuselage and wings

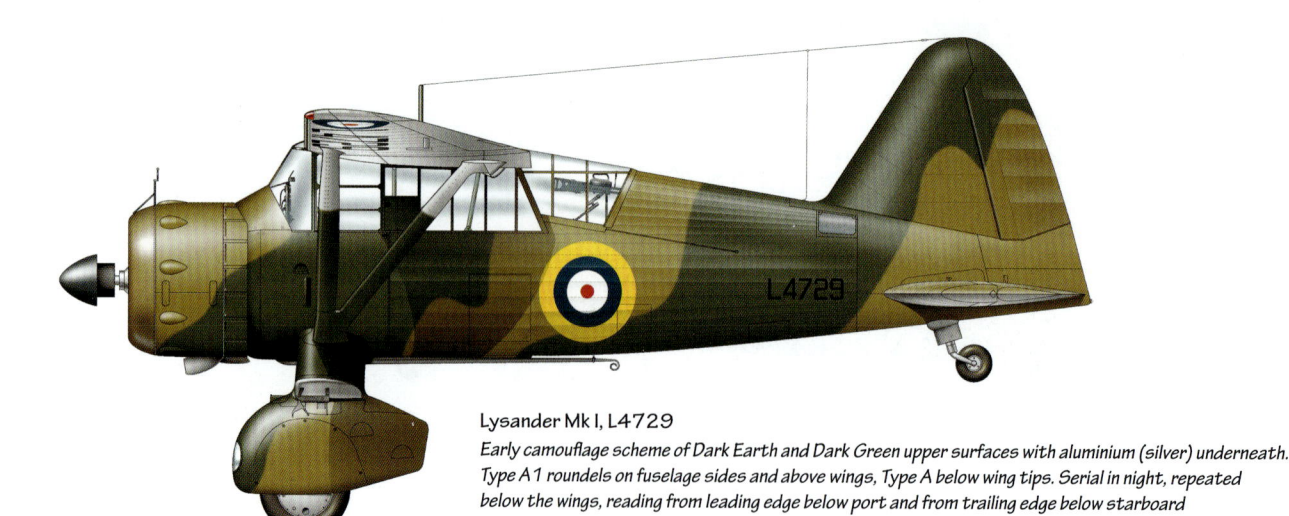

Lysander Mk I, L4729
Early camouflage scheme of Dark Earth and Dark Green upper surfaces with aluminium (silver) underneath. Type A1 roundels on fuselage sides and above wings, Type A below wing tips. Serial in night, repeated below the wings, reading from leading edge below port and from trailing edge below starboard

looking forward under the starboard wing and from the leading edge looking aft under the port.

The only changes with K6128 from K6127 in its later form was that during trials in Cairo it looks to have had a band applied around the rear fuselage, between the roundel and serial number. It is likely this was either black or red.

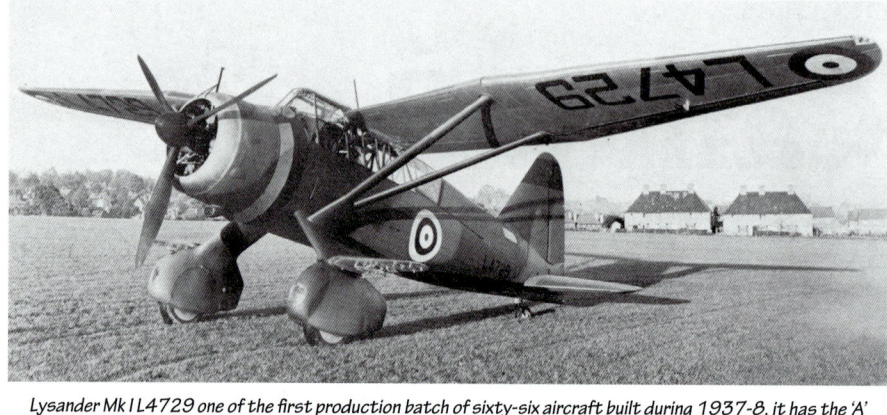

Lysander Mk I L4729 one of the first production batch of sixty-six aircraft built during 1937-8, it has the 'A' pattern camouflage, aluminium undersides and the serial repeated under the wings – note the roundel under the wing right out near the tip (©Air Ministry)

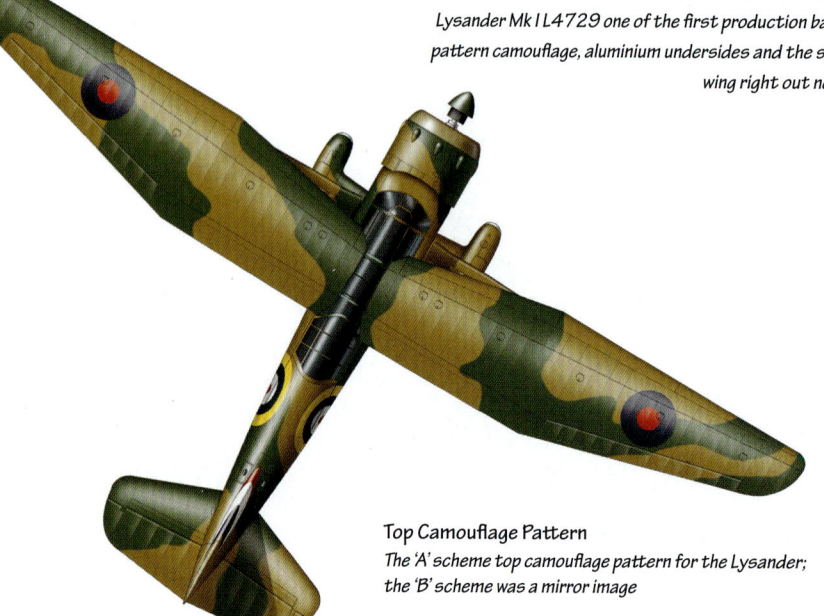

Top Camouflage Pattern
The 'A' scheme top camouflage pattern for the Lysander; the 'B' scheme was a mirror image

outer wing panel, positioned well outboard at the tip. The serial number was applied either side of the rear fuselage in 8in high black characters and was repeated in 30in high versions below each wing. As with the prototypes, these were applied so that it could be read from the trailing edge looking forward under the starboard wing and from the leading edge looking aft under the port. These serials were usually centralised between the tip and wing struts and were located well forward, so the top/bottom edges were along the line of the slats.

In September 1938 with the Munich Crisis the wing undersides were painted Night (black) under the port and white under the starboard; note that the underside of the

Production

Temperate Land Scheme

The initial production batch were painted with Dark Green and Dark Earth disruptive camouflage over aluminium undersides. The camouflage was offered in A and B patterns, the latter being a mirror-image of the former. The markings comprised a 35in diameter Type A1 roundel on either side of the fuselage and a 35in diameter version above each wing, although it should be noted that the larger 49in diameter roundel was sometimes applied above the wings instead. A 30in diameter Type A roundel was applied under each

This port side views of Mk I L4729 shows the standard finish for first production batch in 1938

Lysander Mk I, KJ•M (serial overpainted), No.16 (Army Co-operation) Squadron RAF, Air Component in France, 1939
Dark Green/Dark Earth upper surfaces, wrapped around fuselage; tailplane undersides in aluminium. Port wing Night (with aluminium aileron), starboard wing aluminium (Night aileron). Yellow spinner. B type fuselage roundels; it is believed that no roundels were carried on top of wings

horizontal tailplanes usually remained in aluminium and there are some examples with the starboard wing also in aluminium. The application of squadron codes and revised roundels meant that most machines lacked the serial number on either side of the rear fuselage. At this time the two-character squadron identification code system was introduced. These were applied in Sky Grey characters that were approximately 36in high (many variations exist) and were always forward of the roundel on each side of the fuselage. An individual aircraft identification letter was applied on the other side of the fuselage roundel in the same colour/style. The rather bright Type A/A1 roundels were replaced with the duller Type B version, with a 25in diameter version on either side of the fuselage and a 35in version above and below the wings (some lacked this latter marking). You will find exceptions though, as Nos.2 and 13 squadron aircraft can be seen with either the pre-war underwing colours, serial number or roundels.

Lysander Mk Is of No.16 (Army Co-operation) Squadron in formation, note the serial numbers have been removed and on KJ•M you can see the aileron of the port wing underside that is painted in contrasting aluminium (©Air Ministry)

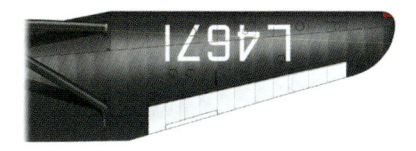

Early RAF style rendering of Night/White underwing finish with aluminium used instead of white sometimes and serial also carried on very early examples

In April 1939 the underwing roundels were deleted, then in November the underwing roundels were reinstated, going back to 36in diameter Type A. At the same time the fuselage Type B roundel was revised to the Type A of the same diameter, however as usual there were various interpretations of the regulations as seen in the accompanying images and profile.

In May 1940 a thin yellow outer ring was added to the fuselage roundel, changing it into a Type A1 and there are numerous variations as units interpreted the new instructions differently. A fin flash of equal vertical bars of red, white and blue was applied over the vertical fin and set at the same angle as the rudder hinge. These stripes were supposed to be the same width as the blue of the fuselage roundel, but were more often 8in or 9in, plus there are those that had the stripes over the entire vertical fin. In August 1940 the fin flash was standardised into 8in wide stripes that were 27in high.

By June 1940 a new colour was introduced

Lysander Mk II of No.13 Squadron in France with temporary tent accommodation, note the small 25in diameter Type A fuselage roundel instead of the prescribed 36in and the ones under each wing right out towards the tip

Airframe Detail No.9 – Lysander

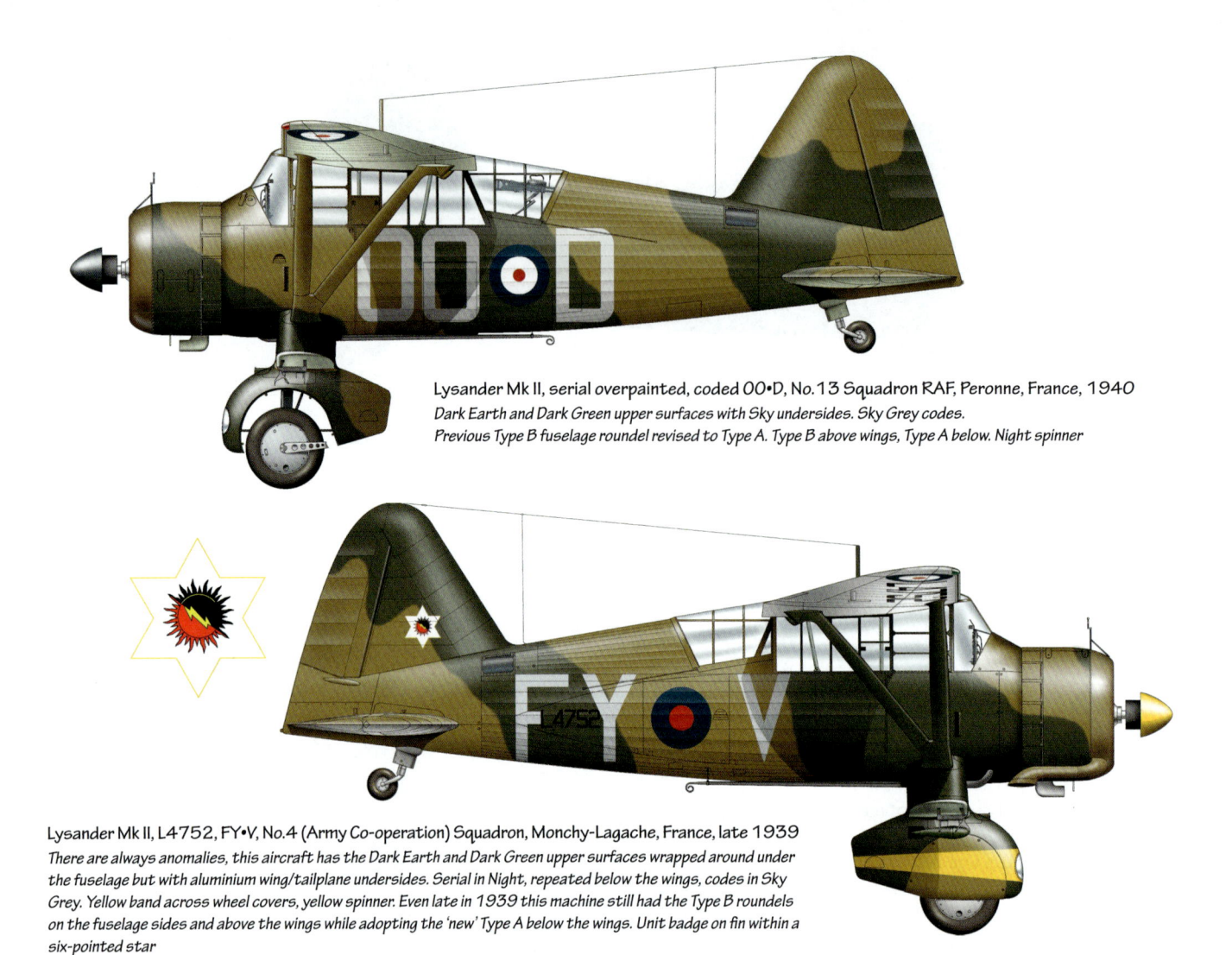

Lysander Mk II, serial overpainted, coded OO•D, No.13 Squadron RAF, Peronne, France, 1940
Dark Earth and Dark Green upper surfaces with Sky undersides. Sky Grey codes.
Previous Type B fuselage roundel revised to Type A. Type B above wings, Type A below. Night spinner

Lysander Mk II, L4752, FY•V, No.4 (Army Co-operation) Squadron, Monchy-Lagache, France, late 1939
There are always anomalies, this aircraft has the Dark Earth and Dark Green upper surfaces wrapped around under the fuselage but with aluminium wing/tailplane undersides. Serial in Night, repeated below the wings, codes in Sky Grey. Yellow band across wheel covers, yellow spinner. Even late in 1939 this machine still had the Type B roundels on the fuselage sides and above the wings while adopting the 'new' Type A below the wings. Unit badge on fin within a six-pointed star

Lysander Mk IIs, N1294, LX•T and L6865, LX•E (nearest) of No.225 Squadron based at RAF Tilshead, Wiltshire, flying in loose formation on a training flight. Note the Type A1 fuselage roundels and the light colour of the undersides of the wings

amendments to the existing regulations, thus resulting in many thinking that Sky Type 'S' was used from the very beginning, when 'duck-egg blue' was the first term used in all official documents. The fact that the later Sky Type 'S' is lighter than duck-egg blue leads to further confusion, but the nature of the regulations at the time led to a rather vague understanding of its nature by both the RAF and paint manufacturers and as you would expect that resulted in numerous shades existing at the time all encompassed by the terms 'Duck Egg Green' or 'Sky'. The roundels under the wings were also dispensed with at this stage and you for the undersides of aircraft that was to be adopted by all in-service aircraft from the 6th and to be applied at the factory on all new production aircraft from the 11th. Here the story gets a bit complicated because those around at the time noted down what they saw (M.J.F. Bowyer), stated that 'pale blue shades' were evident and he went on to say that more commonly this 'sky' tint was meant to be blue but in fact had a shade of green in it and is thus more accurately called 'duck-egg green' (or duck-egg blue). It is certainly the case that the AMO of the time termed the new colour as 'duck-egg blue', but later the term Sky Type 'S' (S = Smooth) was used by the Air Ministry and this was subsequently used in all future

Lysanders of No.225 Squadron, with N1294 nearest showing the post-June 1940 scheme with the lack of underwing roundels, Sky undersurfaces and a Type A1 fuselage roundel. The fin flash highlights the confusion for interpretation of the regulations, as the bands may be 8 or 9in wide, but they are set vertically and not the full fin height, whilst the aircraft in the background has the bands following the angle of the rudder hinge and they are full height (©British Official)

Airframe Detail No.9 – Lysander

Lysander Mk II, L4818, KO•L, No.2 (Army Co-operation) Squadron, 1940
Dark Earth/Dark Green upper surfaces (wrapped around underside of fuselage); Sky undersides of wings, tailplane and winglets. Sky Grey codes. Note Type A fuselage roundel modified to Type A1 with addition of narrow yellow band and gas detection panel on front of wheel fairings

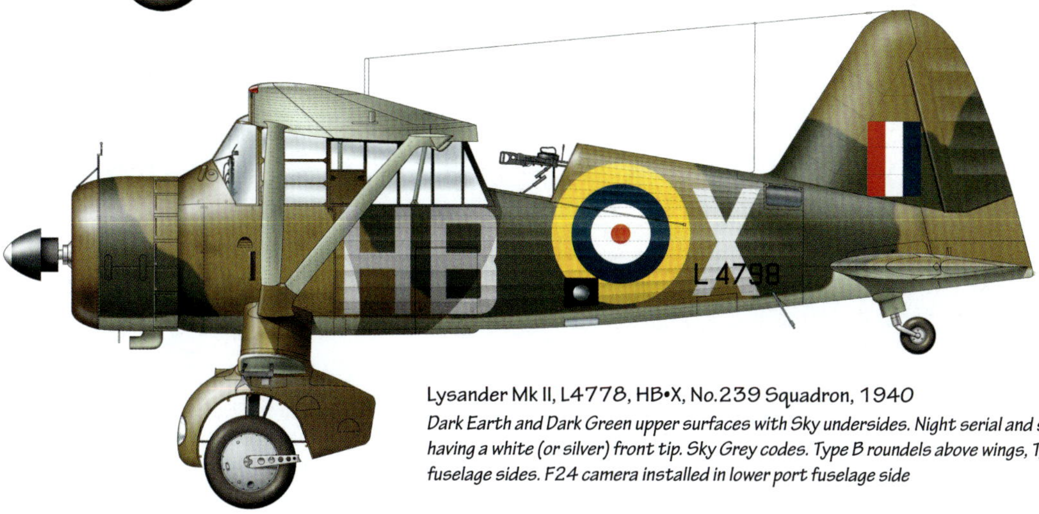

Lysander Mk II, L4778, HB•X, No.239 Squadron, 1940
Dark Earth and Dark Green upper surfaces with Sky undersides. Night serial and spinner, the latter having a white (or silver) front tip. Sky Grey codes. Type B roundels above wings, Type A1 on the fuselage sides. F24 camera installed in lower port fuselage side

will find some machines that had the camouflage applied right round the fuselage, only having Sky underneath the tail and wings.

In May 1942 the Type B roundel was replaced with the new Type C, with a yellow-ringed version (Type C1) for use on dark surrounding colours. On the Lysander this was 30in diameter on the fuselage and 35in for the wings. The fin flash was also changed to Type C, comprising bands of red (front – 11in), white (2in) and blue (11in) and at this stage the fuselage codes changed to Dull Red. By this stage though, Lysander use was very much restricted to ASR/FAA and target towing usage in the UK or standard and Special Duties in the Middle and Far East (see elsewhere for each).

Standard finish for late production batch in December 1941 and see here on Mk IIIA V9602

Lysander Mk II, L4761, AN•B, No.13 Squadron, 1939
While the Dark Earth/Dark Green upper surfaces are standard, this machine has Sky undersides, which weren't common this early and the undersides of port wing is Night (with white serial), while the starboard is white (Night serial) as per the 1938 Munich Crisis regulations. It also has the Type B roundels on the fuselage and above the wings; codes in Sky Grey. Note unit crest in six-pointed star on fin; spinner is red

Airframe Detail No.9 – Lysander

Lysander Mk I, P1684, UG•A, No.16 (Army Co-operation) Squadron RAF Teversham, August 1940
Dark Earth/Dark Green upper surfaces; Sky undersides. Sky Grey codes; flash covers the entire fin and raked at the rudder hinge-line angle. Type A1 roundels on fuselage, and Type B above wings

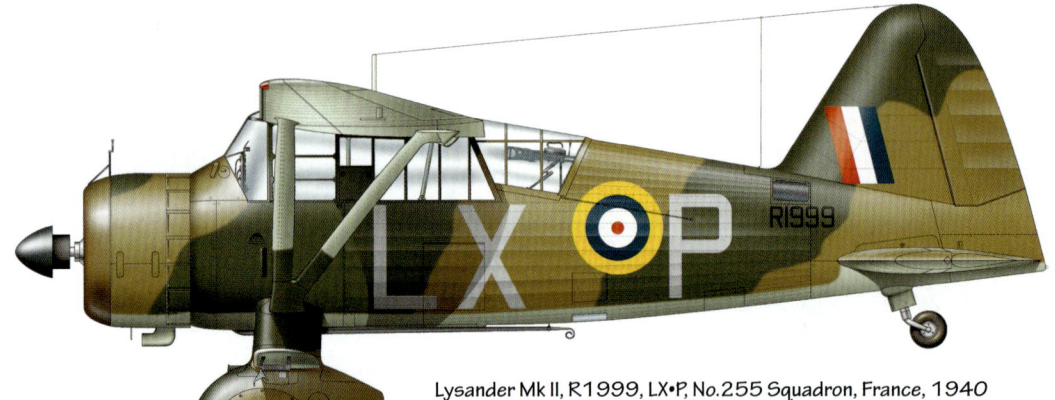

Lysander Mk II, R1999, LX•P, No.255 Squadron, France, 1940
Dark Earth and Dark Green upper surfaces with Sky undersides. Sky Grey codes, Night spinner and serial. Type B roundels above wings, Type A1 on fuselage sides. Note the non-standard fin flash

Lysander Mk III, T1423, No.309 (Polish) Squadron, Scotland, 1942
Dark Green and Dark Earth upper surfaces with Sky undersides. This aircraft has Type B roundels above wings, but even though seen in 1942 it still has Type A1 roundels on the fuselage sides. Serial and spinner in Night. Polish flag aft of fuselage roundel. Shown as operated before being allocated squadron codes

Lysander IIIA, V9576, AR•N, No.309 (Polish) Squadron, RAF Abbotsinch
Dark Earth/Dark Green upper surfaces, with Sky undersides; codes are in Sky Grey. Type A1 roundels on fuselage (followed by the Polish emblem), Type B roundels above wings, none below

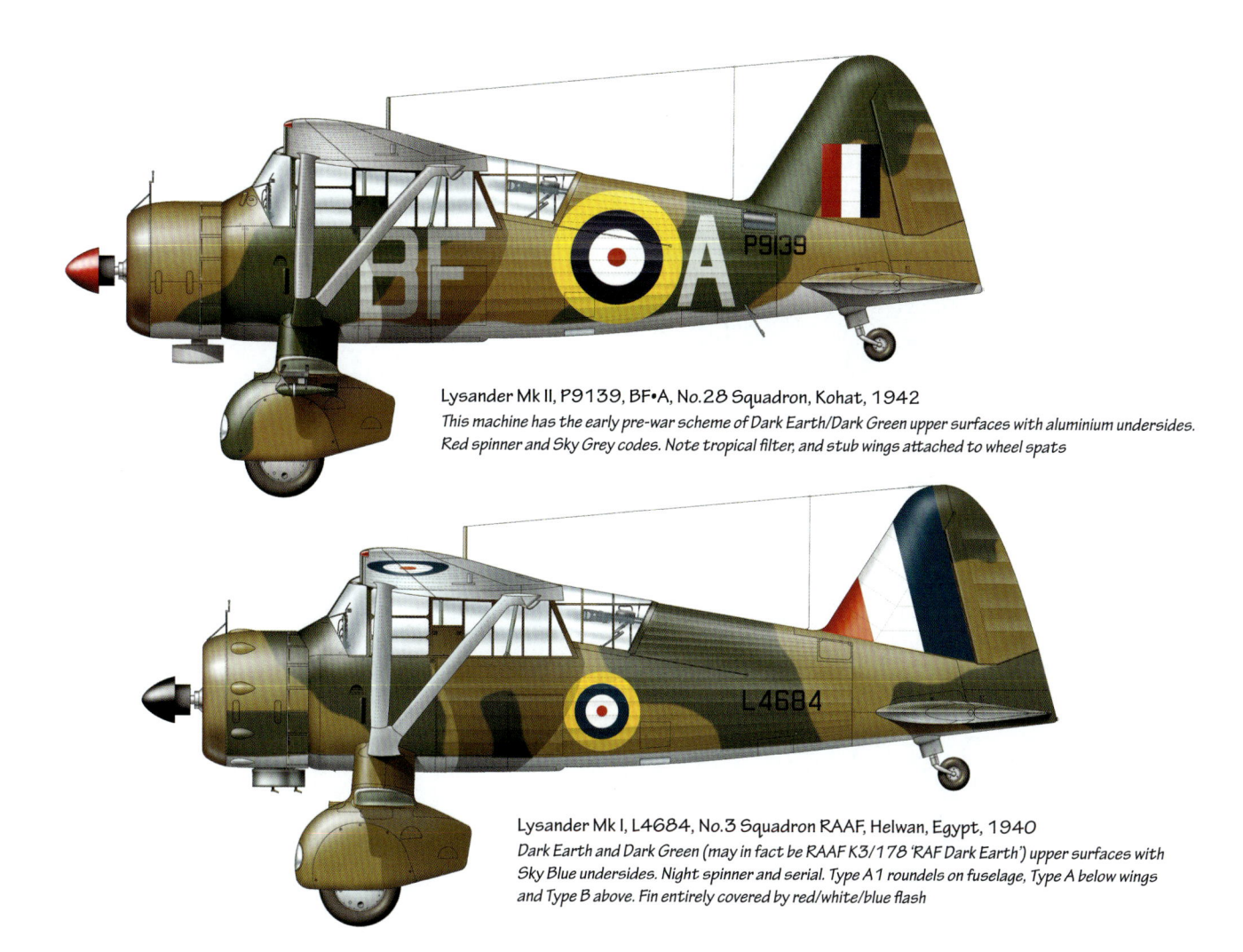

Lysander Mk II, P9139, BF•A, No.28 Squadron, Kohat, 1942
This machine has the early pre-war scheme of Dark Earth/Dark Green upper surfaces with aluminium undersides. Red spinner and Sky Grey codes. Note tropical filter, and stub wings attached to wheel spats

Lysander Mk I, L4684, No.3 Squadron RAAF, Helwan, Egypt, 1940
Dark Earth and Dark Green (may in fact be RAAF K3/178 'RAF Dark Earth') upper surfaces with Sky Blue undersides. Night spinner and serial. Type A1 roundels on fuselage, Type A below wings and Type B above. Fin entirely covered by red/white/blue flash

Middle & Far East

A scheme specific to operations in a tropical environment (Tropical Land Scheme) were considered as early as 1939 as an addenda to AMO A.520/39, although no documents survive to confirm this. It used Dark Green with Light Earth in place of Dark Earth, but from 12th December 1940 (AMO A.926/40) allowed Middle Stone to be used in place of Dark Green, however it was a relatively new colour at this stage, so there were delays in getting supplies into the theatres and thus Light Earth remained in use. From the 10th July 1941 AMO A.513/41 mistakenly authorised the use of Middle Stone and Dark Green and this was corrected shortly afterwards to Middle Stone and Dark Earth, although there may be some machines that used the incorrect scheme? This new scheme was officially designated the Desert Scheme on the 28th August 1941 via AMO A.687/41. Adoption of the correct (or incorrect) new scheme was entirely discretional, so some machines may have retained the Temperate Land Scheme until such times as operational requirements or repairs allowed the aircraft to be repainted. Slow supplies of paint to the Middle East may well have resulted in the adoption of the RAAF colour K3/178 RAF Dark Earth (later renamed Earth Brown) and that may explain why colour images show a very much darker colour that would be expected for Dark Earth on some machines. This is not conclusive however, because the use of Dark Green also gives the same sort of high contrast between the two colours (many sources also state that the Middlestone/Dark Green scheme was never applied to any airframes in the theatre).

The Lysanders supplied to the Middle East were initially supplied in the standard Temperate Land Scheme of Dark Green/Dark Earth/Sky but this soon wore, tended to make the aircraft soak up the heat and was quite visible against the sand and limited shrub of the desert, so they were often repainted during servicing or as a matter of routine by their squadron. Repainted these machines adopted the Tropical Land Scheme of Dark Earth and Middle Stone on the upper surfaces in the same style disruptive scheme as used by Dark Green and Dark Earth. As far as the undersides go, the use of Sky was also supplemented by Sky Blue, but the regulations stipulated Azure Blue for the undersides, however this colour was not liked in the theatre as it was very visible, so Sky Blue was often used. It should be noted that various period photographs show that the entire fuselage was often done in the camouflage colours, whilst only the underside of the tail and

Lysander Mk II, R1992 used to transport General Ginbachan Singh whilst he visited Indian troops in the Middle East

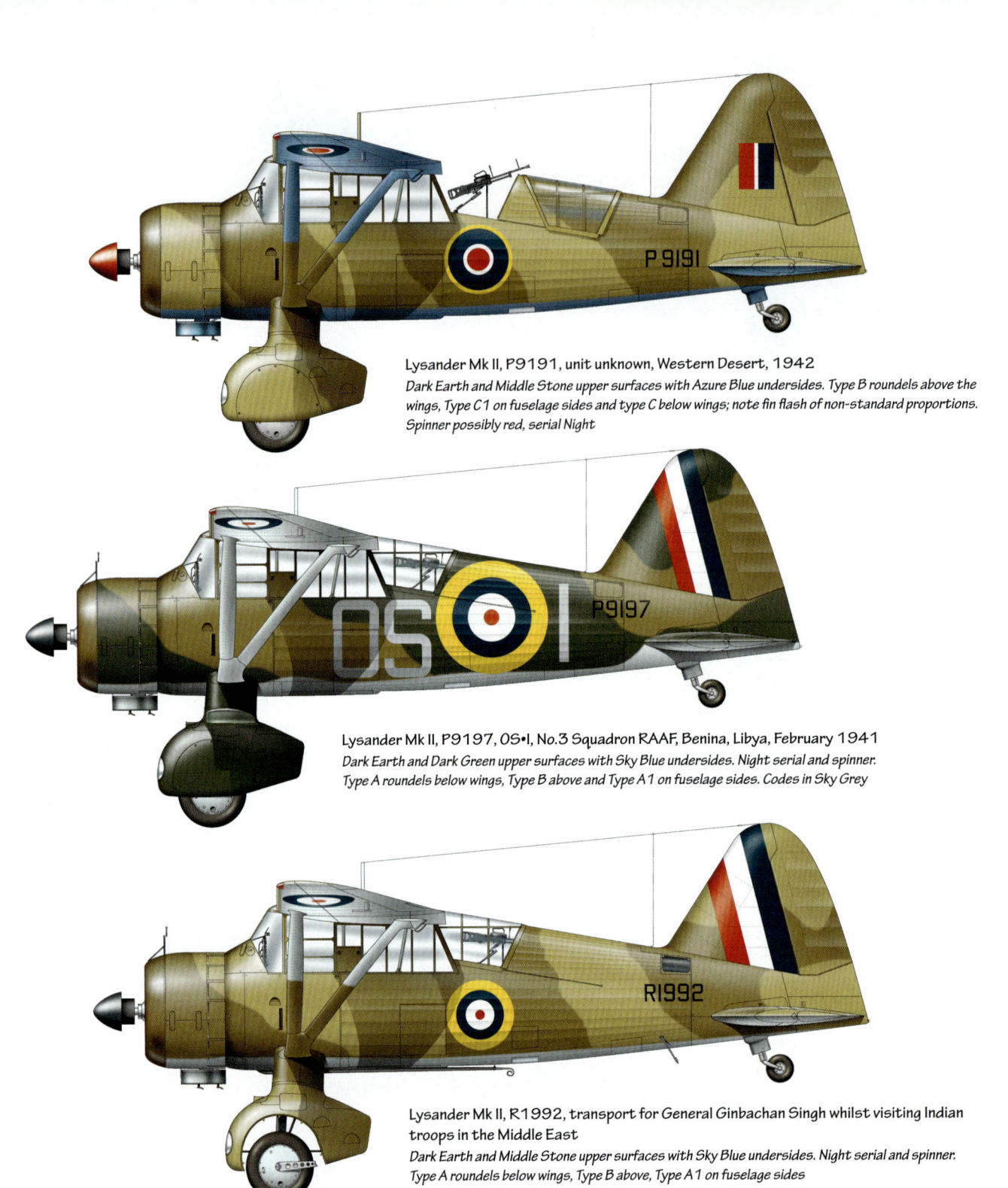

Lysander Mk II, P9191, unit unknown, Western Desert, 1942
Dark Earth and Middle Stone upper surfaces with Azure Blue undersides. Type B roundels above the wings, Type C1 on fuselage sides and type C below wings; note fin flash of non-standard proportions. Spinner possibly red, serial Night

Lysander Mk II, P9197, OS•I, No.3 Squadron RAAF, Benina, Libya, February 1941
Dark Earth and Dark Green upper surfaces with Sky Blue undersides. Night serial and spinner. Type A roundels below wings, Type B above and Type A1 on fuselage sides. Codes in Sky Grey

Lysander Mk II, R1992, transport for General Ginbachan Singh whilst visiting Indian troops in the Middle East
Dark Earth and Middle Stone upper surfaces with Sky Blue undersides. Night serial and spinner. Type A roundels below wings, Type B above, Type A1 on fuselage sides

Lysander Mk III, V9606, No.1433 Flight, Ivato, Madagascar
Dark Earth and Dark Green upper surfaces with Sky undersides. Type C1 markings introduced in May 1942 on fuselage sides with Type C below the wings; Type B above wings. Red spinner, Night serial

80 | Airframe Detail No.9 – Lysander

wings were done in Sky, Sky Blue or Azure Blue. All the markings remained unchanged although you need to check reference images because some have the entire vertical fin in red/white blue, as per the April 1940 regulations, while other adopted the later smaller 24x27in version of the fin flash.

From May 1942 the Type B roundel was replaced with the new Type C, with a yellow-ringed version (Type C1) for use on dark surrounding colours. On the Lysander this was 30in diameter on the fuselage and 35in for the wings. The fin flash was also changed to Type C, comprising bands of red (front – 11in), white (2in) and blue (11in) and at this stage the fuselage codes changed to Dull Red.

Special Duties

The Lysanders operated by the Special Duties Squadron were often painted Special Night RDM 2 or RDM 2A, which was a sooty matt black, while others adopted the standard Night, which was a lot smoother. Squadron codes and the serial number were applied in red, no serial was applied under the wings. On the 15th August 1941 Dark Earth was replaced with Medium Sea Grey for the upper surface camouflage and this change also saw the adoption of the 'A' camouflage pattern for all machines. Special Duties Lysanders after this stage wore the Dark Green/Medium Sea Grey/Night scheme with the codes and serial numbers in Identification (Dull) Red. From May 1942 the Type B roundel was replaced with the new Type C, with the Night undersides of the SD machines requiring a yellow-ringed version (Type C1) to be used to gain contrast. On the Lysander this was 30in diameter on the fuselage and 35in for the wings, while the fin flash was also changed to Type C.

Those machines operating with the SD squadron in the Far East did not adopt the Dark Green/Medium Sea Grey/Night scheme, instead they used a Dark Green and Ocean Grey over Night scheme. The roundels were replaced with the SEAC (South-East Asia Command) versions that were in blue and 'India white'. The latter colour was actually a

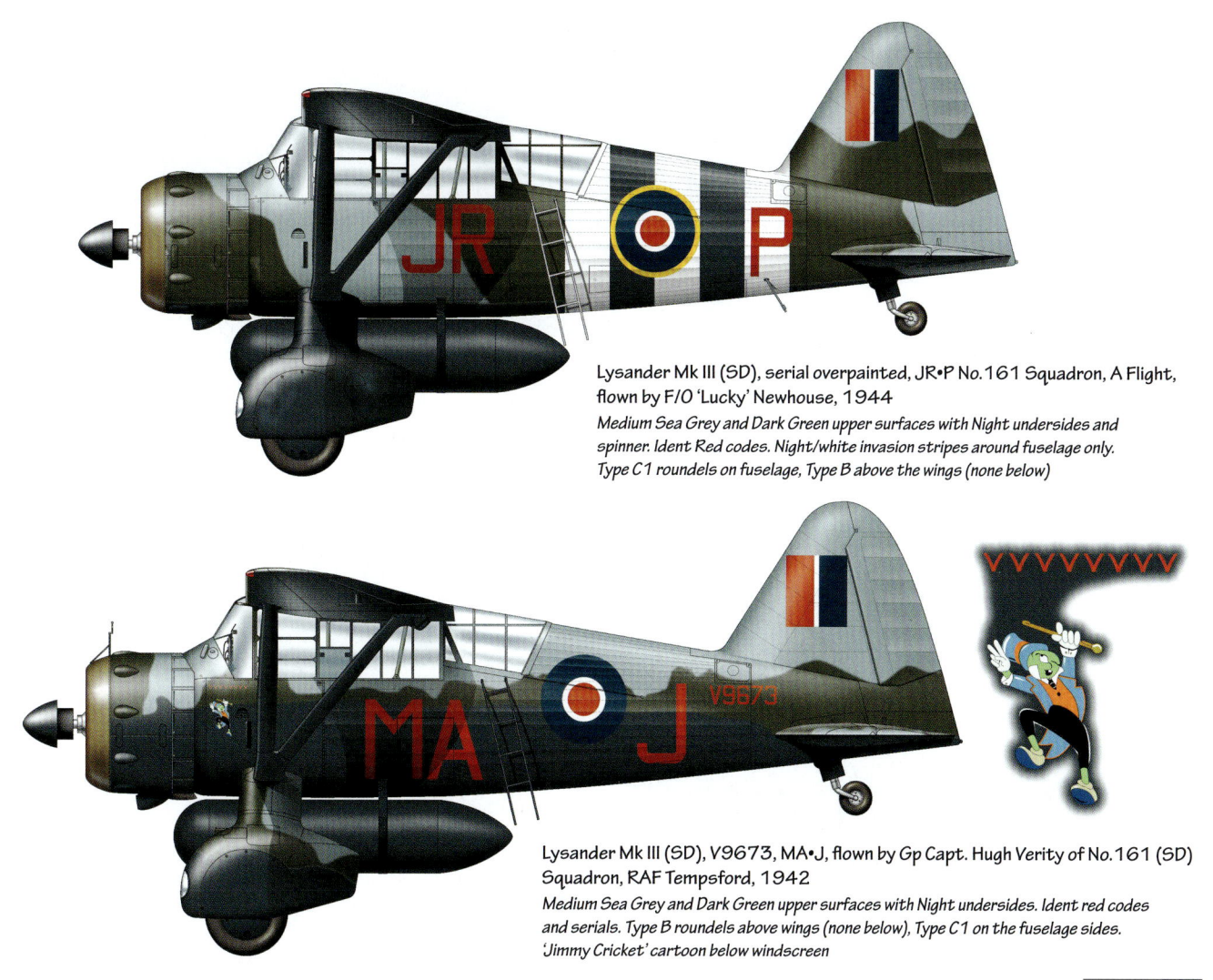

Mk IIIAs of No.1433 Flight, based at Ivato, Madagascar, in flight in starboard echelon formation over typical Madagascar countryside (©British Official)

Lysander Mk III (SD), serial overpainted, JR•P No.161 Squadron, A Flight, flown by F/O 'Lucky' Newhouse, 1944
Medium Sea Grey and Dark Green upper surfaces with Night undersides and spinner. Ident Red codes. Night/white invasion stripes around fuselage only. Type C1 roundels on fuselage, Type B above the wings (none below)

Lysander Mk III (SD), V9673, MA•J, flown by Gp Capt. Hugh Verity of No.161 (SD) Squadron, RAF Tempsford, 1942
Medium Sea Grey and Dark Green upper surfaces with Night undersides. Ident red codes and serials. Type B roundels above wings (none below), Type C1 on the fuselage sides. 'Jimmy Cricket' cartoon below windscreen

mix of white with a bit of Roundel Blue (the official colour for the centre was blue, made by a 50/50 mix of Roundel Blue and white, but there are examples that used less blue and more white). The SEAC roundels on the Lysander were of 16in diameter on both the fuselage and wings and the corresponding fin flash was 16in x 24 with just 8in stripes of the two shades. The serial number was applied in the usual location but in white (or red) instead of black and were often applied with a stencil.

Air-Sea Rescue & FAA

Although most sources state that all Coastal Command ASR squadrons adopted the Temperate Sea Scheme, this is certainly true for the majority, but images exist that shows what seems to be very early machines in the Dark Green/Dark Earth over Sky scheme, with Type B roundels above the wings (none below) and Type A1 on the fuselages. For some reason these images show the code(?) '-ASRS' forward of the fuselage roundel.

These were exceptions however and the vast majority of Lysanders used by the Coastal Command ASR squadrons adopted the Dark Slate Grey and Extra Dark Sea Grey over Sky Temperate Sea Scheme. The squadron codes were applied in Sky Grey (or Medium Sea Grey) and they had a Type C1 fuselage roundel and fin flash, with a Type B roundel above and Type C below the wings.

There were also those machines that adopted the 'fighter' scheme of Dark Green and Ocean Grey over Medium Sea Grey. The squadron codes could be applied in Sky Grey or Medium Sea Grey and they had a Type C1 fuselage roundel and fin flash, with a Type B roundel above the wings but none underneath.

Mk IIIA (SD), V9707, •G, of No.148 (Special Duties) Squadron, surrounded by partisans after landing in a field near the town of Cortemilia, south of Asti in northern Italy, to evacuate three wounded partisans to the Allied-held area (©British Official)

A Japanese soldier passes a pack to another in the back of Mk IIIA, V9818 of No.357 (SD) Squadron at Mingaldon airfield, they would later be dropped into remote areas to tell Japanese soldiers there that the war was over. Note how little contrast the outer blue ring of the roundel gives against the Night background and the serial, applied in red using a stencil (©Australian War Memorial)

This is probably Mk III, V9597, BA•E No.277 (ASR) Squadron with crew rushing to it, this staged press shot has all signs of codes (you can just make out the 'B' and 'E' though) and serial removed, but you can still see the Type C1 roundels and fin flash (©British Official)

Lysander Mk IIIA, V9289, •C, C Flight Special Service, 14th Army, South East Asia
Ocean Grey/Dark Green upper surfaces with Night undersides. Blue/Light Blue roundels on fuselage and above wings; note black 'spider' on fuselage roundel. 14th Army emblem carried on forward fuselage; spinner is yellow. Serial on fuselage in white, repeated under fin flash in Ident Red

The Lysanders used by Fleet Air Arm (FAA) units were in the standard RAF Dark Green/Dark Earth upper surface camouflage, but due to their usage (gunnery and bombing training), the undersides were in the black and yellow stripes seen on the target towing machines (see elsewhere in this section). The serial was reapplied in smaller (6in) black characters slightly forward of their original location and with the legend 'Royal Navy' above it. These machines adopted a complex identification numbering system comprising three characters on the fuselage sides, directly forward of the roundel and thus under the canopy mid and aft sections (e.g. W6-I) with the last character repeated on either side of the engine cowling (and often on the vertical fin), all usually done in Sky Grey.

Mk IIIA, V9618 with No.754 NAS at RNAS Tayside in 1941, it lacks any roundels under the wings and has no squadron codes, just an individual aircraft letter on either side of the cowling (©British Official)

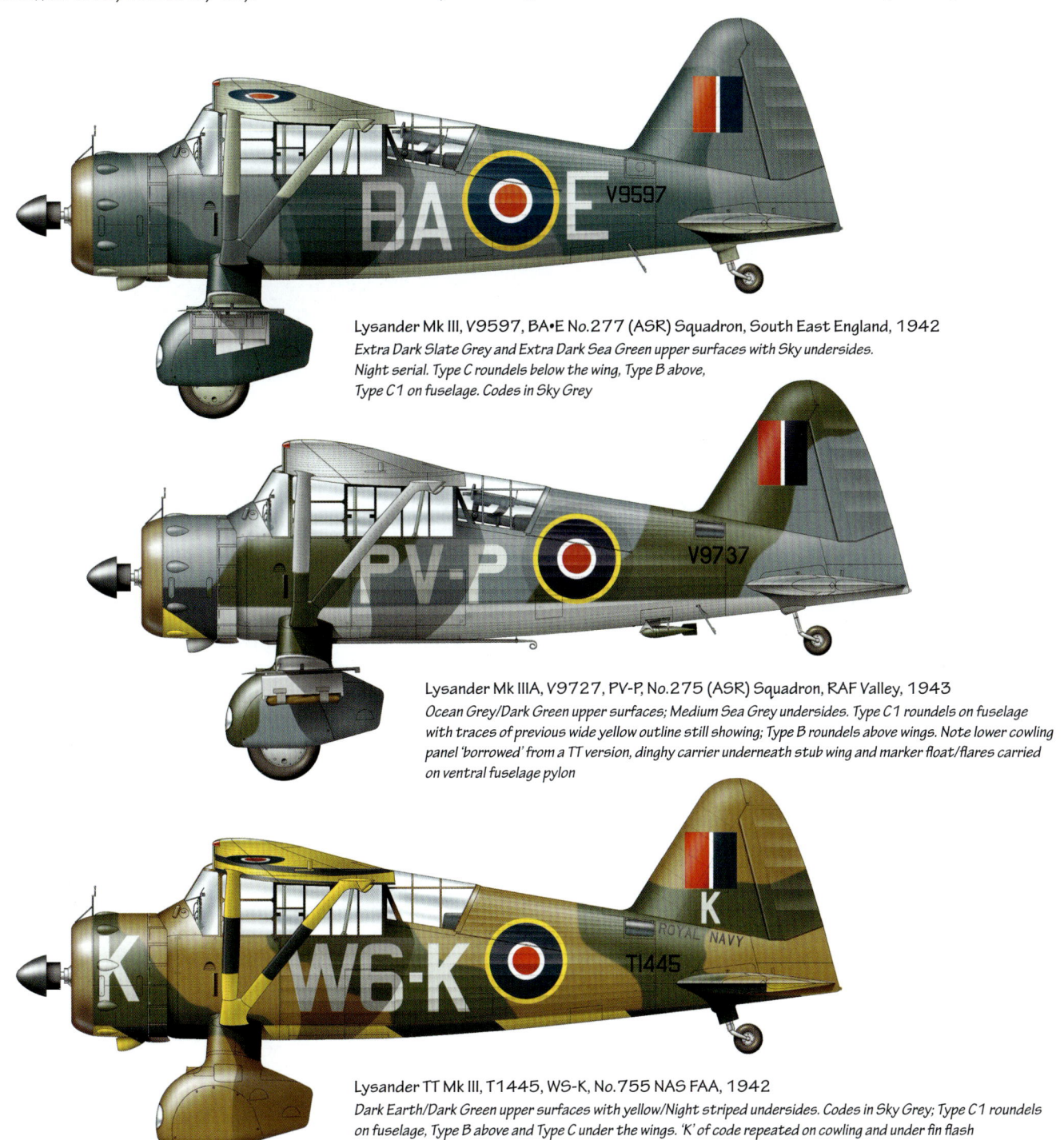

Lysander Mk III, V9597, BA•E No.277 (ASR) Squadron, South East England, 1942
Extra Dark Slate Grey and Extra Dark Sea Green upper surfaces with Sky undersides. Night serial. Type C roundels below the wing, Type B above, Type C1 on fuselage. Codes in Sky Grey

Lysander Mk IIIA, V9727, PV-P, No.275 (ASR) Squadron, RAF Valley, 1943
Ocean Grey/Dark Green upper surfaces; Medium Sea Grey undersides. Type C1 roundels on fuselage with traces of previous wide yellow outline still showing; Type B roundels above wings. Note lower cowling panel 'borrowed' from a TT version, dinghy carrier underneath stub wing and marker float/flares carried on ventral fuselage pylon

Lysander TT Mk III, T1445, WS-K, No.755 NAS FAA, 1942
Dark Earth/Dark Green upper surfaces with yellow/Night striped undersides. Codes in Sky Grey; Type C1 roundels on fuselage, Type B above and Type C under the wings. 'K' of code repeated on cowling and under fin flash

Airframe Detail No.9 – Lysander

Lysander TT Mk IIIA, V9905, prior to delivery to No.58 Operational Training Unit, Grangemouth, Stirlingshire
Ocean Grey and Dark Green upper surfaces with yellow undersides superimpose with Night angled bands. Type A1 roundels on fuselage sides, Type B above wings and Type A underneath. Night spinner and serial

Target Towing

Lysanders converted to this role usually retained the Dark Green/Dark Earth upper surfaces but had yellow undersides with black stripes, with new-build Mk IIIs adopting Dark Green and Ocean Grey (although some sources incorrectly quote Dark Sea Grey) disruptive camouflage on the upper surfaces and yellow and black stripes on the undersides. These stripes were of 36in wide black bands on a yellow background, 72in apart. The stripes usually extended over the control surfaces, but the tailplanes were done with the horizontal tailplane in black and the elevators in yellow. The fuselage roundels are often Type A with an outer ring of yellow the same width as the other red/white/blue rings. These machines also usually had the Type A roundel applied once again under each wing, usually of about 35in diameter.

The codes on the fuselage were in Sky Grey to give contrast and the units operating the type in the role this often comprised just a letter and number combination, e.g. G•5, with it applied the same orientation, regardless of the side it was applied to.

Lysander TT Mk III, T1444, G-5, of No.5 Air Observers School at Jurby, as a conversion this machine retained its original green/brown upper camouflage combined with new hi-vis yellow/black undersides (©British Official)

TT Mk IIIA, V9905, on the ground at Westlands before delivery to No.58 Operational Training Unit at Grangemouth, Stirlingshire. The hi-vis nature of the markings combined with the black and yellow underside are all very prominent in this shot. The cowl gills look to be unpainted at this stage and the wing struts have a complex transition from yellow (top) through black (middle) to the camouflage colour of the undercraft, with an odd demarcation on the wheel spats themselves. Note that the upper camouflage colours on this machine are reversed from the usual pattern, with the Dark Green where the Ocean Grey should be and vice versa (©Air Ministry)

Lysander TT Mk III, T1444, G-5
Dark Earth and Dark Green upper surfaces with yellow undersides superimposed with Night angled bands. Sky Grey codes, Night serial. Spinner is probably Sky Grey. Type A1 fuselage roundels, Type A below wings, Type B above

84 Airframe Detail No.9 – Lysander

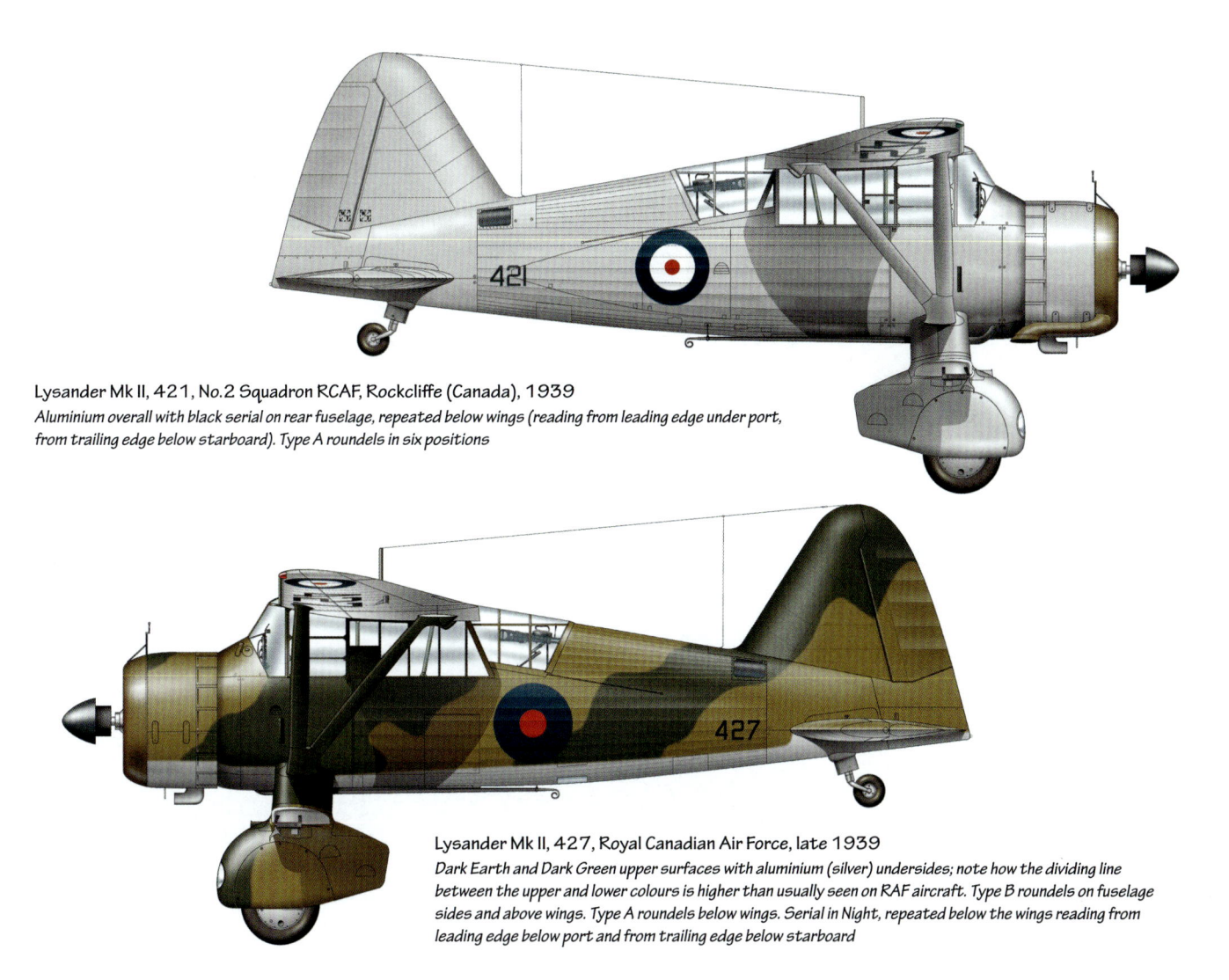

Lysander Mk II, 421, No.2 Squadron RCAF, Rockcliffe (Canada), 1939
Aluminium overall with black serial on rear fuselage, repeated below wings (reading from leading edge under port, from trailing edge below starboard). Type A roundels in six positions

Lysander Mk II, 427, Royal Canadian Air Force, late 1939
Dark Earth and Dark Green upper surfaces with aluminium (silver) undersides; note how the dividing line between the upper and lower colours is higher than usually seen on RAF aircraft. Type B roundels on fuselage sides and above wings. Type A roundels below wings. Serial in Night, repeated below the wings reading from leading edge below port and from trailing edge below starboard

Canadian-built

Initially all the Canadian machines were aluminium overall, later though they adopted RAF camouflage. Most retained the Type A roundels and fin flash and had a serial that just comprised numbers and this was applied either side of the rear fuselage and under each wing in the same style/location as used on RAF post-war machines.

By December 1939 the type adopted the Dark Earth/Dark Green over aluminium scheme, with a Type B roundel above the wing, a Type A below (near the tip) and a Type B either side of the fuselage, with the serial number applied under the wings and either side of the rear fuselage as below.

Lysander Mk II 421 was photographed on the 17th November 1939 in overall aluminium at Ottawa (©Library and Archives Canada)

Lysander Mk II 427 photographed on the 14th December 1939 resplendent in camouflage; as others were photographed on the 17th November 1939 (see previously image of '421') still in overall aluminium, the change took place retrospectively and pretty quickly for the very early production machines (©Library and Archives Canada)

By late 1941 machines adopted the Type A1 roundel on the fuselage while keeping a Type B above the wings and a Type A roundel underneath each wing, right out by the tip. The fuselage demarcation on both styles is often slightly higher than seen on RAF examples and tended to be a straighter (soft) line, whilst the RAF machines had a slight undulation. The wing struts were always in the upper surface camouflage colours, whilst the wheel spats had the inner faces in the underside colour with this wrapping round ever so slightly at the front/lower edge.

Target towing machines adopted the black and yellow striped scheme overall with the

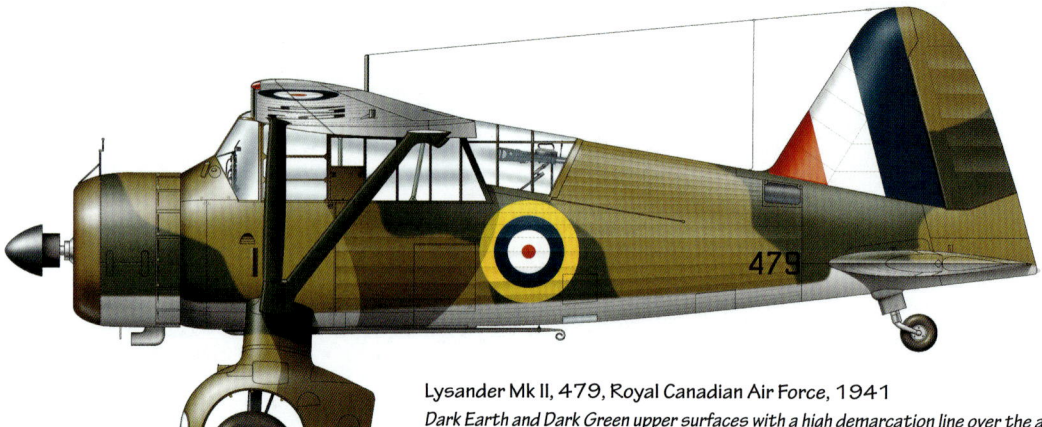

Lysander Mk II, 479, Royal Canadian Air Force, 1941
Dark Earth and Dark Green upper surfaces with a high demarcation line over the aluminium (silver) undersides. Night serial, repeated below the wings, reading from leading edge below port and from trailing edge below starboard. Type A1 roundels replaced the earlier Type B on the fuselage, with those above and below wings remaining in Type B and A respectively. Whole fin is covered in fin flash colours. Note that RCAF Lysander wheel spats were painted silver on their inner faces

horizontal tailplanes in black and elevators in yellow. This was known as the 'Oxydol scheme', after the packaging at that time of a brand of soap flakes! There were equal-width vertical stripes of red, white and blue covering the entire vertical fin, with them set at the same angle as the rudder hinge. Type A roundels were applied to the fuselage and above and below the wings, the latter positioned right out at the tip. The serial number was applied in a colour that contrasts with the background, so on black it was yellow and vice versa. This serial was repeated under each wing, as per the pre-war RAF markings, again with each element in the colour that contrasted with its background. If the type had an RAF serial, only the last four numbers were applied, all Canadian-built examples had a serial that only comprised numbers, so these were applied in their entirety.

Lysander Mk II 473 photographed on the 1st November 1941 with the Type A1 roundel on the fuselage and straight demarcation along the fuselage. Note the entire vertical fin covered with the flash (©Library and Archives Canada)

Mk II 425 prepares for a flight, circa 1940
(©Library and Archives Canada)

Lysander TT Mk III 2307 of the No.4 Bombing and Gunnery School, Ontario in the overall yellow with black stripes scheme; the fuselage roundel is Type A, the central dot is just washed out in this image
(©Library and Archives Canada)

Lysander 416 at Patricia Bay BC 11th January 1941
(©CFB Shearwater, RCAF)

Lysander TT Mk III, 9353/53, No.8 Bombing and Gunnery School, Lethbridge, Alberta, Canada, 1942
Yellow/Night stripes overall with large red/white/blue fin flashes; Type A1 roundels in six positions. Serial, repeated under wings, is yellow over black areas, and black over yellow areas. '53' repeated in yellow in large digits below rear cockpit

Lysander TT Mk III, V9323, No.8 Gunner/Bombing School, Lethbridge, Alberta, Canada, 1943
Yellow/Night stripes overall with large red/white/blue fin flashes; standard Type A roundels in six positions. Serial, repeated under wings, in yellow over black areas, and black over yellow areas

Colour Specifications

- Aluminium (for metal): There is no BS 381C match for this colour (nearest FS595B match is 17178)
- Dark Green: BS 381C-641
- Dark Earth: BS 381C-450
- Light Earth:
- Middle Stone:
- Sky Blue (Duck Egg Blue): BSS 381 (1930) No.1, DTD 63A & 260A
- Eau-de-Nil (Duck Egg Green): BSS 381 (1930) No.16, DTD 63A & 260A
- Sky (or Sky Type S): BS 381C-240
- Medium Sea Grey: BS 381C-637
- Extra Dark Sea Grey: BS 381C-640
- Dark Sea Grey: BS381C-638
- Sky Grey: Has no Ministry of Supply colour code (nearest FS 595B match is 36463)
- Night: BS 381C-642
- Special Night RDM 2 or RDM 2A: Has no Ministry of Supply (MoS) colour code (No BS or FS 595B equivalent)
- Dull Red: There is no MoS colour code nor BS 381C equivalent for this colour (nearest FS 595B match is 30109)
- White: There is no BS 381C or FS 595B match for this colour, nor was it included in the MofS colour range
- Roundel Blue: There is no BS 381C match for this colour, nor was it included in the MofS colour range (nearest FS 595B match is 35048)
- Yellow: Ministry of Supply Aircraft Finish No.2, but there is no BS 381C match for this colour (nearest FS 595B match is 33538)

Note: Each of the above colours, except Special Night RDM 2 or RDM 2A, would have been specified to DTD 63 for Cellulose and DTD 260 for synthetic pigments

Westland Lysander
Stencil Marking Details

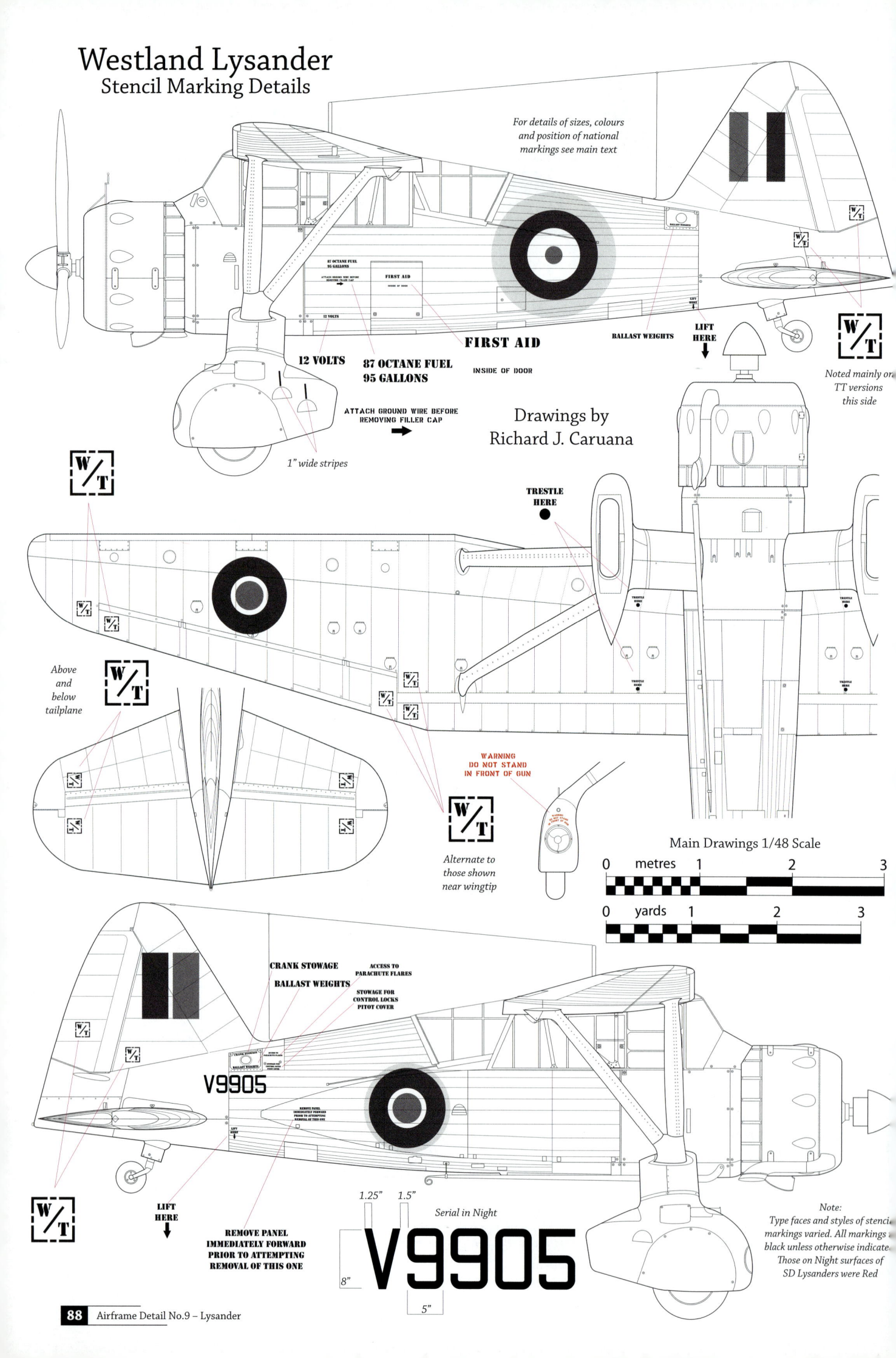

For details of sizes, colours and position of national markings see main text

87 OCTANE FUEL
95 GALLONS

ATTACH GROUND WIRE BEFORE REMOVING FILLER CAP

FIRST AID
INSIDE OF DOOR

BALLAST WEIGHTS

LIFT HERE

Noted mainly on TT versions this side

12 VOLTS

FIRST AID

Drawings by Richard J. Caruana

ATTACH GROUND WIRE BEFORE REMOVING FILLER CAP

1" wide stripes

TRESTLE HERE

Above and below tailplane

WARNING
DO NOT STAND IN FRONT OF GUN

Alternate to those shown near wingtip

Main Drawings 1/48 Scale

0 metres 1 2 3
0 yards 1 2 3

CRANK STOWAGE
BALLAST WEIGHTS
ACCESS TO PARACHUTE FLARES
STOWAGE FOR CONTROL LOCKS
PITOT COVER

V9905

LIFT HERE

REMOVE PANEL IMMEDIATELY FORWARD PRIOR TO ATTEMPTING REMOVAL OF THIS ONE

1.25" 1.5"

Serial in Night

V9905

8"
5"

Note:
Type faces and styles of stencil markings varied. All markings black unless otherwise indicated. Those on Night surfaces of SD Lysanders were Red

88 Airframe Detail No.9 – Lysander

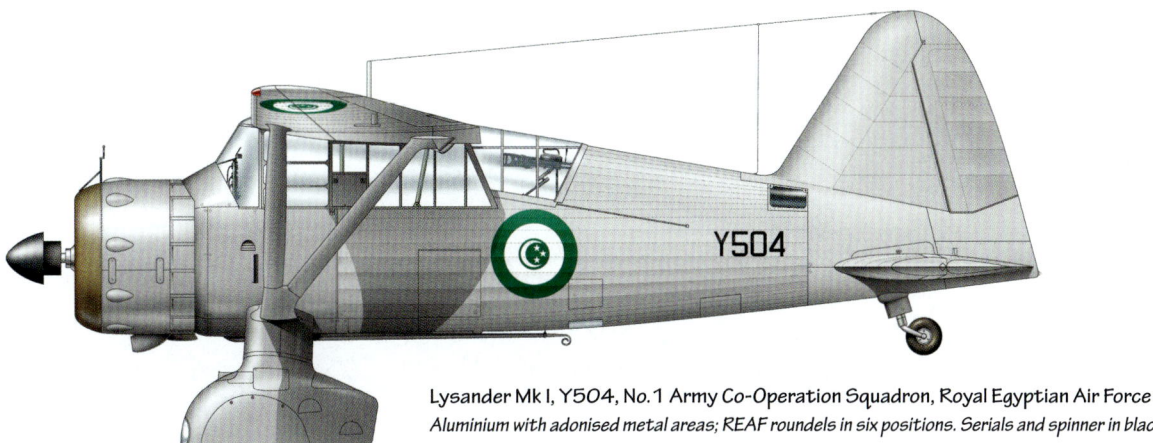

Lysander Mk I, Y504, No.1 Army Co-Operation Squadron, Royal Egyptian Air Force
Aluminium with adonised metal areas; REAF roundels in six positions. Serials and spinner in black

Foreign Service

Egypt

The aircraft supplied to the Royal Egyptian Air Force were supplied in a bright aluminium overall. The only markings were REAF roundels above and below the wings and either side of the rear fuselage. The wing roundels were positioned at a point equal to mid-way along the aileron and were sited slightly aft, so they were not actually central to the wings chord at that point. Those below the wings were situated well outboard towards the tip, like RAF examples and the serial number (Y500 to Y518) was applied in the same style as pre-war RAF ones were. This serial number was repeated in black on either side of the rear fuselage, again very much like RAF machines, albeit using slightly larger characters.

Finland

Initially all the first batch (LY-114 to LY-122) being ex-RAF were supplied in the standard Dark Earth and Dark Green camouflage pattern on the upper surfaces, with aluminium undersides. The serial number was applied in black characters either side of the rear fuselage between the national insignia and the tailplane. The national insignia comprised a blue swastika on a white disc and this was ap-

Y517 was the penultimate Lysander supplied to Egypt and is seen here at Yeovil prior to delivery finished in full RAEF markings (©British Official)

LY-123 of Lentolaivue 12 at Kauhava in August 1940, this was ex-L4681 and is seen here in its original RAF camouflage

Lysander Mk I, LY-121, LeLv 16, Värtsilä, Finland, August 1941
Aircraft in delivery scheme of Dark Earth and Dark Green with aluminium undersides. Black spinner and serial. National markings in six positions. Underside of wing tips and rear fuselage band in yellow

plied above and below each wing at mid-span between the wing struts and tip and either side of the rear fuselage. These were of large diameter, being dictated by the space available between the leading edge slat and the aileron hinge line on the wings (the same diameter was used on the fuselage).

At some stage in 1940/41 the scheme was revised and aircraft were repainted in Musta (black) and Vihreä (olive green) upper surface camouflage over Alta Vall.harmaa (Light Grey) undersides.

From June 1941 a yellow theatre band was applied around the rear fuselage and under each wing tip to a point halfway between the wing support struts and the tip. This colour was officially supposed to be Unica 2, a deep yellow previously used to mark some interior equipment, but stocks were too limited, so Unica 12 (a brighter yellow)

Good old LY-120 again, this time showing it at Värsilä with the yellow theatre band around the rear fuselage and under each wing tip (©SA-Kuva)

Lysander Mk I, LY-118, 2 LeLv 16, Finnish Air Force, 1942
Musta (black) and Vihreä (light olive green) upper surfaces with Alta Vaal.harmaa (light grey) undersides. Yellow rear fuselage band and undersides of wing tips. National markings in six positions. Unit badge on fin. Serial in black with part of '8' on the black area being in green

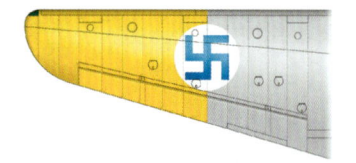

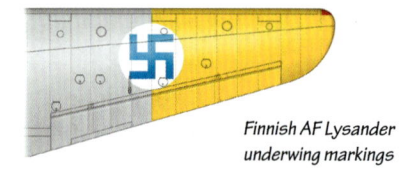

Finnish AF Lysander underwing markings

was used instead; this marking was finally deleted by mid-September 1944 with the end of the Continuation War. The national insignia was applied in the same positions as the earlier scheme, but the diameter was reduced and the serial number was applied in the same manner, but the yellow band meant that it was usually applied in part across it. Machines from 2./LeLv.16 carried the unit's emblem, a stylised 'Diana the huntress', on either side of the vertical fin in white.

The winter camouflage applied to LY-116 in 1942/43 is often quoted as being white distemper over the base camouflage, but it was actually ground chalk mixed with glue. This was blotchy in its application and wore off quite quickly. The demarcation was soft along the fuselage sides and oddly did not follow that of the original camouflage demarcation, while the inner faces of each undercarriage spat/leg was not covered with the white, so stayed Alta Vaal.harmaa (light grey).

From the 1st September 1941 a 50cm wide band in Dicca 6 yellow was applied around the engine cowling of all aircraft. At this stage the national marking on the fuselage seems to have been toned down by removing the white

LY-120 of 2/LeLv 16 at Nurmoila in June 1942 (©SA-Kuva)

90 Airframe Detail No.9 – Lysander

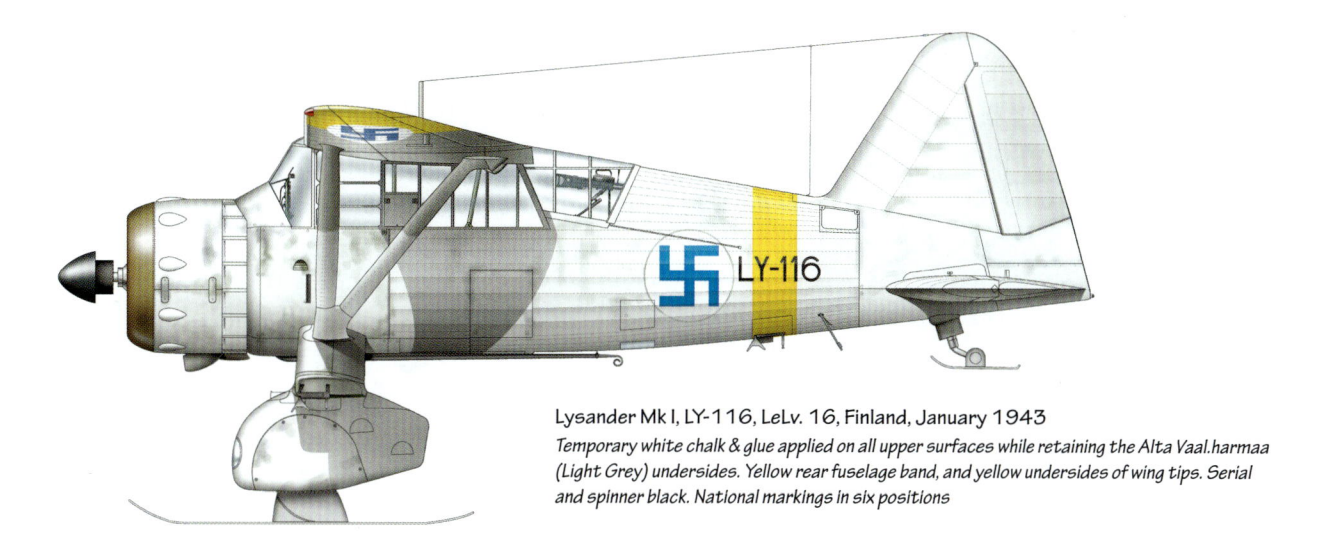

Lysander Mk I, LY-116, LeLv. 16, Finland, January 1943
Temporary white chalk & glue applied on all upper surfaces while retaining the Alta Vaal.harmaa (Light Grey) undersides. Yellow rear fuselage band, and yellow undersides of wing tips. Serial and spinner black. National markings in six positions

Not the greatest quality image, but this does show LY-116 of 2./LeLv 16 at Hirvas (some state Äänislinna) on 16th January 1943 fitted with skis and with white chalk and glue applied. The yellow fuselage band appears black in this shot, plus the canopy frames are left in the original camouflage colours, while the inside of the undercarriage spats looks to have the removeable cover in Alta Vaal.harmaa (light grey) and the rest in camouflage?

Lysander Mk I, LY-119, 2 LeLv 16, Finnish Air Force, 1942
Musta (black) and Vihreä (light olive green) upper surfaces with Alta Vaal.harmaa (light grey) undersides. Yellow band around rear fuselage; Yellow cowl and undersides of wingtips. Fuselage national marking is outlined in white. Serial in black on yellow band and green areas, in green on black area. Unit badge on fin

Lovely shot of LY-119 outside the residential buildings with the church of Viiksjärvi visible in the background. This machine seems to have the lower section of each wheel spat painted in a combination of two or more lighter shades, the exact colours are unknown though (©SA-Kuva)

Airframe Detail No.9 – Lysander

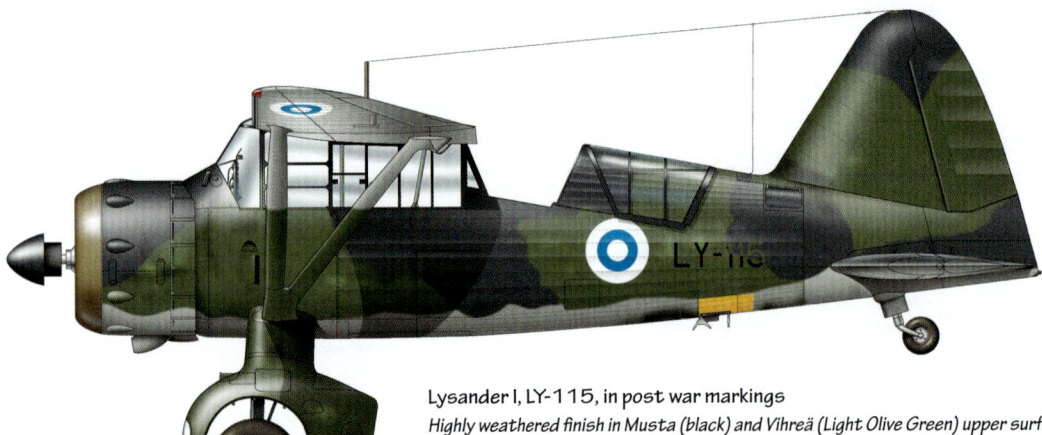

Lysander I, LY-115, in post war markings
Highly weathered finish in Musta (black) and Vihreä (Light Olive Green) upper surfaces with Alta Vaal.harmaa (Light Grey) undersides; note remnant of previous yellow fuselage band below rear fuselage. Post-war insignia of white/blue/white roundels in six positions. Serial is black on green areas, green on the black areas

disc background and just leaving a narrow white border around the blue swastika.

The upper section of the yellow nose band was ordered removed when the Russian offensive started on the 9th June 1944 and this was completed by all units, repair depots and factories by the 21st of the month.

With the end of hostilities, the remaining Lysanders used for communications duties or as hacks retained their wartime camouflage, but adopted the new national insignia, which was a roundel comprising a white disc with a blue ring in the middle and this was applied either side of the rear fuselage and above and below the wings.

France

The single example ordered by France prior to their country's surrender was simple marked as '01'. It was painted Armée de l'Air Khaki overall with the engine cowling and collector ring left in bare metal. French roundels were applied above and below the wings, both positioned well outboard near the tip in RAF fashion. No roundels were applied to

Not the best quality, but the only image we could find showing a Lysander with the post-war roundels applied, this is LY-115 of HLeLv 21 visiting Pori in the autumn of 1945 (via K. Stenman)

The single Lysander Mk II (note smooth cowling and square carburettor intake of the Perseus) ordered by France before the fall of that Nation, '01' is seen here at Yeovil prior to delivery

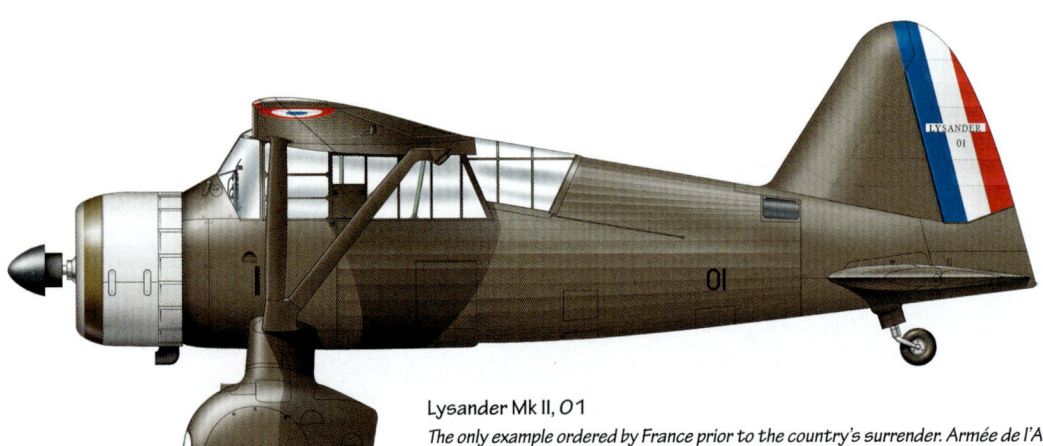

Lysander Mk II, 01
The only example ordered by France prior to the country's surrender. Armée de l'Air Khaki overall with engine cowling in natural metal. Black spinner and serial on aft fuselage. French roundels in four wing positions. Tricolour on rudder carried the lettering 'Lysander' in black on a white band, and '01' also in black underneath

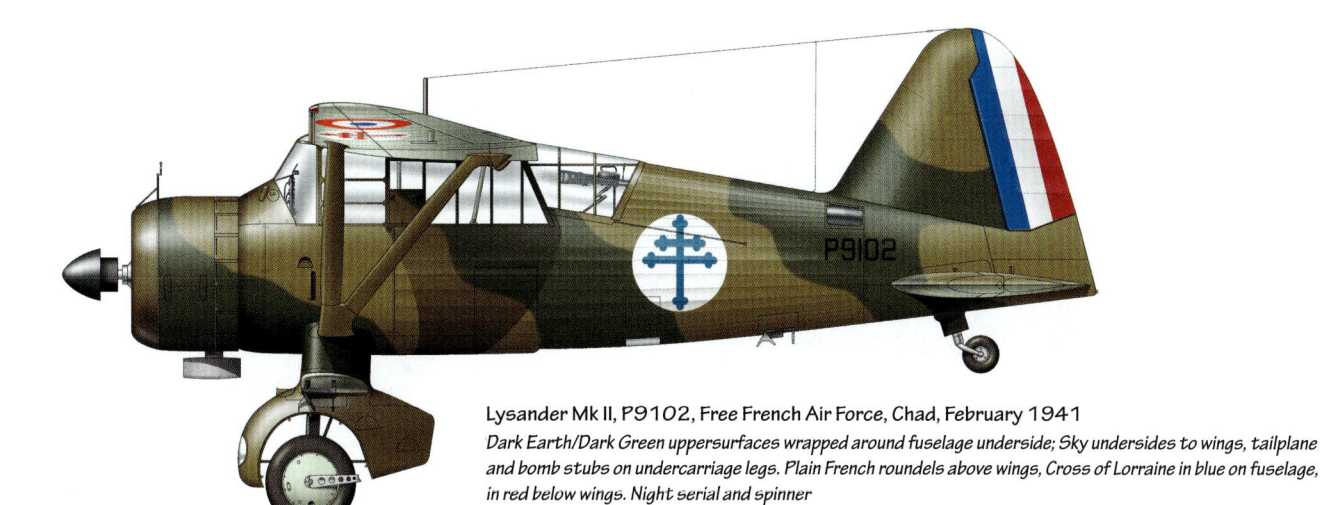

Lysander Mk II, P9102, Free French Air Force, Chad, February 1941
Dark Earth/Dark Green uppersurfaces wrapped around fuselage underside; Sky undersides to wings, tailplane and bomb stubs on undercarriage legs. Plain French roundels above wings, Cross of Lorraine in blue on fuselage, in red below wings. Night serial and spinner

Free French Air Force underwing markings; only the tri-colour roundel was used above the wings

Although not the best quality, this unique image shows P1735 one of first to join the Gabonese and Middle Congo Detachment in the early summer 1940 complete with RAF roundel and simplified Cross of Lorraine on the fuselage and no cross under (and we assume above) the wing

the fuselage sides and the entire rudder was painted in the French tricolour of light blue (front), white and red. Superimposed over this in a white oblong was the title 'LYSANDER' in a block typeface very much of the era and below this, just on the white of the rudder marking, was '01'. The '01' was repeated in larger black characters on either side of the rear fuselage, just aft and below the rearmost end of the rear canopy rail.

The Lysanders that served with the Free French units in West Africa were all in standard RAF Dark Green and Dark Earth that wrapped around the fuselage, while the undersides of the wings, stub wings and tailplanes were Sky. French roundels were applied above and below the wings. A Cross of Lorraine was also applied in red on a white disc under (not always on the white disc) each wing, inboard of the roundel and on either side of the fuselage in blue in place of a roundel (or alongside it for early machines –

Lysander Mk II P1738 of the Free French Air Force photographed in Cameroon in 1940. Note the Cross of Lorraine under the wings lack the white disc, but have a thin white outline instead

P9181 from the Rennes Flight seen in Chad in March 1942 with what looks like a sand colour applied over the base green/brown camouflage. Only a Cross of Lorraine is applied to the fuselage sides, sadly you can't see what markings are applied above or below the wings, but the remnants of the fin flash has been truncated, there is a squadron badge on the vertical fin and the serial number has obviously been re-applied, as it is in a stencil style (via J-J Petite)

see accompanying image). The rudder carried the blue/white/red stripes seen on '01' and you will find images of machines with a unit badge painted on the vertical fin, on top of a darker patch of paint that we assume was used to obscure the RAF fin flash.

There are also a few images, showing machines that operated with the Rennes Flight in Chad and neighbouring countries that seem to have adopted the Luftwaffe technique of applying a sand colour over the base camouflage.

There are images of French machines after the liberation that show them still in the same overall camouflage scheme but with black undersides and French roundels below (and we presume above) the wings and

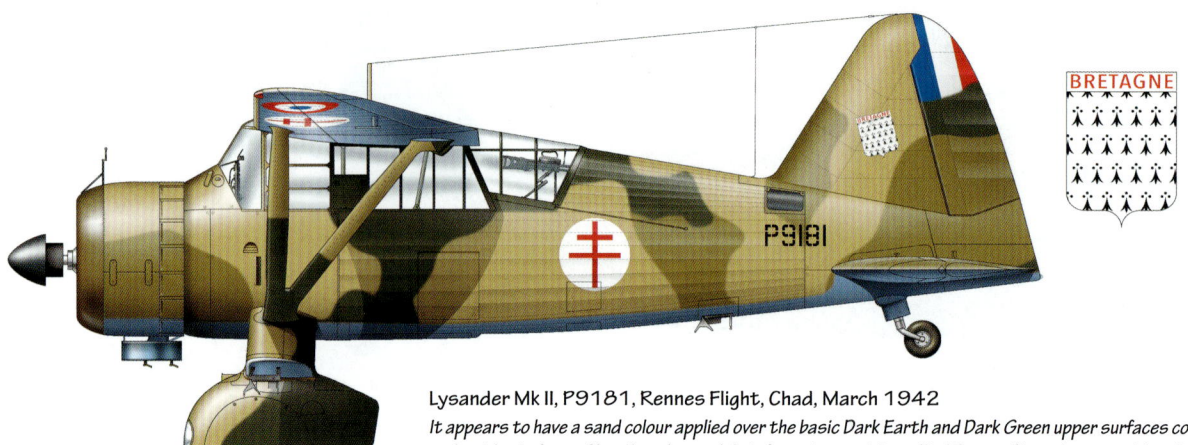

Lysander Mk II, P9181, Rennes Flight, Chad, March 1942
It appears to have a sand colour applied over the basic Dark Earth and Dark Green upper surfaces colours; undersides in Azure Blue. French roundels in four wing positions. Red Cross of Lorraine on a white disc on fuselage sides and below the wings. Night spinner and serial, the latter in stencilled form. Tricolour rudder markings have been painted over leaving only the top section visible. 'Bretagne' Coat of Arms carried on the fin

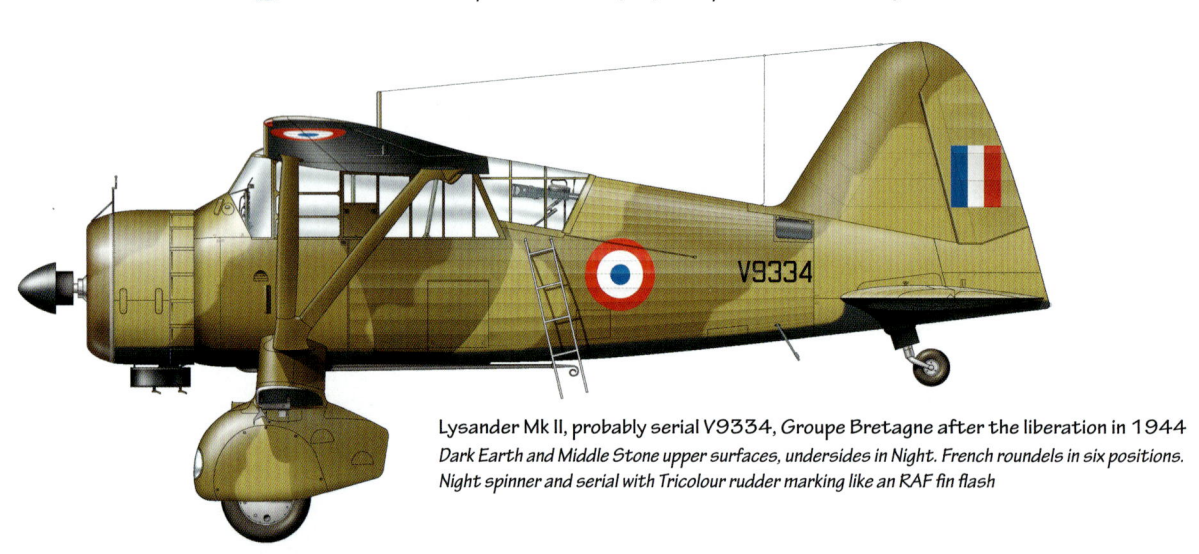

Lysander Mk II, probably serial V9334, Groupe Bretagne after the liberation in 1944
Dark Earth and Middle Stone upper surfaces, undersides in Night. French roundels in six positions. Night spinner and serial with Tricolour rudder marking like an RAF fin flash

A well known image, showing a Lysander operated by a French unit in Europe after the liberation, the small French roundel can just be made out under the port wing; note that this machine carried a P-38 drop tank under the fuselage

The same machine as seen in the previous image, this time in colour and from the side, so you can see the roundel on the fuselage and the flash applied to the rudder, the serial number is pretty illegible, but it ends with 334?

either side of the rear fuselage. The tricolour however, is applied on the rudder as a block, like an RAF fin flash and probably of about the same size (24x27in).

Ireland

The Mk IIs supplied to the Irish Air Corps were in RAF Dark Green and Dark Earth camouflage that wrapped around the fuselage, with a light grey used in place of aluminium for the undersides of the wings and tailplanes. The roundels on the fuselage and above the wings were replaced with the Irish version (green Titanine T.E.32 and orange Titanine T.E.78), with green/white/orange stripes in place of the roundels on the underside of each wing. No fin flash was applied and the serial number (61 to 66) was applied in black characters either side of the rear fuselage and aft of the roundel in much the same way as RAF machines, but using much larger characters.

Portugal

Only a couple of images have ever come to light showing the Mk IIIAs (V9309, V9321, V9363, V9439, V9555, V9594, V9705 and V9729) sent to this country. They all seem to show a machine in Dark Green and Dark Earth upper surface disruptive camouflage, with the lower surfaces in Sky, although many claim this was light blue. A three digit serial

Lysander Mk II, '62', Irish Air Corps
Dark Earth/Dark Green upper surfaces, wrapped around underside of fuselage; Light Grey undersides to wings and tailplanes. Two-colour roundel on fuselage sides and above wings; tricolour stripes under wings, with Orange towards wing tip

number from 361 to 368 was applied in white characters on either side of the rear fuselage, directly below the clear inspection panel just below the vertical fin leading edge fillet junction. The Portuguese cross was applied by itself on either side of the fuselage and again above and below the wings, although these were superimposed onto a white disc. The national colours (green [forward] and red) were applied in a fin flash on either side of the vertical fin, but the red portion was twice the width (same height) of the green.

Turkey

The Mk IIs supplied to this country were sent in standard RAF colours of Dark Green/Dark Earth disruptive camouflage that wrapped around the fuselage and was above the tail and wings, with Sky below the wings and tail. The Turkish national insignia was applied under and above each wing, with the serial number (3101 to 3136) applied inboard of it in black orientated in the same manner as pre-war RAF machines. The serial was repeated on either side of the rear fuselage, positioned so it started by the forward frame of the rear sliding canopy and with all of it on the removeable panel. The only other marking was that the entire rudder was red with the crescent moon and star motif superimposed on top – the moon always pointed (open) aft, so that the star was always at the trailing edge of the rudder.

Later some machines had the last two of the serial number (e.g. '22' of 3122) applied in white characters instead of black (which the first two remained in) on either side of the rear fuselage, all other markings remained unchanged (see profile pg 96).

The six Lysanders ordered for the IAC serial numbers 61 to 66 seen prior to delivery (©Westlands)

We have only ever seen two images of Portuguese Lysanders, this is the 'better' one(!), but it at least gives an overall view of the markings

Lysander Mk IIIA, 'White 366', Portuguese Army Aviation, Reconnaissance and Liaison Squadron BA3, Tancos, 1943
Dark Earth and Dark Green upper surfaces with Sky undersides. National markings on fuselage sides, and in four wing positions, the latter over a white disc. Serial in white

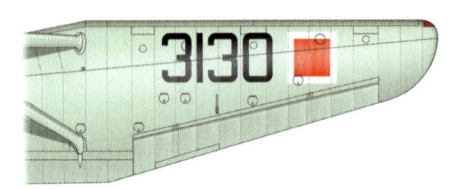

Lysander Mk II, '3130', Turkish Army, 1944
Dark Earth/Dark Green upper surfaces, wrapped round underside of fuselage; Silver undersides. Code is black (31) and white (30), repeated in black under the wings inboard of square red/white markings, the latter repeated above the wings. Rudder in red with crescent and star in white

Turkish Air Force underside markings; red/white square markings repeated above wings

USAAF

The Mk IIIAs and TT Mk IIIAs allocated to the USAAF were all supplied in standard RAF camouflage, but as most were used for gunnery training, they adopted the black and yellow undersides of target towing examples (see elsewhere in this section). RAF roundels were retained above and below the wings, but the fuselage one was replaced with a white star superimposed on an Insignia Blue disc that had a very thin yellow outline giving it the same overall size as the original RAF roundel underneath. The serial number remained on either side of the rear fuselage, as did the Type C flash on either side of the vertical fin.

We would also recommend the following titles for those wishing to read more on the subject of post-war RAF camouflage and markings:
- British Aviation Colours of World War Two, RAF Museum Series Vol.3 (Arms & Armour Press ©1976, ISBN: 0-85368-271-2)
- Fighting Colours: RAF Fighter Camouflage and Markings 1937-1969 by M.J.F. Bowyer (ISBN: 85059 041 8 Patrick Stephens Ltd 1969)

3112 one of the 36 ordered by Turkey and delivered during February-March 1940, seen here factory fresh prior to delivery

V9817 that was assigned to the 3rd Gunner and Tow Target Fight in March 1944. The RAF upper wing roundels are just still visible, as is the Type C fin flash, while the underside black and yellow are less prominent from this angle (©USAAF)

Lysander TT Mk III, V9817, No.3 Gunnery & Tow Target Flight, 8th Air Force (USAAF), spring 1944
Dark Earth/Dark Green upper surfaces; yellow/Night striped undersides. Standard RAF style B roundels above wings, with C type underneath; US star insignia, outlined yellow, on fuselage sides

Section 3

Little Lizzie

Dora Wings 1/72nd
Lysander Mk III (SD)
by Libor Jekl

There have not been that many kits of the Lysander produced over the years, but there are examples in all three of the major scales, so what follows is a superb build of the new 1/72nd scale example from Dora Wings by Libor Jekl. Apologies for not covering the type in 1/48th scale, but Steve A. Evans did an excellent build of the Eduard/Gavia kit in our Airframe Extra Series (No.6 The Continuation War, ISBN 978-0-9935345-4-6)* which is still available from us and in 1/32nd scale there is only the old Matchbox kit, which is currently unavailable even in its reissued form by Revell.

All photos Libor Jekl ©2020

Technical Specifications
Scale: 1/72nd
Manufacturer: Dora Wings
Kit No.: DW 72023
Material: IM
UK Price: £23.95

Dora Wings are quite a new name in the hobby market, and they are mostly focusing on lesser known aircraft types in which the mainstream manufacturers are usually uninterested. However, in case of the Lysander it's not an unfamiliar name, though its importance is not comparable with the likes of the Spitfire or Hurricane. Perhaps the best known episode in its service was the 'special duty' deployment with the SOE (Special Operations Executive) picking up and dropping off agents and equipment behind enemy lines.

This is the very first attempt by Dora Wings at the Lysander in a planned series. The kit consists of five sprues in mid grey-coloured plastic, one transparent, an etched fret, a single resin item, canopy masks, decal sheet and full colour instructions, the components equating to one hundred and twenty plastic and seventeen etched. All the plastic parts are moulded with decent quality and the amount of flash and defects are limited to a minimum. However, the mould separation seam line is apparent on smaller parts, so cleaning up the cockpit tubular framework and similar components won't be a 'fun' part of the build, I suspect. The panel lines along with covers and fasteners are done via fine engraved lines, which seem to be too shallow in places, e.g. on the tailplanes, but a few strokes with a scribing tool should address

this. The rendition of the fabric on the wing and fuselage looks fine and realistic, without excessive representation of the ribs or fabric sag. The ailerons, rudder and landing flaps are moulded separately which is all fine how-

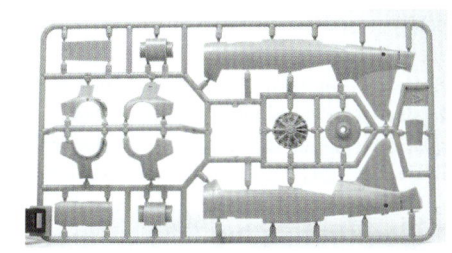

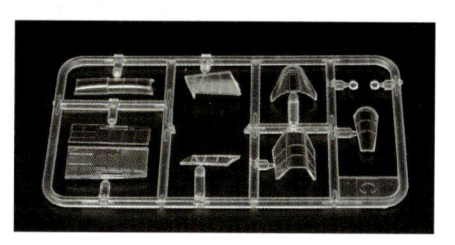

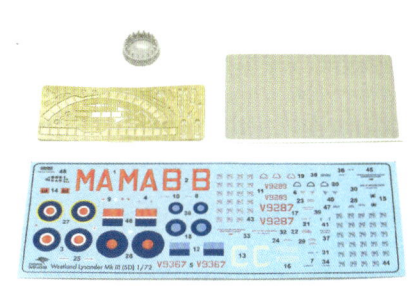

Airframe Detail No.9 – Lysander 97

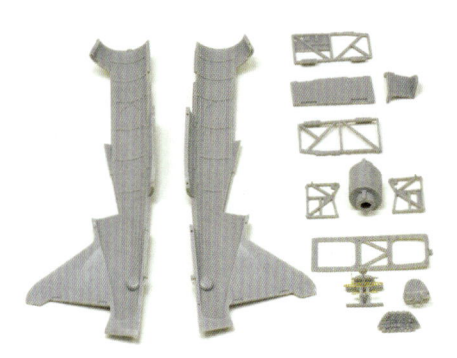

Layout of the interior components and fuselage halves

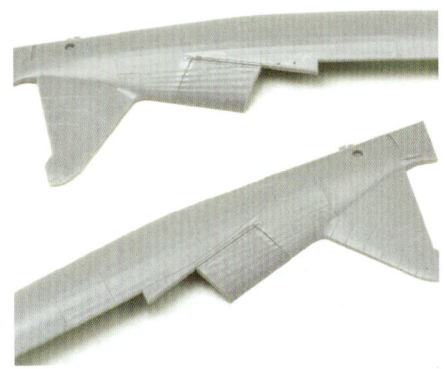

Oddly, the decking aft of the cockpit is a separate insert, so attach them whilst the halves are separate, so you can ensure they are all level etc.

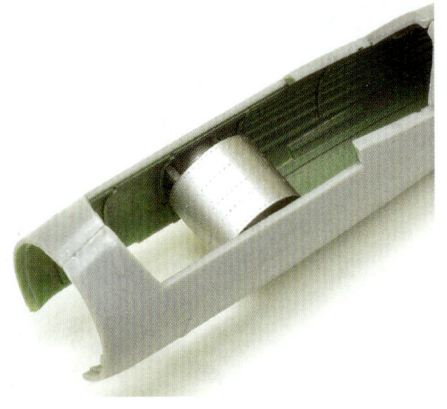

The main fuel tank was painted aluminium and some rivet detail added in the still soft paint

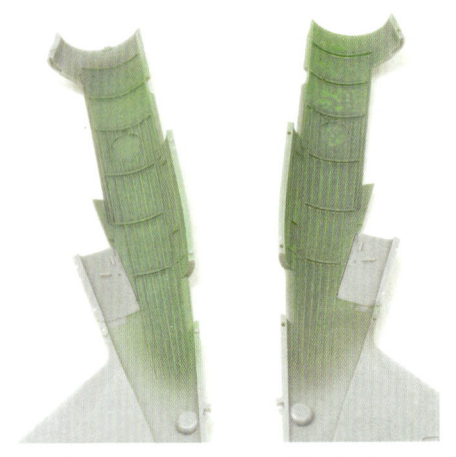

The interior was sprayed black then Interior Grey-Green to give some shading

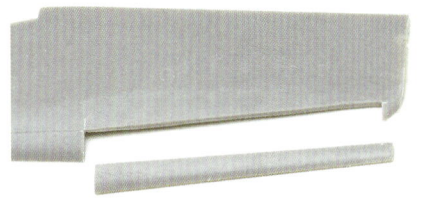

The inboard slats were cut away from the wings

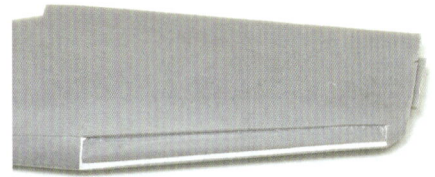

The slats that were cut out were then trimmed a bit and put back inside the wing halves to create a recess

ever, the latter items were inter-connected with the slats on the inner parts of the wing leading edge, so whilst the flaps were extended, the slats must be extended too but the kit does not provide separate slats, so the flaps should only be put in the closed position (and the instructions suggest doing so, which makes me curious why the manufacturer bothered with the separate flaps?) My initial good feeling about the surface quality deteriorated a little by the inclusion of a separately moulded rear fuselage spine (the reason for this remains unclear to me), as its joint lines could not be easily filled and sanded because the surrounding fabric will most likely get damaged in the process.

The cockpit is well detailed with many nice looking components, as is the multi-part framework with control boxes and radio, wire-type pilot seat, control column and system of internal wing supports; the other small parts can be found on the etched fret although oddly some of them are not shown on the instructions (e.g. the seat belts). The instrument panel has fine raised dials detail with the bodies of the individual instruments moulded on the back and the dials themselves are included on the decal sheet. For the SD version there is the external additional ex-Harrow fuel tank, however the upper additional extra gravity-feed fuel tank sandwiched between the wing sup-

porting structure in the canopy is omitted. For this version you should also leave out all equipment connected with the armament in the rear cockpit, such as the gun mount and sight, as the SD variant had all this removed, except the radio. The canopy is split into several parts and it looks a little bit thick, but crystal clear; (its robustness does matter, as the canopy creates a firm attachment point for the wing halves). The engine consists of plastic, etched and resin parts and looks great, however with its assembly I do not recommend following the instructions, which will bring you to a dead-end, but more on that later. The landing gear covers are designed both as fully closed and partially open, with the latter though you may need to add some of the other visible internal

All interior parts were painted prior to assembly

details such as the mud scrapers and braces because these are not included in the kit. The external fuel tank is nicely detailed and comes with its supports while the etched fret includes the ladder for the rear cockpit.

The kit provides marking for three machines: two from No.161 (SD) Squadron operating from the United Kingdom (V9287 and V9367) plus an example from No.357 Squadron operating in Burma (V9289). Photographs of the originals can be found and even without detailed analysis there are certain discrepancies compared to the camouflage schemes depicted in the instructions. V9287 should have the black extended to the fuselage sides approximately up to the level of the bottom of the canopy frame, and the landing gear spats were not completely black, but partially camouflaged. The same applies for the machine from the Burmese theatre, which lacked the serial number (but this is included on the decal sheet), and it had a tropical filter unit fitted to the air intake, which is omitted from the kit. The decal sheet is printed by Decograph and has very good quality, they are thin with perfect register and have matt carrier film. It also provides a set of stencils.

Construction

At the beginning you need to carefully remove the sprue attachments from the

98 Airframe Detail No.9 – Lysander

No additional fuel tank was included for the SD version, so the tank from the Airfix Swordfish was used instead, with details added from tape etc.

The bulge at the back of the upper tank along with the feed pipe to starboard was added from plasticard and tube

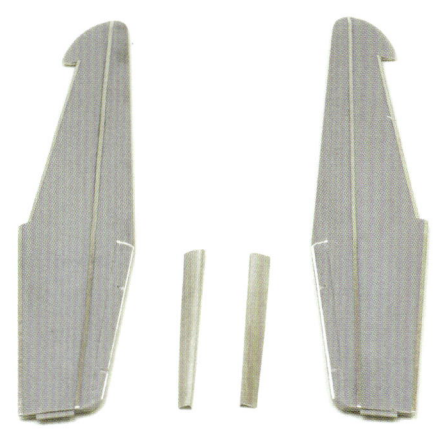

New inboard slats were made from aluminium sheet and the raised spar was reproduced with tape

Filler will be needed to blend everything ahead of the windshield

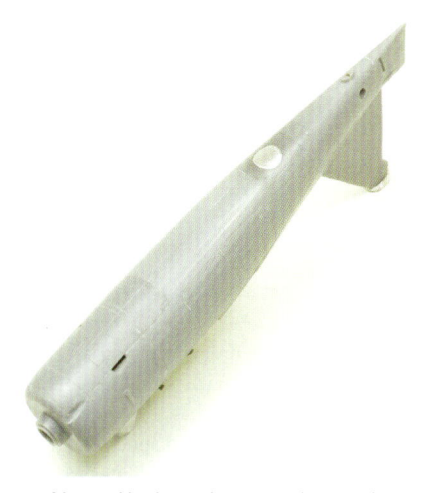

Take care blending in the joints, otherwise the fabric effect will be damaged

cemented the windshield to the fuselage and levelled the joint with some Superfine Milliput (white) as there were some small gaps. The fuselage halves could be then closed with the two separately moulded front and rear covers and on the latter part I glued on a new circular fairing cut from self-adhesive foil as I damaged it whilst sanding the joints. In the next step I progressively installed the clear parts, working from the pilot side to the back, the parts were first dry-fitted it to either fuselage half and gradually add the rest of the components as this technique offers better control of the overall fit and the possibility to adjust the parts as needed. The instructions suggest the assembly of the complete interior first before sandwiching it between the fuselage halves, which will create difficulties if you are not precise enough. The fuel tank could be left in the framework loose, without applying glue, and fixed later through the open ventral section. I continued with the attachment of the instrument panel along with the compass console, while the gunsight could be left out for now. Lysanders of this version usually had an additional gravity feed fuel tank located inside the wing supports between the front and rear cockpit, but this is not provided in the kit. I found a suitable basis for it in the Airfix Fairey Swordfish kit, which was similar in shape it just needed slight reshaping with a file and detailing with some plasticard and copper wire. I also added its triangularly-shaped end part with interconnecting piping to the ventral tank. From thin self-adhesive foil I cut the reinforcing strips and eventually painted it with the interior colour. I

various tiny interior parts and clean them up, fortunately the plastic is not fragile and is thus very workable. I do not recommend you strictly follow the instructions and continue in a traditional way instead, which means you skip the first seven building steps depicting the engine, external fuel tank and tailplanes and start with the interior. Before that however, it seems more convenient to attach the separate spine halves to the fuselage as they can be better aligned than on an already assembled fuselage. This step will require careful alignment of the parts as any unnecessary filling and sanding will cause damage to the surrounding fabric detail (on the real aircraft there was no such panel lines). Then I assembled the plastic interior components and added the etch before gluing the asymmetric fuselage fuel tank in place (remember its sharper end points forward). I tested the fit of the tank between the fuselage halves and once all looked fine, I painted it aluminium, while the interior was sprayed using Mr Color 364 Interior Grey Green. On assembling the tubular framework, I recommend that you install half of

and then secured in situ with extra thin Mr Cement S. Eventually, all the joints were sealed with Gator's Grip white hobby glue. All the components matched each other with minimum tolerances, so in the end this originally feared assembly was straightforward. I continued with the landing gear assembly, with each spat created from ten pieces, including the landing lamp, so it again required a lot of trial fitting and a careful approach. You should not use excessive force here as the tiny L-shaped load-bearing wheel brace can easily be bent or broken. The wheels are

The canopy is made up in sections, so work slowly and logically

Each undercarriage leg is made up of multiple parts and although the side panels are separate, there is no internal detail, so they can't be left off

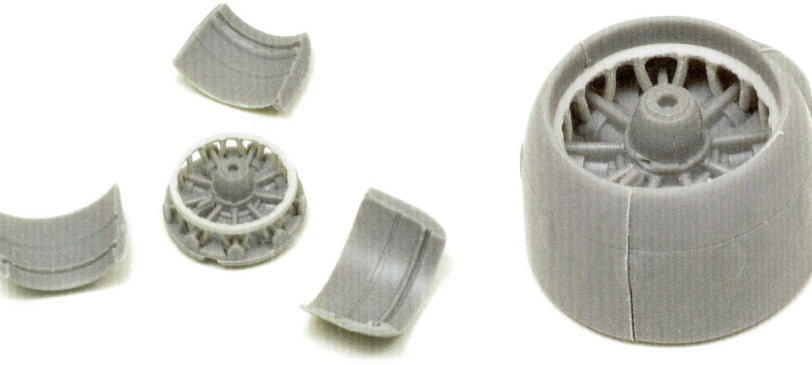

The engine is made up of plastic and resin components

You will have to do adjustments and test-fits before you can finally assembly the engine unit

The clear parts were attached with Mr Cement S and any gaps filled with Gator's Grip PVA

Once the undercarriage is secured the stance of the Lysander becomes apparent

A tape ring was added to the rear of the engine cowling to later accept the etched cowl flaps

The cowl gills are etched, so need to be curved before fitting

Once in place the cowl gills look effective

designed as built-in unit so they can't be inserted separately, which would have made painting easier, but this has to be done with a brush later. The completed spats were then cleaned up, any damaged panel lines were rectified with a fine razor saw and then fixed to the fuselage.

While checking the slats on the wing leading edge I thought I would try and model them in the extended position. It looked like it would not mean a vast amount of surgery to the kit parts and it would give the correct 'feel' to my Lysander. First, I removed the slats with a fine razor saw, sanded each down a bit and inserted them back in the wing leading edge, which created shallow openings for the slats. Small imperfections were levelled with Superfine Milliput and new slats were pre-shaped from thin aluminium sheet over the wing's leading edge. Final adjustments to the required size and dimensions were then made with modelling scissors. Also, I felt that the main spar was not prominent enough on the wing surface, so it was added from a strip of self-adhesive tape and in the same way I made the reinforcements along the flap and aileron hinge lines. Now I could attach each wing half to the canopy, where it was immediately supported with the spar. Thanks to good fit all this went smoothly without any real problems and while the glue set, the completed airframe created a firm and stable base. Due to the extended flaps I had to modify the attach-

The wings assemble solidly thanks to the tabs

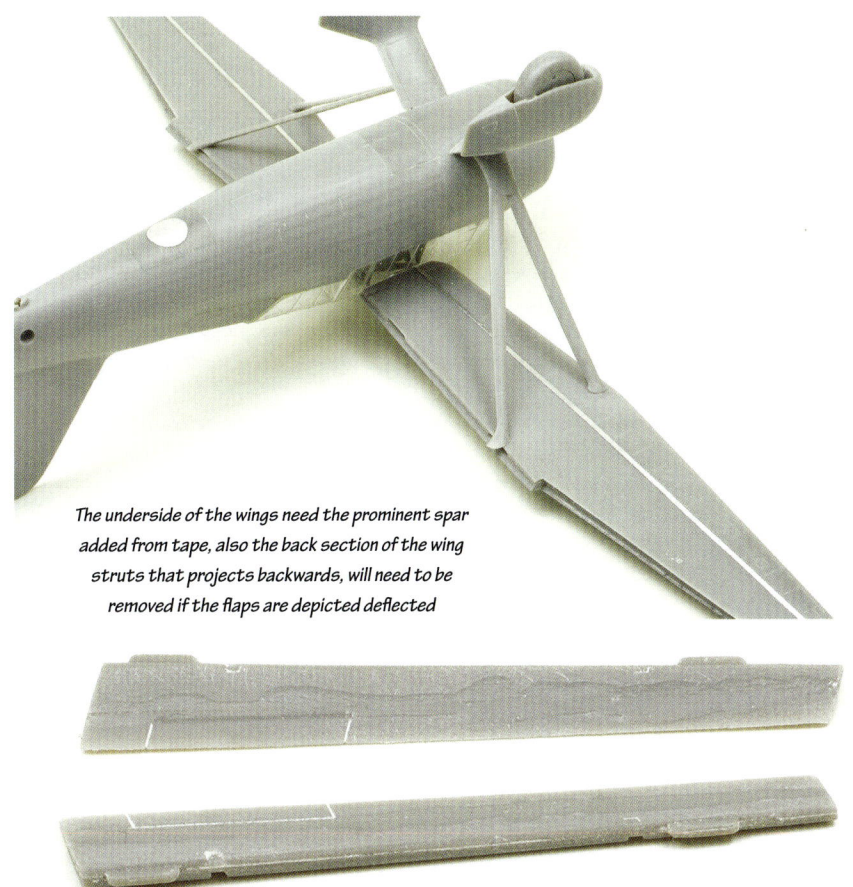

ments of the rear pair of braces, from which I cut off the end parts and glued them on to the flaps; a good close-up photograph may help to understand how this worked on the real thing. Some extra effort was needed for the assembly of the ailerons which were assembled from two halves each, but they did not fit well, so I ended up sealing the visible joint line with thicker cyanoacrylate and sanded it all smooth. All control surfaces were then attached, so I could now turn my attention to the engine.

As already mentioned, I warn you against following the instructions for the first assembly steps shown in diagram 4, since once the cowling is closed you won't be able to insert the completed engine inside along with its resin exhaust collector and braces. It is mandatory to start by dry-fitting the main parts and after a few rounds of fine tuning the cowling sections can be assembled with the engine, inner collector ring and outer ring without using any glue. The engine was painted with Alclad II Jet Exhaust, while the gear casing was airbrushed gloss black. The inner braces and other small bits were left off until the final assembly. The cooling flaps are provided as closed or fully extended, so you can choose your preferred option. For a firmer attachment I glued them inside the cowling with a 2mm wide stripe of self-adhesive tape onto which I placed each flap (they can be bent to shape using the round handle of a modelling knife) and finally secured them with cyanoacrylate. The completed engine unit was then glued to the fuselage and its correct position ensured by a series of tabs. I added the tailplanes, which needed some filler on the bottom to create a flush transitions, and added their respective etched root plates.

Camouflage & Markings

For masking off the canopy, I used the masks provided in the kit. The vinyl material is

The underside of the wings need the prominent spar added from tape, also the back section of the wing struts that projects backwards, will need to be removed if the flaps are depicted deflected

The flaps have tabs that ensure they sit in a neutral position, so these are cut off to allow them to be deflected slightly

The tailplanes need filler on the undersides for a smooth transition

The self-adhesive masks included in the kit were used to masked off the canopy, which was then sprayed with Interior Grey-Green

Mr Surfacer 1000 was used to prime the model

Airframe Detail No.9 – Lysander **101**

sufficiently flexible and I had no trouble with the masks' adhesion either, as they firmly stuck to the rounded contours. However, some of the masks did not completely match their respective canopy shapes and had to be trimmed with a scalpel or extended with strips of Tamiya tape. The framing was overpainted with the interior colour and the kit was then primed with couple of thin layers of Mr Surfacer 1000 (grey). The painting session started with the exhaust collector ring and that was airbrushed with a mix of black and brown to simulate heated metal. For the lower wing surfaces and fuselage sides I used H77 Tire Black, which is less intense than pure black and followed period photographs in spraying this colour up to the canopy bottom sill line. The upper surfaces were painted next, using H72 Dark Green and AK Real

Black and brown was used to reproduced the heated metal of the collector ring

Tyre Black is used for the undersides, as its more appropriate then standard black

modelling scissors, this being determined by the mounting holes on the fuselage, and then painted it black. To the fuselage I fixed the 150 gal external tank and added some fuel leaks and paint weathering using a mix of various light grey colours applied by airbrush. From a plastic profile I cut four identical bearers for the slats, fixed them in the leading edge and adjusted their size and shape with a scalpel. Eventually, I painted on the position lights because they are missing using transparent acrylics and from a piece

The upper surfaces of Dark Green (H73) and Ocean Grey (RC288) were applied freehand

Once glossed, the decals were applied, although only a limited number of stencils were used, as that seemed accurate for the depicted example going from period photographs

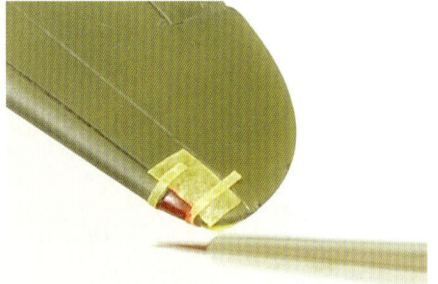

The tip lights are not depicted, so they were reproduced with transparent red and green paint

Colors RC288 Ocean Grey. After sealing the surface with Mr Color GX 100 Super Clear varnish I applied the decals, which were of high quality and responded well to Mr Mark Softer. Judging by the period photographs it seems that not all of the stencilling was applied on the black painted areas, so I left out most of them off my model.

Final Details

I bent to shape the external ladder using a brush handle and trimmed it to size using

The slats, ladder, external fuel tank and propeller were all painted before being secured

of stretched sprue I added the bottom antenna wire.

Conclusion

Overall, this is a precise rendition of a unique subject that at last replaces the aged or too difficult to build kits from Frog, Matchbox or Pavla Models, respectively. However, this kit is intended for more experienced modellers, mainly due to complex assembly and rather confusing instructions in certain areas.

Little Lizzie

The next release has already been announced by Dora Wings, so we can look forward to Mk III and most likely earlier versions at a later date as well.

Paints Used
AK Real Colors:
• RC288 Ocean Grey
GSI Creos (Gunze-Sangyo) Mr Aqueous Hobby Color:
• H73 Dark Green
• H77 Tire Black
• Mr Surfacer 1000 (Grey)
GSI Creos (Gunze-Sangyo) Mr Color:
• 364 Interior Grey Green
• GX100 Super Clear

Our thanks to Albion Alloys, the UK importer of Dora Wings, for the review sample.

Airframe Detail No.9 – Lysander **103**

Appendix i

Lysander Kits

Below is a list of all static scale construction kits produced to date of the Lysander. This list is as comprehensive as possible, but if there are amendments or additions, please contact the author via the Valiant Wings Publishing address shown at the front of this title.

All are injection moulded plastic unless otherwise stated

1/100th or smaller

- Fox One Design Studio [res] 1/144th Westland Lysander Mk I #A014 (N/K) – *Finnish Air Force*
- Fox One Design Studio [res] 1/144th Westland Lysander Mk II #A015 (N/K) – *RAF & Turkish Air Force*
- Fox One Design Studio [res] 1/144th Westland Lysander Mk IIIA #A021 (N/K) – *RAF & Portuguese Air Force*
- Fox One Design Studio [res] 1/144th Westland Lysander Mk IIISD #A022 (N/K) – *Royal Air Force*
- Fox One Design Studio [res] 1/144th Westland Lysander Mk I Skis #A027 (N/K) – *Finnish Air Force*

1/72nd Scale

- Airfix Lysander #Pattern No.1385 (1956) – Also included in 'The Airfix Historical Air Fleet' boxed set #1370 in 1956 (with Bristol F.2b, Gladiator, Spitfire and Whirlwind helicopter). Reissued with full-colour header card (still #Pattern No.1385) in 1959, relabelled as a Lysander Mk II #Patt. No.84 in 1962 (listed in 1969 catalogue as such), This kit was retooled and reissued as #01004-5 in late 1972 (this allowed Mk I and Mk III versions to be built), reissued as #02053-9 in 1974, as #02053-0 in 1975, again as #903052 in 1985, in 1986 as #02053, in 1998 as #02053, again (same kit number) in 2005, renumbered in 2008 as #A02053
- AMT (ex-Frog) Westland Lysander #A-607-80 (1967-1970s)
- Ark Models (ex-Frog) Lysander Mk I/III Spotter/Spy Plane #72018 (2011)
- Continental Models (ex-Airfix) Westland Lysander #N/K (late 1950s)
- DFI* (ex-Frog) 1/72nd Lysander Mk I/III #U-3140 (1980s) – *This is the Donetsk Toys Factory*
- Dora Wings Westland Lysander Mk III (SD) #DW72023 (Announced 03/2019, released 05/2020)
- Dora Wings Westland Lysander Mk III #DW72024 – *Due 2020*
- Eastern Express (ex-Frog) Lysander Mk I/III #72285 (2000) – Reissued, same item number, 2014
- Frog Lysander Mk 1 or Mk 3 'Spy Plane' #F193 (1968 – 1972) – Reissued, as #F420 in 1972-1974 (header bag), then again as #F193 in 1974 only (white box)
- Frog 'Penguin' Westland Lysander II #50P (1939-1941) – Reissued as #050P (1946-1947)
- Hasegawa (ex-Frog) Lysander Mk1/3 #JS-042 (1967-1973/4)
- Lotnia (ex-Frog) Westland Lysander #N/K – *Production ceased by the late 1980s*
- Matchbox Lysander #PK-7 (1973) – Reissued under Revell's control in 1982 and 1983 (#PK-7) and in 1991 as #40007 'Lysander Mk II'
- NovoExport (ex-Frog) 1/72nd Lysander Mk I/III #76021 (1977-1980) – *Only a small quantity of each kit (2000) were produced for export and firm liquidated in 1980*
- Pavla Models Lysander Mk II #72048 (2004)
- Plasty (ex-Airfix) 1/72nd Lysander #1640-16 (1956)
- Revell (ex-Matchbox) Lysander Mk II 'Revell Classics' #00001 (2008) – *Limited edition, only 5,000 worldwide*
- Special Hobby Lysander Mk I #SH72142 – *Planned 2005, not released to date*

1/48th Scale

- Eduard (ex-Gavia) Mk III 'ProfiPACK' #8083 (2003) – Reissued in 2011 as #8290 and again in 2016
- Eduard (ex-Gavia) Mk III 'In Ilmavoimat service' #1138 (2008) – *Limited edition – Reissued in 2011*
- Gavia Lysander Mk III #007/0401 (2001)
- Gavia Lysander Mk III SD #008/0901 (2001)
- Hawk Lysander Mk II/III 'Completely chrome plated' #216-200 (1968)
- Hawk Lysander Mk II #563-100 (1967), also 563-130 & 563
- Hawk Lysander #HL410 (2014) – *Reissue under new ownership of the Hawk brand*
- Italaerei/Testors (ex-Hawk) Westland Lysander Mark III #804 (1979) – *Firm changed name from Italaerei to Italeri in 1980*
- Italeri (ex-Hawk) Westland Lysander Mk III #804 (1994)
- Lindberg (ex-Hawk) Westland Lysander Mk II #410 (N/K) – *Under the new ownership of Round 2 Models*
- Testors (ex-Hawk) Westland Lysander Mk II 'Plated' #216 (1987)
- Testors (ex-Hawk) Westland Lysander Mk III #563 (1987)

1/32nd Scale

- Matchbox Lysander Mk I/III #PK-504 (1979) – Reissued, presume same number, in 1987 and reissued under Revell's control in 1991 as #40504
- Revell (ex-Matchbox) Lysander Mk I/III #04710 (1998) – Reissued, same kit number, in 2007
- Revell (ex-Matchbox) Lysander Mk I/III 'Shuttleworth Collection 75 Years' #04710 (2003-5) – *Special limited edition only available via the Shuttleworth Trust shop with decals for their machine for an extra £1*

Notes

inj	–	Injection Moulded Plastic
ltd inj	–	Limited-run Injection Moulded Plastic
pe	–	Photo-etched metal
res	–	Resin
vac	–	Vacuum-formed Plastic
3dp res	–	3D Printed Resin
(1999)	–	Denotes date the kit was released
(1994->)	–	Date/s denote start/finish of firm's activities, the exact date of release of this kit is however unknown
ex-	–	Denotes the tooling originated with another firm, the original tool maker is noted after the '-'

Airfix 01004-5

Airfix 02053 (1998)

Airfix Patt No 1385 (2nd ed)

Airfix Patt No 84

Airfix Pattern No 1385 (1st issue)

Airmodel No 128

Ark Models 72018

Dora Wings DW72024

Eduard 11138

Eduard 1138

Eduard 8083 (2003)

Frog F193 (white box)

Matchbox PK-504

Matchbox PK-7

Pavla Models 72048

Revell 00001

Revell 04710

Appendix ii

Lysander Accessories, Masks & Decals

As there are relatively few accessories, decals and masks for the Lysander we thought it best to combine these in one Appendix. Below therefore is a list of all accessories, paint masks and decals for static scale construction kits produced to date for the type. This list is as comprehensive as possible, but if there are amendments or additions, please contact the author via the Valiant Wings Publishing address shown at the front of this title.

Accessories

1/72nd

- Airmodel [vac] Westland Tandem Wing Lysander (P.12 Delanne) Conversion #218 {Frog}
- Dujin [res] Westland P.12 Twin Lizzie conversion #DC7209
- Falcon [vac] RAF World War II (Part 4) Clear-Vax Set No.22 – *Included canopy for Lysander* {Matchbox}
- Kora Models [res] Lysander Mk I/III Conversion #DS 7250 {Matchbox/Revell or Pavla}
- Kora Models [res] Lysander Mk I Finnish Service Ski Set #DS 7263
- PlusModel [pa] Lysander Mk I Instrument Panel #None
- PlusModel [pa] Lysander Mk IIIa Instrument Panel #None
- Yahu Models [pe] Lysander Instrument Panel (pre-painted) #YMA7288 {Pavla}

1/48th

- Aires [res] Lysander Mk III Control Surfaces #4703 {Gavia/Eduard}
- CMK [res/pe] Lysander Mk III Detail Set #4130 {Gavia/Eduard}
- Eduard [pe] Lysander Mk III Detail Set #48-203 {Gavia/Eduard}
- Eduard [pe] Lysander Detail Set #48-367 {Gavia/Eduard}
- Eduard [pe] Lysander Seat Belts – Steel #FE1089 {Gavia/Eduard}
- Eduard [pe] Lysander Upgrade Set #481015 {Gavia/Eduard}
- Eduard [res] Lysander Mk III Instrument Panel 'LööK #644 054 {Gavia/Eduard}
- Final Connections [res] Lysander Detail Set #N/K {Hawk/Italeri/Testors}
- Final Connections [res] Lysander Cowl Bumps #48-006 {Hawk/Italeri/Testors}
- Part [pe] Lysander Mk III Detail Set #S48-091 {Gavia/Eduard}
- Part [pe] Lysander Mk III Canopy Frames #S48-092 {Gavia/Eduard}
- Quickboost [res] Lysander Exhaust #QB48587 [Gavia/Eduard}
- Squadron [vac] Lysander Canopy #9578 {Hawk/Italeri/Testors}
- True Details [res] Lysander Mk I/II/III Wheel Set #48079

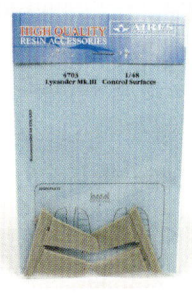

Aires 4703

CMK 4130 Lysander Detail Set

Quickboost QB48587 Lysander Exhausts

Final Connections Lysander Detail Set

1/32nd

- Engines & Things [res] Bristol Aero Engine – Mercury for Lysander, Blenheim, Gladiator etc. #32031 {Matchbox/Revell}

Masks

1/72nd

- KV Models [ma] Lysander Mk II canopy & wheel masks #72904 {Matchbox/Revell}

1/48th

- Cutting Edge Modelworks [vma] Lysander wheel hub masks #CEBM48128 {Testors}
- Cutting Edge Modelworks [vma] Lysander canopy & wheel hub masks #CEBM48303 {Gavia/Eduard}
- Eduard [vma] Lysander canopy & wheel hub masks #XF109 {Gavia/Eduard}
- Montex [vma] Lysander Mk III canopy & marking option masks #K48111 {Gavia/Eduard}
  LY-118, 2/LeLv 16. Finnish Air Force, 1941
  AR•M, No.309 (Polish) Squadron, 1942
- Montex [vma] Lysander Mk III canopy & marking option masks #K481127 {Gavia/Eduard}
  T Mk III, V9323, Royal Canadian Air Force
  T Mk III, USAAF, 1944
- Montex [vma] Lysander Mk III canopy & wheel hub masks #SM482428 {Gavia/Eduard}

1/32nd

- Cutting Edge Modelworks [vma] Lysander canopy & wheel hub masks #CEBM32042 {Matchbox/Revell}
- Montex [vma] Lysander Mk III canopy & wheel hub masks #SM32058 {Matchbox/Revell}
- Montex [vma] Lysander Mk III canopy & marking option masks #K32096 {Matchbox/Revell}
  Same options as #K48111

Notes
- 3dp – 3D Printed
- br – Brass
- fb – Fabric
- ma – Die-cut Self-adhesive Paint Masks [tape]
- pa – Paper (laser-cut)
- pe – Photo-etched Brass
- PP – Pre-painted (photo-etched)
- res – Resin
- SA – Self-adhesive
- vac – Vacuum-formed Plastic
- vma – Vinyl Self-adhesive Paint Masks
- wm – White-metal (including Pewter)
- {Academy} – Denotes the kit for which the set is intended

- Montex [vma] Lysander Mk III canopy & marking option masks #K32097 {Matchbox/Revell}
  Same options as #K48112

Decals

1/72nd

ABT
#100 Westland Lysander Mk I
- Unidentified Free French example

#42
Inc. Egyptian Air Force Lysander 'Black Y517'

AML Decals
#72002 Westland Lysander
- LY-120, 2/LeLv 16, Nurmola airfield, June 1942
- LY-119, 2/LeLv 16, Viiksjärvi, February 1942
- LY-116, 2/LeLv 16, January 1943 in winter camouflage
- LY-118, 2/LeLv 16, during visit to Tiiksjärvi on the 5th August 1942

Black Cat Decals
#BC72005 Lysander Mk III
- '361' of the Portuguese Air Force, Base 3, Tancos, 1944

Blackbird Models
#BMD72017 Operation Overlord Pt.1
Inc:
- Mk IIA, JR•P, No.161 Squadron, RAF Tempsford, June 1944

Carpena
#72.49 FAFL 1ere Partie Free French Air Force
Inc:
- P9184, Free French Air Force, Fort Lamy, N'Djamena, Tchad, 1941

Esci
#No.33 Lysander & Blenheim
Inc:
- Free French Air Force example
- OO•F, No.13 (Army Co-Operation) Squadron, France, 1939
- Mk III (SD), V9289, •C, No.357 (Special Duties) Squadron, Burma, 1945

Kora Decals
#DEC 72.388 Lysander Mk I Estonian Service
Inc.
- Aircraft 'White 167' in camouflage and 'Black 168' in overall aluminium of unidentified Estonian Air Force unit

L Decals Studio
#LSD 72004 Lysander Mk I, II and III
- Mk I, L4723, No.208 (Army Co-operation) Squadron, Qasaba, Egypt, summer 1939
- Mk I, KJ•L, No.16 (AC) Squadron, Old Sarum, autumn 1938/early 19391938
- Mk II, 'Black 3130', Turkish AF, July 1940
- Mk II, Escadrille 'Rennes', Groupe Bretange, CRB 1, Free French Air Force, Fort-Lanny, Chad, 1941-2
- Mk I, LY-121, 2./LeLv 16, Värtsilä, Finland, 1941
- TT Mk III, 1587 (ex-V9285), Royal Canadian Air Force, December 1942

Max Decals
#72-002 Irish Air Corps 1938-1948
Inc:
- Lysander, 'Black 66', Irish Air Corps, circa 1942 (camouflage)
- Lysander, 'Black 66', Irish Air Corps, circa 1945/46 (silver)

Plastic Planet Club
#PPD-72005 Allied Bombers in the Battle of Greece
Inc:
- Lysander Mk I, L4719, No.208 (Army Co-Operation) Squadron, based at Larissa

Print-Scale
#72-129 Westland Lysander
- Mk III (SD), V9289, •C, No.357 (Special Duties) Squadron, Burma, 1945
- Mk III, L4761, AN•B, No.13 Squadron, 1935
- Mk II, OO•D, No.13 (Army Co-Operation) Squadron, Peronne, France, 1939
- Mk IIA, V9618, •E, No.754 NAS, RNAS Arbroath, September 1941
- Mk II, 'Black 461' GV•C or either No.3 or 32 OTU, Canada, 1942
- Mk IIA, V9347, AR•B, No.309 (Polish) Squadron, 1942-3
- TT Mk III, V9817, 3rd Gunnery and Target Towing Flight, 8th AF, USAAF, UK, 1944
- Mk II, P9134, Group Bretagne, Free French Forces, Tunisia, 1941-2
- Mk II, 'Black 3122', Turkish Air Force, 1940
- Mk I, R2649, •C, No.208 (Army Co-operation) Sqn, Siwa Oasis, Egypt, November 1940

Protransfer Decalques
#72008 Westland Lysander Mk IIIa
- 'White 361' or '366' of the Portuguese AF

Techmod
#7235 Westland Lysander Mk III
- Mk IIIA, R9125, LX•L, No.54 OTU, as preserved by the RAF Museum, Hendon
- V9644, AR•O, No.309 (Polish) Squadron

Travers
#72-015 Westland Lysander
- P9134, Group Bretagne, Free French Forces, Tunisia, 1941-2
- P1674, HB•T, No.239 Squadron, Hatfield, September 1940

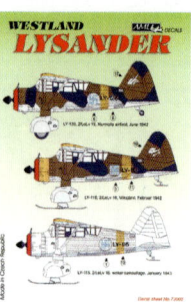

AML 72002

L Decals Studio LDS 48004

Max Decals 3201

Blackbird Models 48008

- V9367, MA•B, as operated by the Shuttleworth Trust
- T1444, G•5, No.15 Air Observer's School
- LY-120, 2/LeLv 16, Finnish Air Force, Nurmola airfield, June 1942
- LY-118, 2/LeLv 16. Finnish Air Force, 1941

Xtradecals
#X039-72 Normandy Invasion Aircraft
Inc.
- Lysander Mk III, serial unknown, JR•P, No.161 (SD) Squadron

#X72-127 RAF No.6 Sqn History 1931-2010
Inc:
- Lysander Mk II, L6878, JV•D, Palestine, 1939

#X72-148 RFC/RAF 100 Years of No.4 Sqn
Inc:
- Lysander Mk II, L4792, FY•V, No.4 Squadron, Monchy Lagache, France, late 1939

#X72-150 RAF No.2 Squadron History 1920-2002
Inc:
- Lysander Mk III, T1532, KO•D, RAF Sawbridgeworth, 1941

1/48th

Aeromaster
#48-257 Lysander Collection Pt.I
- Free French example
- 'Black 62' Irish Air Corps
- LY-118, 2/LeLv 16. Finnish Air Force, 1941
- L4761, RAF

#48-258 Lysander Collection Pt.II
- Mk II, P9134, Group Bretagne, Free French Forces, Tunisia, 1941-2
- Mk III (SD), V9289, •C, No.357 (Special Duties) Squadron, Burma, 1945
- Unidentified Free French example
- V9816, RAF

Blackbird Models
#BMD48008 Operation Overlord Pt.1
Same option as #BMD72017

L Decals Studio
#LSD 48004 Lysander Mk I, II and III
Same options as LDS 72004

Max Decals
#48-001 Irish Air Corps 1922-1997
Same options as #72-002 Irish Air Corps 1938-1948

#4803 Exotic Lysanders
- 'Black 3106', Turkish Air Force, 1939
- Y513, No.1 Army Co-Operation Squadron, Royal Egyptian Air Force, 1940 (plus a special markings version from 1941)
- 'White 361', Grupo de Recohecimento e Informacao, Portuguese Air Force, 1943
- T1445, K-W6-K, No.755 NAS, Royal Navy, 1941-2
- V9817, No.3 Gunnery & Towed Target Flt, 8th AF, USAAF, March 1944

Print-Scale
#48-083 Westland Lysander
- Mk III (SD), V9289, •C, No.357 (Special Duties) Squadron, Burma, 1945
- Mk III, L4761, AN•B, No.13 Squadron, 1935
- Mk IIA, V9618, •E, No.754 NAS, RNAS Arbroath, September 1941
- Mk IIA, V9347, AR•B, No.309 (Polish) Squadron, 1942-3
- Mk I, R2649, •C, No.208 (Army Co-operation) Squadron, Siwa Oasis, Egypt, November 1940
- Mk II, OO•D, No.13 (Army Co-Operation) Squadron, Peronne, France, 1939

Xtradecals
#X48-106 RFC/RAF 100 Years of No.4 Sqn
Same option as #X72-148

#X48-109 RAF No.2 Squadron History 1920-2002
Same options as #X72-150

1/32nd

Kora Decals
#DEC 3243 Lysander Mk I Estonian Service
Same options as #DEC 72388

Max Decals
#3201 Exotic Lysanders Pt.1
- Y513, No.1 Army Co-Operation Squadron, Royal Egyptian Air Force, 1940 (plus a special markings version from 1941)
- 'White 361', Grupo de Recohecimento e Informacao, Portuguese Air Force, 1943

#3202 Exotic Lysanders Pt.2
- 'Black 3106', Turkish Air Force, 1939
- T1445, K-W6-K, No.755 NAS, Royal Navy, 1941-2
- V9817, No.3 Gunnery & Towed Target Flt, 8th AF, USAAF, March 1944

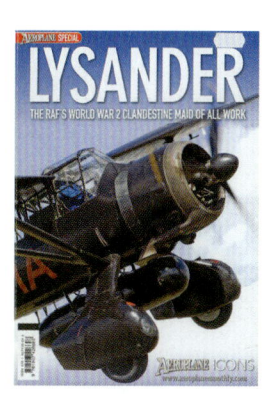

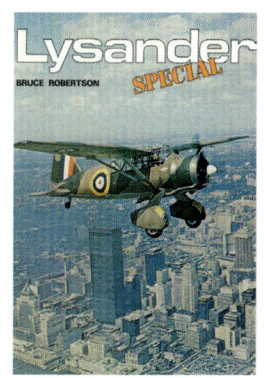

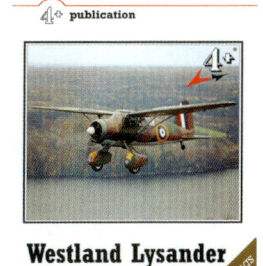

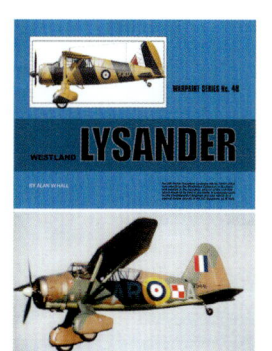

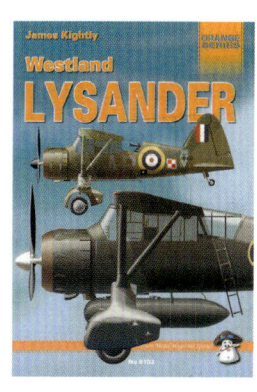

Appendix iii

Bibliography

The list of Lysander related publications below is as comprehensive as possible, but there are bound to be omissions so if you have amendments or additions, please contact the author via the Valiant Wings Publishing address shown at the front of this title.

Official Documents

Lysander Mk I – Air Publication 1582A
Lysander Mk II – Air Publication 1582B
Lysander Mk III/IIIA – Air Publication 1582C
Lysander TT – Air Publication 1582ABC

Publications

- Pilot's Notes for Lysander III & IIIA – Air Publication 1582C – P.N. (Air Data Publications)
- Aircraft Archive – Classics of World War Two (Argus Books 1989 ISBN:0-85242-985-1)
- Aircraft of World War II by C. Chant (Dempsey Parr, 1999)
- Eyes of the Phoenix: Allied Aerial Photo-Reconnaissance Operations South-East Asia 1941-1945 by G.J. Thomas (Hikoki Publications 1999 ISBN: 0-9519899-4-4)
- Finnish Air Force 1939-1945 by K. Keskinen & K. Stenman (Squadron/Signal Publications 1998 ISBN: 0-89747-387-6)
- Flying the Westland Lysander by Dave Hadfield
- Les Avions Britanniques aux Coleurs Françaises by J-J Petit (Avia Editions 2003 ISBN: 2-915030-04-9)
- Lysander – De La Tourmente au clair de lune by J-M Legrand (Foundation Les Sabena Old Timers 1998)
- Lysander – De La Tourmente au clair de lune [From hell to moonlight] by J-M Legrand (Vario 2003)
- Lysander Pilot – Secret Operations with 161 Squadron by James Atterby McCairns
- Lysander Special by Bruce Robertson (Ian Allan Ltd 1977 ISBN: 0-7110-0764-0)
- Lysander: The RAF's World War 2 Clandestine Maid of all Work, Aeroplane Icons (Kelsey Publishing Ltd 2013 ISBN: 987-1-907436-69-8)
- Polish Air Force 1939-1945 by Dr J. Koniarek (Squadron/Signal Publications 1994 ISBN: 0-89747-324-8)
- RAF & RCAF Aircraft Nose Art in World War II by C. Simonsen (Hikoki Publications 2001 ISBN: 1-902109-20-1)
- Sticky Murphy (Alan Michael 'Sticky' Murphy DSO and Bar, DFC & Croix de Guerre): Love of Life by James H. Coley
- The Long Drag: A Short History of British Target Towing by D. Evans (Flight Recorder Publications 2004 ISBN: 0-9545605-4-X)
- The Lysander Passenger by Peter Clements
- The Secret Years: Flight Testing at Boscombe Down 1939-1945 by T. Mason (Hikoki Publications 1998 ISBN: 1-951899-9-5)
- We Landed by Moonlight: The Secret RAF Landings in France 1940-1944 by Hugh Verity (Crécy Publications)
- Westland Aircraft since 1915 by D.N. James (Putnam ©1991 & 2001 ISBN: 0-85177-847-X)
- Westland Lysander by F.K. Mason, Profile No.159 (Profile Publications 1967)
- Westland Lysander by J. Knightly, Orange Series No.8103 (Mushroom Models Publications 2005 ISBN: 978-83-917178-4-4)
- Westland Lysander in Indian Air Force Service by P.V.S. Jagan Mohan (Warbirds India 2011)
- Westland Lysander – Mks I, III/IIIA, III(SD), IIIA(SD), TT Mks I, II & III by M. Ovcacik & K. Susa (4+ Publications 1999 ISBN: 80-902559-1-4)
- Westland Lysander by T.J. Drewnik, Samalot Wielozadaniowy No.179 (Bellona I Agencja Wydawnicza CB 1997)
- Westland Lysander by A.W. Hall, Warpaint Series No.48 (Warpaint Books Ltd 2004)
- Westland Lysander 1936-46 (all marks), Owner's Workshop Manual by Edward Wake-Walker (Haynes Publishing Ltd 2914 ISBN: 978-8-85733-395-7)

Periodicals & Part-works

- Aeroplane Monthly, September 1979, June 1990, July 1990, December 1992, May 2010 & September 2012
- Aero Modeller, December 1967
- Air Classics, January 1975
- Air Enthusiast No.22 & Vol.3 No.1 July 1972
- Air International, January 1975 and Vol.26 No.1 January & Vol.26 No.2 February 1984
- Air News, November 1943
- Air Pictorial, May 1967, July 1971 & January 1985
- Airfix Magazine, October 1975
- Fana de l'aviation No.228 (1988)
- Flight International, 8th August 1974 & 12th May 1979
- Flug Revue 2/1975
- Mach 1 No.143/23
- Modelaid International, September 1986
- Model Airplane News, March 1958
- Popular Aviation April 1937
- Scale Aircraft Modelling Vol.4 No.4 January 1982 and Vol.17 No.3 May 1995
- Scale Aviation Modeller International Vol.9 Iss.6 June 2003
- Scale Models, Vol.1 No.2 November 1969, Vol.5 No.2 February 1974, Vol.10 No.119 August 1979 & Vol.10 No.120 September 1979
- Replic No.33 (May 1994) & No.119 (July 2001)
- Wonders of World Aviation, Part 7

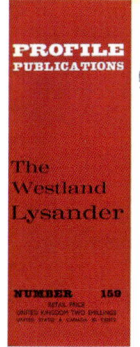

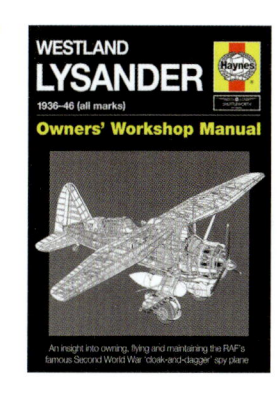

Appendix iv

Lysander Squadrons

To list in any detail the operational use of the Lysander would be a massive task, well beyond the scope of this title. Instead what we will offer here is a list of all Lysander squadrons and units along with a brief history of each during their time operating the type.

Royal Air Force

No.II (Army Co-operation) Squadron

This squadron first operated the Mk I from July 1938 from RAF Hawkinge and moved to Abbeville/Drucat on the 29th September 1939. The Mk Is were replaced with Mk IIs in February 1940 with detachments to Senon, Ronchin and Labuissiere. Moved to Labuissiere on the 15th May 1940 with a detachment to Wevelghem, then moved to Boulogne on the 19th May 1940, to Lympne and then on to Bekebourne on the 20th May 1940 and on to Hatfield on the 8th June 1940 and Cambridge with a detachment at Sawbridgeworth on the 1st August 1940. The unit re-equipped with the Mk III in September 1940 and moved to Sawbridgeworth on the 24th October 1940, then on to Fulbeck on the 19th July 1941, back to Sawbridgeworth on the 23rd July 1941, then to Weston Zoyland on the 4th August 1941 and back to Sawbridgeworth on the 10th August 1941. The unit re-equipped with the Curtiss Tomahawk Mk I and II at some stage in August 1941.
Codes: KO & XV

No.4 (Army Co-operation) Squadron

The squadron operated the Mk I from Odiham, Mons-en-Chaussée, Ronchin, Aspelaere, Clairmarais, Dunkirk, Detling, Ringway and Linton-on-Ouse between December 1938 to September 1940, with the Mk III from Clifton from September 1940 to July 1941 and with the Mk IIIa from May 1941 to June 1942.
Codes: TV & FY

Although this period image is damaged, it shows Mk III, T1532 KO•D, of No II (Army Co-operation) Squadron based at RAF Sawbridgeworth, Hertfordshire, in flight while making a practice attack on a road convoy at Odiham, Hampshire (©Air Ministry)

Mk II, JV•E, of No.6 (Army Co-operation) Squadron based at Ramleh, Egypt, makes a low-level 'attack' on Australian infantry during an anti-aircraft exercise in the Western Desert (©British Official)

Lysander of No.4 (Army Co-operation) Squadron line-up including L4752 (FY•V) and L4753 (FY•W) at RAF Odiham in 1939 (©Air Ministry)

Mk I L4808 KJ•H of No 16 (Army Co-operation) Squadron at Old Sarum (©Air Ministry)

No.6 (Army Co-operation) Squadron

The squadron operated the Mks I & II from Ramleh, Qasabam Siwa, Tobruk, Aqir, Helipolosi, Agedabia, Antelat, Msus, Marawa, Derna, El Gubbi East, El Gubbi West and Maaten Bagush from September 1939 to June 1941 and from Wadi Halfa with a detachment at Kufra from the August 1941 to January 1942.
Codes: JV

No.13 (Army Co-operation) Squadron

The squadron operated the Mk II from Odiham, Mons-en-Chaussée, Flamicourt, Douai, Abbeville, Clairmarais, Châteaubriant and Bekesbourne between January 1939 to January 1941 and the Mk III from Hooton Park and Speke from November 1940 until July 1941.
Codes: AN & OO

No.16 (Army Co-operation) Squadron

The squadron operated the Mk I from Old Sarum from May 1938 to April 1939, then re-equipped with the Mk III and operated that until November 1940 with moves to Hawkinge on the 17th February 1940, Amiens on the 13th April 1940, Bertangles on the 14th April 1940 and Lympne on the 19th May 1940. Reverted to the Mk I in May 1940 and moved to Redhill on the 3rd June 1940, to Cambridge on the 29th June 1940 and Okehampton with a detachment to Cambridge on the 3rd August 1940 and then to Weston Zoyland on the 15th August 1940. The unit re-equipped with the Mk III in October 1940 with detachments to Okehampton, Roborough, Tilshead, St. Just and Bolt Head, before adopting the Mk IIIA in May 1941. It moved to Okehampton on the 4th June 1941, Weston Zoyland on the 6th June 1941 with a detachment to Lee-on-Solent and Tilshead before moving to Okehampton on the 9th September 1941 and Weston Zoyland again on the 11th September 1941. The unit moved to Thruxton on the 25th September

1941 and back to Weston Zoyland on the 3rd October 1941 with a detachment to Farnborough, then moved to Lympne on the 23rd November 1941 and Weston Zoyland with a detachment at Okehampton on the 27th October 1941 before re-equipping with the North American Mustang Mk I in April 1942.
Codes: KJ, EE & UG

No.20 (Army-Co-operation) Squadron
The squadron operated the Mk II from Begumpet from December 1941 then moved to Peshawar on the 2nd March 1942, to Chakilia on the 1st May 1942 and Jamshedpur with detachments to Tezpur, Dinjan, Feni, Imphal and Chittagong on the 5th May 1942. It moved to Charra on the 11th December 1942 with detachments to Imphal, Chittagong and Maungdaw before re-equipping with the Hawker Hurricane Mk IIB in January 1943 but not finally relinquishing its Lysanders until April 1943.
Codes: HN

No.26 (South African) Squadron
The squadron operated the Mk III alongside the Curtiss Tomahawk Mk II from West Malling from November 1940 with moves to Weston Zoyland on the 14th July 1941, Leconfield on the 18th July 1941, Gatwick on the 22nd July 1941, Detling on the 4th August 1941, Gatwick again on the 8th August 1941, Warmwell on the 29th August 1941, Gatwick again on the 1st September 1941, Barton Bendish on the 27th September 1941, Twinwood Farm on the 30th September 1941, Upwood on the 1st October 1941, Snailwell and Honington on the 2nd October 1941, back to Gatwick on the 3rd October 1941, Manston on the 12th October 1941, back to Gatwick on the 15th October 1941 with a detachment to Manston before permanently being based there from the 22nd November 1941. It returned to Gatwick on the 30th November 1941 and swapped the Tomahawks for North American Mustang Mk Is, then moved to Weston Zoyland on the 8th February 1942, back to Gatwick on the 23rd February 1942 with a detachment to Madley, then to West Malling on the 19th May 1942, back to Gatwick on the 31st May 1942 where it finally relinquished its Lysanders.
Codes: HL & RM

No.28 Squadron
The squadron operated the Mk II at Kohat from September 1941, then moved to Lashio on the 31st January 1942 with detachments to Zayatkwin and Port Blair before moving to Magwe on the 8th February 1942 with a detachment to Mingladon. It moved to Asansol on the 6th March 1942, to Lahore on the 7th March 1942 and Ranchi with detachments to Dum Dum and Jamshedpur on the 7th April 1942 before moving to Kohat again on the 18th July 1942 and Ranchi on the 31st August 1942 where it re-equipped with the Hawker Hurricane Mk IIb in December 1942.
Codes: BF

No.116 Squadron
The squadron formed with the Mk III at Hatfield in February 1941 then moved to Hendon on the 24th April 1941. It added Hawker Hurricane Mk Is in November 1941 and moved to Heston on the 20th April 1942 where it also gained the D.H. Hornet Moth, Tiger Moth, Avro Anson Mk I, Spitfire Mk Va/Vb and Airspeed Oxford Mk II before moving to Croydon on the 12th December 1942 and relinquished the Lysander there in March 1943.
Codes: II

No.138 (Special Duties) Squadron
Formed at Newmarket by renumbering No.1419 Flight on the 25th August 1941 operating the Lysander Mk IIIa, A.W. Whitley Mk V and H.P. Halifax Mk II, moved to Stradishall on the 16th December 1941 and Tempsford on the 11th March 1942 by which time it had relinquished the Lysander.
Codes: NF

L4773, RM•B of No 26 (South African) Squadron seen shortly after capture after forced-landing during a reconnaissance mission around Calais on the 20th May 1941 (via Internet)

Mk IIIA (SD), V9673, MA•J, of No.161 (Special Duties) Squadron on the ground at Tempsford, Bedfordshire. This aircraft was flown by Squadron Leader Hugh Verity

Mk II, P9139, BF•? of No.28 Squadron photographed in 1941

Airframe Detail No.9 – Lysander 109

No.161 (Special Duties) Squadron
Formed at Newmarket on the 15th February 1942 from No.138 Squadron and the King's Flight operating the Lysander Mk IIIA, Lockheed Hudson Mk I and A.W. Whitley Mk V. Moved to Graveley on the 1st March 1942, then Tempsford on the 8th April 1942 with a Lysander detachment to Tangmere in October 1942 and another to Winkleigh in September 1943 before disbanding on the 2nd June 1945.
Codes: MA

No.173 Squadron
Formed at Heliopolis on the 9th July 1942 with the Hawker Audax, Lysander Mk II, Hawker Hart, Hurricane Mk I, Bristol Blenheim Mk IV, Airspeed Oxford, D.H. Moth Major, Percival Gull Six, Miles Magister Mk I, Douglas Boston Mk III, Lockheed Electra, Percival Proctor Mk I, Lockheed Lodestar, Fairchild Argus and D.H. Dragon Rapide plus captured Savioa-Marchetti SM.79s. The unit continued to operate the Lysander until July 1943.
Codes: None

No.208 Squadron
The squadron operated the Mks I and II at Heliopolis from January 1939, then moved to Mersah Matruh on the 26th February 1942, back to Heliopolis on the 16th March 1939, then back to Mersah Matruh on the 7th August 1939. It moved again to Qasaba on the 1st September 1939 and Maaten Bagush on the 23rd October 1939, returning to Qasaba on the 28th October 1939. It went back to Heliopolis on the 15th November 1939 with detachments to Qasaba and Mersah Matruh, then moved to Qasaba on the 9th June 1940 with detachments to Sidi Barrani, Bir Kanayis and Siwa. Hawker Hurricane Mk Is joined the squadron in November 1940 and operated alongside the Lysander, then the unit moved to Gambut on the 10th June 1941, Tmimi on the 22nd June 1941 with a detachment to Mechili and Agedabia, then on to Marawa on the 4th February 1941, Barce on the 6th February 1941 and back to Heliopolis on the 3rd March 1941. It moved to Mersah Matruh again on the 5th April 1941 and on to Kazalar with detachments to Larissa and Pharsala on the 6th April 1941. It moved once again to Amphiklia on the 17th April 1941, Kalamaki on the 18th April 1941, Elevsis on the 19th April 1941 with detachments to Amphiklia and Kalamaki, then to Argos on the 22nd April 1942, Maleme on the 24th April 1942, then Aboukir on the 28th April 1941 and Gaza on the 1st May 1941 where it added Hawker Audaxes to its strength with detachments to Habbaniyah, Annan, H.4 and Haifa. On the 21st June 1941 it moved to Ramleh with detachments to Haifa, Muqueibila, Rosh Pinna, H.4, Rayak and Del-es-Zor then on to Aqir on the 29th September 1941 and LG.10 on the 19th October 1941 with detachments

Mk Is, L4721, L4728 and L4715, of No.208 Squadron, based at Heliopolis, Egypt, entering a starboard turn after flying over the Suez Canal (©British Official)

to Gabr, Saleh and LG.75. Then followed a period of moves to landing grounds, with LG.112 on the 14th November 1941 with a detachment at LG.134, followed by being based at LG.134 from the 21st November 1941, on to LG.123 on the 24th November 1941, LG.128 on the 28th November 1941 with a detachment at LG.134, back to LG.134 on the 30th November 1941 and then to El Gubbi on the 10th December 1941 with detachments to LG.131 and LG.134. The unit moved to Tmimi on the 19th December 1941 with detachments to Mechili, Antelat, Msus, Benina and Martuba, then on to Acroma on the 3rd February 1942, Sidi Azeiz on the 8th February 1942 with detachments at Acroma, Bir el Regal and el Adem and then on to Moascar on the 27th March 1942 where it relinquished the Lysander in May 1942 having re-equipped with the Curtiss Tomahawk Mk IIB in April and Hawker Hurricane Mk IIa and IIb in May 1942.
Codes: None

No.225 Squadron
The squadron was reformed at Odiham on the 9th October 1940 from B Flight No.614 Squadron and moved to Old Sarum on the 9th June 1940, then Tilshead on the 1st July 1940 with detachments to Okehampton, Shoreham, Pembrey, Exeter and Staverton. It re-equipped with the Lysander Mk III in September 1940 and moved to Thruxton on the 29th July 1941 with detachments to Weston Zoyland and Dumfries. The squadron gained Hawker Hurricane Mks I and IIc in January 1942 and moved to Abbotsinch on the 13th May 1942 and Thruxton on the 19th May 1942 where it added some N.A. Mustang Mk Is and finally relinquished the Lysander in June 1942.
Codes: LX & WU

No.231 Squadron
The squadron reformed at Aldergrove on the 1st July 1940 from No.416 Flight and operated the Lysander Mk II. It moved to Newtownards on the 15th July 1940 and re-equipped there with the Lysander Mk III in November 1940 with a detachment sent to Maydown. The Lysander was replaced with the Curtiss Tomahawk Mk I and IIb in October 1941.
Codes: VM

No.237 (Rhodesian) Squadron
The squadron operated the Mks I and III from Gordons Tree from November 1940 with a detachment at Blackdown. It moved to Umtali on the 30th January 1941 with a detachment at Blackdown and Agordat, then to Barentu with a detachment at Agordat from the 9th March 1941 where Gloster Gladiators joined the squadron strength. It moved to Umritsar on the 27th March 1941 and Asmara on the 7th April 1941, then on to Wadi Halfa on the 30th May 1941 with a detachment at Kufra. It then moved to Kasfareet on the 24th August 1941 and Hawker Hurricane Mk Is were added, then on to LG 'Y' on the 21st September 1941 and LG.10 on the 30th October 1941, where it relinquished the Lysander in November 1941.
Codes: None

No.239 Squadron
The squadron reformed at Hatfield on the 18th September 1940 from Nos.16 and 225 Squadrons. It operated the Lysander Mk II with detachments at Gatwick and Cambridge, then moved to Gatwick on the 22nd January 1941 where Lysander Mk IIIs were added in April 1941 and Curtiss Tomahawks in June 1941. It moved to Weston Zoyland on the 6th July 1941, Gatwick again on the 13th July 1941, Netheravon on the 26th September 1941, Kidlington on the 30th September 1941 and Gatwick again on the 3rd October

Mk II, R1999, LX•P, of No.225 Squadron, undergoing maintenance at Tilshead, Wiltshire (©British Official)

1941. In January 1942 it received Hawker Hurricane Mks I and IIc and ceased operating the Lysander the same month.
Codes: HB

No.241 Squadron
The squadron was reformed at Longman on the 25th September 1940 from A Flights of Nos.4 and 614 Squadrons. It operated the Lysander Mk II and had the Blackburn Roc added in November 1940, but these did not remain with the unit and left the same month. The Lysander Mk III was adopted from December 1940 and the unit moved to Bury St. Edmunds on the 11th April 1941, then Bottisham on the 1st July 1941 where it took on some Curtiss Tomahawk Mk IIas in August 1941. The unit had detachments to Snailwell, Macmerry, Henlow and Docking before adding the N.A. Mustang Mk I in March 1942 and ceasing to operate the Lysander in May 1942, probably just after relocating to Ayr on the 2nd of that month.
Codes: RZ

No.267 Squadron
The squadron reformed at Heliopolis on the 20th August 1940 and operated the Lysander Mk I and II from January 1941 alongside many other types and continued to do so from this base until June 1942 .
Codes: KW

No.268 Squadron
The squadron was reformed at Bury St. Edmunds from crews of Nos.2 and 26 Squadron on the 30th September 1940. It operated the Lysander Mk II with a detachment to Cambridge, then added the Mk III to its strength in February 1941. It moved to Snailwell on the 1st April 1941, Ipswich on the 26th April 1941 and back to Snailwell on the 28th April 1941 during which month it ceased using the Lysander Mk II but added the Curtiss Tomahawk Mk IIa during May 1941. It moved to West Raynam on the 20th June 1941, Barton Bendish on the 21st June 1941, Snailwell on the 25th June 1941, Weston Zoyland on the 21st July 1941, then back to Snailwell on the 27th July 1941, to Penshurst on the 4th August 1941 and back to Snailwell on the 8th August 1941. On the 28th September 1941 it moved to Barton Bendish again then on to Twinwood Farm on the 30th September 1941, back to Snailwell on the 1st October 1941, Barton Bendish on the 25th October 1941, Snailwell on the 26th October 1941, Weston Zoyland on the 24th November 1941 and Snailwell from the 8th December 1941 with detachments to Docking and Ibsley. It ceased using the Lysander Mk III in March 1942 and re-equipped with the N.A. Mustang Mk I in April 1942
Codes: NM

No.275 (ASR) Squadron
The squadron formed at Valley on the 15th

Although it lacks any squadron codes and it not the clearest shot, this image shows Mk I L4677 of No.267 Squadron in North Africa

October 1941 with detachments at Andreas and Eglington operating the Lysander Mk III and Supermarine Walrus. In May 1942 it added the B.P. Defiant Mk I (but these were gone again by June 1943), followed in March 1943 by the Avro Anson Mk I and ceased operating the Lysander in September 1943.
Codes: PV

No.276 (ASR) Squadron
The squadron reformed at Harrowbeer on the 21st October 1941 operating the Lysander Mk IIIA, then added the Hawker Hurricane Mk I in November 1941 and Supermarine Walrus in January 1942. The unit had detachments to Roborough, Portreath, Warmwell, Perranporth and Fairwood Common, when it added the Spitfire Ml IIa and Defiant Mk I in May 1942, followed by the Avro Anson Mk I in March 1943. It ceased using the Lysander in May 1943.
Codes: AQ

No.277 (ASR) Squadron
The squadron formed at Stapleford Tawney on the 22nd December 1941 operating the Lysander Mk III and Supermarine Walrus, followed by the B.P. Defiant Mk I from May 1942. It moved to Gravesend on the 7th December 1942 with detachments to Hawkinge, Martlesham Heath and Shoreham, then received the Spitfire Mk IIa in February 1943 and Supermarine Sea Otter in November 1943. It moved to Shoreham on the 15th April 1944 with detachments to Martlesham Heath, Warmwell, Hurn and Hawkinge and added the Spitfire Mk V to its strength in April 1944 before ceasing to operate the Lysander from June 1944.
Codes: BA

No.278 (ASR) Squadron
The squadron formed at Matlask from No.3 ASR Flight on the 1st October 1941 operating the Lysander Mk IIIa and Supermarine Walrus with a detachment at North Coates. It moved to Coltishall on the 21st April 1942 with detachments to North Coates, Woolsington, Acklington, Hutton Cranswick, Ayr, Drem, Castletown, Peterhead and Sumburgh. It replaced the Lysander with the Avro Anson Mk I in February 1943.
Codes: MY

No.285 Squadron
The squadron formed at Wrexham on the 1st December 1941 operating the Bristol Blenheim Mk I, Lockheed Hudson Mk III and Lysander Mk III and continued to operate the Lysander there until June 1942.
Codes: VG

No.287 Squadron
The squadron formed at Croydon from No.11 Group AAC Flight on the 19th November

Mk IIIA, V9437, AR•V of No.309 (Polish) Squadron having the oblique F.24 camera installed prior to a mission (©British Official)

1941 operating the Bristol Blenheim Mk IV, Lockheed Hudson Mk III, Hawker Hurricane Mks I, IIB and IV and Lysander Mk III and it continued to operate the Lysander there until April 1942.
Codes: KZ

No.288 Squadron
The squadron formed at Digby from No.12 Group AAC Flight on the 18th November 1941 operating the Bristol Blenheim Mk IV, Lockheed Hudson Mk III, Hawker Hurricane Mk I and Lysander Mks II and III and it continued to operate the Lysander there until March 1942.
Codes: RP

No.289 Squadron
The squadron formed at Kirknewton from No.13 Group AAC Flight on the 18th November 1941 operating the Bristol Blenheim Mk IV, Lockheed Hudson Mk III, Hawker Hurricane Mks I, IIc and IV and Lysander Mk III and it continued to operate the Lysander there until March 1942.
Codes: YE

No.309 (Polish) Squadron
The squadron formed at Abbotsinch on the 7th October 1940 and operated the Lysander Mk III from November 1940. It moved to Renfrew with detachments to Perth/Scone on the 6th November 1940 and to Dunino on the 8th May 1941 where it replaced the Mk IIIs with the Mk IIIa. It operated from Dunino with detachments at Gatwick, Longman and Findo Gask until re-equipping with the N.A. Mustang Mk I in August 1942 having ceased using the Lysander a month previous.
Codes: AR & ZR

No.400 (City of Toronto) Squadron
The squadron formed at Odiham from No.110 (Army Co-operation) Squadron RCAF on the 1st March 1941 operating the Lysander Mk III with detachments at Redhill and Gatwick. It added the Curtiss Tomahawk Mks I, IIa and IIb in April 1941 and moved to Bottisham on the 18th June 1941, then Odiham from the 25th June 1941 with detachments to Gatwick and Weston Zoyland. It ceased operating the Lysander at some stage during December 1941.
Codes: SP

No.414 (Sarnia Imperials) Squadron
The squadron formed at Croydon on the 12th August 1941 operating the Curtiss Tomahawk Mks I and II and Lysander Mk III and it continued to operate the Lysander there until June 1942 when both types were replaced by the N.A. Mustang Mk I.
Codes: RU

No.510 Squadron
The squadron formed at Hendon from a nu-

Crews run to their Mk IIs of No. 400 (Canadian) Squadron at RAF Odiham (©Air Ministry)

cleus of No.24 Squadron on the 15th October 1942 operating the Lysander Mk I alongside various other types and it continued to do so until June 1943.
Codes: None

No.516 Squadron
The squadron formed at Dundonald from No.1441 Flight on the 28th April 1943 operating the Lysander Mk III alongside a number of other types and continued to operate it until December 1943.
Codes: None

No.598 Squadron
The squadron formed at Peterhead from Nos.1479 and 1632 Flights plus a detachment of No.289 Squadron on the 1st December 1943 operating the Lysander Mk IIIA alongside various other types. It had detachments to Longman, Skaebrae, Sumburgh, Montrose and Turnhouse and ceased operating the Lysander in January 1944.
Codes: None

No.613 (City of Manchester) Squadron
The squadron started to operate the Lysander Mk II from April 1940 when the unit was based at Odiham with detachments at Weston Zoyland and Hawkinge. It moved to Netherthorpe on the 30th June 1940 and Firbeck on the 7th September 1940 with detachments to Clifton, Netherthorpe, Sutton Bridge, Doncaster and Martlesham Heath. In June 1941 it re-equipped with the Lysander Mk IIIa and moved to Doncaster on the 8th July 1941 where it received the Curtiss Tomahawk Mk II the next month. It moved to Andover on the 26th September 1941 and Doncaster on the 6th October 1941 with detachments to Odiham and Weston Zoyland, then on to Twinwood Farm on the 15th April 1942 where the Tomahawks were replaced with N.A. Mustang Mk Is. The unit moved to Ouston on the 28th August 1942 with detachments to Odiham and Gatwick and finally relinquished its Lysanders in September 1942.
Codes: ZR & SY

No.614 (County of Glamorgan) Squadron
The squadron started to operate the Lysander Mk II from Pengam Moors in July 1939 and moved to Odiham on the 2nd October 1939 with a detachment at Weston Zoyland. It moved to Grangemouth on the 8th June 1940 with detachments to Evanston, Montrose, Longman, Dumfries and Tangmere, then to Macmerry on the 5th March 1941 with detachments to Westhampnett, Dalcross, Elgin and Clifton. It re-equipped with the Lysander Mk III in April 1941 and added the Bristol Blenheim Mk IV in July 1941 with detachments to West Raynham, Odiham and Thruxton, but had ceased operating the Lysander by January 1942.
Codes: YX & LJ

Mk IIIA, V9374, ZR•F of No.613 (City of Manchester) Squadron being decontaminated during an exercise (©British Official)

Lysander Mk III, LJ•P of No.614 (County of Glamorgan) Squadron based at Macmerry, East Lothian, airborne on a photographic-reconnaissance flight (©Air Ministry)

No.695 Squadron
The squadron formed at Bircham Newton from Nos.1611, 1612 and 1626 Flights on the 1st December 1943 operating the Lysander Mks I and II alongside numerous other types and it continued to operate the Lysander there until January 1944.
Codes: 4M

Other Units

Air Gunnery School (AGS)
- Nos.1, 2, 3, 4, 7, 8, 9, 10 and 13 plus No1. AGS (India)

Air Observer School (AOS)
- Nos.1, 2, 4, 5 & 9

Armament Practice Camps (APC)
- Nos.1, 2, 3, 4, 11 and 16

Anti-Aircraft Practice Camps (AAPC)
- Montrose & Locking plus Nos.2, 3, 4, 6 & 8

Observers Advanced Flying Unit (O)AFU
- Nos.2, 3, 4, & 9

Anti-Aircraft Calibration Unit (AACU)
- No 1 (A, B, D, F, H, M, O & P Flights), Nos. 2, 3, 4

Flights
- No.1414 Flight, No.416 (Army Co-operation) Flight, Nos.419 & 1419 (Special Duties) Flight, No.1416 (Reconnaissance) Flight, No.1424 (Air Observation Post) Flight,, No.1433 Flight, No.1441 (Combined Operations Development) Flight, No. 1447 Flight, No. 1480 (Anti-Aircraft Co-operation) Flight, Nos. 1481, 1482, 1483, 1484, 1485, 1486, 1487, 1488, 1489, 1490, 1491, 1492, 1493, 1494, 1495, 1496, 1497, 1498 & 1500 (Target Towing) Flight, Nos.4 & 1504 (Beam Approach Training) Flight, No.1568 Meteorological Flight, Nos.1601, 1625, 1626, 1627, 1628, 1630, 1631, 1632, 1633 & 1634 (Anti-Aircraft Co-operation) Flight, Flying Training Command Communications Flight, The Lysander Flight, No.5 Group Training Flight, Army Co-operation Command Communications Flight, Special Duty Flight & Transport & Communications Flight

Anti-Aircraft Co-operation Flight
- Nos.9, 10, 11, 12 and 13 Group

Communications Flight
- Nos.2, 3, 4, 5, 8, 9, 14, 15, 16, 18, 19, 82, 201, 204 & 221 Group
- Aden, Bengal, Khartoum & Lydda,
- West Africa Communications Squadron
- Communications Flight, Air Headquarters Western Desert/Communications Unit, Western Desert

Station Flights
- Algerdrove, Andover, Asansol, Beaulieu, Boscombe Down, Bottisham, Catfoss, Catterick, Coltishall, Coningsby, Driffield, Dundonald, Eastchurch, Fairwood Common, Gibraltar, Goxhill, Hawkinge, Hutton Cranswick, Inverness, Kaldadames, Kenley, Lydda, Manston, Mildenhall, Netheravon, Newmarket, Northolt, Odiham, Old Sarum, Pembrey, Perranporth, Portreath, Reykjavik, Ringway. Roborough, Salmesbury, Talbenny, Tangmere, Warmwell, Weston Zoyland, West Raynham, White Waltham & Wyton

(Coastal) Operational Training Unit
- Nos.1, 2, 3, 4, 8, 9 & 132

Operational Training Unit
- Nos.5, 6, 7, 10 to 16, 18 to 32, 34, 36, 41, 42, 43, 51, 53, 54, 55, 56, 58, 59, 60, 61, 70 (Middle East), 71, 74, 81, 102 (Glider) and 151 (Fighter)
- No.1 AD

- No.1 Air Armament School
- No.1 Combat Training Wing
- No.1 Ground Defence Gunners School
- No.1 Operational Training Unit (India)
- Nos.1 & 3 RAF Regiment School
- Nos.1 & 2 Torpedo Training Unit
- Nos.1 & 2 School of Army Co-operation
- No.3 Civil Maintenance Unit
- No.3 School of General Reconnaissance
- No.5 Glider Training School
- Nos.7 & 31 Bombing & Gunnery School
- No.10 Flying Training School
- No.21 Airborne Forces Experimental Establishment
- No.31 Service Flying Training School (Canada)
- No.239 Wing
- Nos.1333 and 1653 Conversion Unit
- Air Headquarters India Communications Unit
- Air Headquarters Levant Communications Unit
- Air Transport Auxiliary (Training) Ferry Pool
- Army Co-operation Pool
- Central Gunnery School (Canada)
- Central Landing Establishment
- Central Navigation School

TT Mk IIIA GW-U of No.755 NAS having its radio tested by WREN radio mechanics (©Admiralty)

Mk IIIA V9618 of No.754 NAS at Tayside in 1941

Airframe Detail No.9 – Lysander

Fleet Air Arm

754 NAS
This squadron operated eighteen TT Mk IIIAs from June 1941 to March 1944 at RNAS Abroath, disbanding in March 1944
Code: W5

755 NAS
Operated the TT Mk III and TT Mk IIIa from July 1941 to October 1944 from RNAS Worthy Down, disbanded 31st October 1944
Code: W6

757 NAS
Operated the Mk III from April to December 1942 from RNAS Worthy Down, disbanded 1st December 1942
Code: X6

771 NAS
Operated the TT Mk III from July to December 1943 from RNAS Twatt

792 NAS
Operated the Mk III from March to May 1942 from RNAS St. Merryn

Mk II, P9197, of No.3 Squadron RAAF photographed at Benina in February 1941 (via Internet)

Foreign Service

Australia – Royal Australian Air Force
- No.3 Squadron – operated the Mk II from August 1940 to Jan 1941
- No.451 Squadron – Operated the Mk I & II during 1941/42 from Kasfareet, Aboukir, Qasaba, Landing Ground (LG) 75, 132, 128, 145 and 146, El Gubbi, LG 131 & 148, Sid Azeiz, Helioplois, Rayak and Estabel

Burma Volunteer Air Force
- The group operated the Mk II from March to December 1942 from Mingaladon, Kyaikto, Syriam, Megui, Pokpyin and Lekokon

Finland – Finnish Air Force (*Ilmavoimat*)
- LLv.12, LLv.14, LLv.16 LLv.30 & HLeLv 21 all operated the Mk III from 1940 through to 1945

France – Free French Air Force (*Forces Aériennes Françaises Libres*)
- D.A.C. – *Detachement Du Cameroun*
- *Detachement Du Moyen Congo et du Gabon*
- D.A.T – *Detachement Permanend Des Forces Aeriennesdu Tchad*
- Free French Flight
- *Escadrille Rennes, Groupe Bretagne*
- *Arras Escadrille, Groupe Artoi*
- *Béthune Escadrille*
- *3e and 4e Escadrille, Groupe de Bombardment 1*
- *Escadrille Spéciale 56*
- *Groupe de Bombardement Bretagne*

Ireland (Irish Air Corps)
No.1 (Fighter) Squadron operated the Mk II from July 1939 to April 1947 from Baldonnel

Portugal – Portuguese Air Force (*Força Aérea Portuguesa*)
The Mk IIIA was operated by the Portuguese Army Aviation's reconnaissance & liaison squadron BA3, based at Tancos and 361 *Grup de Reconhecimento e Informacao.*

Turkey – Turkish Air Force (*Türk Hava Kuvvetleri*)
Little is known about the operation service of the Mk IIs purchased by Turkey, other than they operated from Yesilkoy airfield.

United States of American – USAAF
Over twenty-five Mk IIIAs were allocated to the USAAF 8th AF in the UK and these were operated by the following units: 330th Bomber Squadron, 457th Bomber Squadron, 496th Fighter Training Group, 2025th and 2031st Gunnery Flight and the 3rd Gunnery & Towed Target Flight.

The Silver Diana on the fin is emblem of 2/LeLv 2 seen here on LY-118 at Tiiksjärvi 5th August 1942

LY-121 of LLv 30 at Pori in June 1941 still in RAF Dark Earth/Dark Green over Aluminium